Oriental Memoirs

Oriental Memoirs

Selected from a Series of Familiar Letters Written During Seventeen Years Residence in India

James Forbes

A new introduction by W.H. SIDDIQUI

In 4 Vols.

VOL. IV

GYAN PUBLISHING HOUSE
Delhi-110 007

GYAN PUBLISHING HOUSE
Publishers of Books on Human Civilization
5, Ansari Road, Daryaganj, Delhi

First Published in 1813 (London)
First reprint in India, 1988

ISBN: 9788121201117 (Set)
ISBN: 9788121201841 (Vol 4)

Published by Smt. Gayatri Garg for Gyan Publishing House, Delhi-110007, and Printed at Goyal Offset Printers, Delhi-110035

XR 4

CONTENTS.

CHAPTER XXXVII.

CHAPTER XXXVIII.

CONTENTS.

CHAPTER XXXIX.

CHAPTER XL.

CONTENTS.

CHAPTER XLI.

CHAPTER XLII.

CHAPTER XXXVII.

CONTINUATION OF THE JOURNEY FROM SURAT TO CALCUTTA, CONTAINING THE TRANSACTIONS FROM OOJEN TO AGRA, WITH A DESCRIPTION OF THOSE CITIES.

1785.

> " Let other lands the potent blessings boast
> Of more exalting suns—Let India's woods,
> Untended, yield the vegetable fleece :
> And let the little insect artist form,
> On higher life intent, its silken tomb.
>
> " From the prone beam let more delicious fruits
> A flavour drink, that in one piercing taste
> Bids each combine—Let Arabia breathe
> Her spicy gales, her vital gums distil.
> —Come, by whatever sacred name disguis'd,
> Oppression, come ! and in thy works rejoice !"

CONTENTS.

wealthy individuals—mausoleum of Akber—Mahomed Gose and Tanseine—account of that extraordinary musician—luxurious fête of Akber—Mhadajee Sindia's treachery in obtaining Gwalier from the rajah—bravery of some of the rajah's troops—attachment to his queen—and heroic death of that princess—cruel fate of the rajah—Nourabad—occurrences—bridge over the Gumbeer—Serai at Jajew—singular Hindoo tombs—arrival at Agra—dreadful situation of that ancient capital—a chaos of ruin and desolation—Taje Mahal appropriated for the residence of the embassy—that magnificent fabric, with the gardens, fountains, and tombs, particularly described.

CHAPTER XXXVII.

On our arrival at Oojen, the capital of Mhadajee Sindia's territory in Malwa, we found our tents pitched in a pleasant situation on the banks of the Sepra, not far from its western walls. The next morning, the 11th of April 1785, an officer and suitable attendants, came by Sir Charles Malet's desire to conduct us within the gates, and also to view the suburbs. Our first visit was to Mhadu-Ghur, called also Byro Ghur, a fortress a mile and a half north of Oojen, by a road running on the banks of Sepra. At the entrance of Mhadu Ghur, is a large Hindoo temple; the outer walls and towers are irregular; within is another fort, or citadel, of an exact square, with four gates, leading to a palace of good dimensions, in an unfinished state. The Sepra, as before observed, flows on the western side of the fortress, and part of its channel is to be conducted into a deep ditch, now forming round the remainder. It is altogether a place of little strength; the walls and towers appearing more like those round an oriental pleasure ground than a fortification. The whole is a recent work, commenced by order of Mhadajee Sindia, not yet finished, nor likely to be.

Our guides then conducted us to a very extraordinary building, at Kallea Déh, about a mile and a half further, said to have been erected by a king of the Goree dynasty, as a place of luxurious retirement. The Sepra running on the east, in its natural bed, has been conducted by a channel to the western side of the structure; where the stream rushes through the arches of a bridge into two large reservoirs, and is, from thence, led to numerous small ones, with fountains and other ornaments. On the right is a range of buildings divided by arches, each leading to a square apartment, with a roof partly projecting inward to form a colonnade round a fountain and small tank, bordered with chunam. This was open to the sky, while the company sat beneath a piazza round the water. Under the roof, throughout all the apartments, are iron rings, from which the tattees, or screens of sweet-scented grass, were suspended. These when sprinkled with water, convert the hottest wind into a cool and fragrant breeze. This range of apartments, the bridge, and large central building, form three sides of a square: on the fourth, which is open to the rest, the river divided into five streams, rushes down as many artificial cascades, into a general receptacle, which loses itself at the foot of a neighbouring hill. The central building, immediately fronting this pleasing scene, consists of a square apartment, covered by four domes, but has no private chambers; it seems to have been intended for the duan konna, or eating room; where the company assembled to take refreshment, and enjoy a view of the lake and cascades below. This structure still remains in high preservation; the excellent materials, especially the fine chunam, having hitherto resisted the effects of time, and the elements. In front of the whole are the remains of a wall, enclosing about three miles of ground; which was formerly a park belonging to this royal villa.

From a Persian history of the province of Malwa, Sir Charles Malet collected the following account of this extraordinary work: "Sultaun Nasir al Deen Ghilzey, son of Ghias al Deen, ascended the throne of Malwa, in the 905th year of the hejira, and reigned eleven years and four months. This prince was tyrannical and cruel: he caused the buildings, the fountains, the reservoirs, and the cascades, to be constructed at Kallea, Déh, and Saadunpore. Having contracted an insufferable heat in his habit, by the use of fixed quick-silver, he had recourse to these watery abodes; there he spent his time, and transacted the business of his kingdom." By this account the water-works and subaqueous edifices are three hundred years old A. D. 1785; and from the excellent state of their present preservation, deservedly claim our admiration. I would remark that the people of India have extraordinary ideas of the invigorating and stimulating powers of fixed mercury. I am told the above prince caused similar places to be constructed in other parts of his dominions; and that there are very fine ones at Mando, about twenty-six coss from Oojen. C. W. M.

From Kallea Déh we returned to the city through the suburbs, where we passed several Hindoo temples, rather pretty than grand; and one most beautiful well, belonging to a merchant of Oojen. The suburbs are extensive and very dusty, most of the houses being built with mud. The city is large, and extremely populous; the streets, broad, airy, paved, and clean; the houses generally good. The most striking public structures are a temple built by Ranojee Sindia, father of Mhadajee; the palace not yet completed for Mhadajee Sindia; a mausoleum erecting in memory of a celebrated Gosannee devotee; and another containing the ashes of Ranojee Sindia. The two latter, with others of less importance, adorn the bank of the Sepra, from whence several large flights of steps lead to the river; the whole produces a good effect. Oojen is infested by swarms of Hindoo mendicants and a prodigious number of courtezans, of more effrontery than usual; in passing through the public streets the dancing-girls beckoned from their doors and windows, and seemed less under the restraint of modesty than any women I have seen in India.

Oojen is a very ancient city, said to have been founded by the great rajah Bicker Maje, who gave an æra to the Hindoos still current in a great part of India, this year, A. D. 1785, being 1842 in their calendar. The city with a large proportion of Malwa province has been about fifty years in the possession of the Mahratta family of Sindia.

We spent the afternoon at a pleasant garden belonging to Kaunna Khan, a Patan general, in great favour with Mhadajee Sindia, and now with him and the army. It was laid out, like most oriental gardens, in a formal manner, divided by narrow gravel walks, bordered with chunam, on which there was room only for one person to walk; this takes off from its utility as a public garden, for which it seems to be intended; at least the citizens have free access to it during the absence of the proprietor. It contains some remarkably fine cypresses, and abundance of apple-trees, figs, mulberries, and sweet lemons: a profusion of roses and jessamin surrounds immense beds of various coloured poppies, closely sown; which having the appearance of a richly variegated carpet, forms a partérre much liked by the Indians. While we were enjoying our tea and hookas, fanned by the evening breeze on one of the garden terraces, a set of dancing-girls, with their duenna and musicians, unexpectedly made their appearance, requesting to have the honour of amusing us. The principal dancers were two sisters; the eldest a pretty girl not sixteen, the other about a year younger; both performed with an elegance and grace beyond the generality of these courtezans.

Every attention was paid to the embassy during its stay at Oojen, and on the 12th the governors waited on Sir Charles, by whom they were handsomely received, and presented with the usual tokens of friendship.

On the 14th of April we left the Malwa capital, attended by an honorary escort as far as Shah-Jehan-pore, to repair as soon as possible to Mhadajee Sindia, then with his army near Agra; which, with its castle, had lately surrendered to him; and Shah Aalum, the Mogul emperor, was then a sort of state prisoner in his camp. After a pleasant journey of twenty-two miles we arrived at Turrana, a tolerable town, with a neat fort. We passed the Chota Colla Sind, about four coss from Turrana: this river had now a plentiful stream, flowing over a rocky bottom; it falls into the Chumbul. We crossed several smaller rivulets in this march, which lay generally through a cultivated tract of country, partly belonging to Sindia, and the rest to Holcar, another great Mahratta chieftain, in whose dominions Turrana is situated.

We proceeded the next day to Shàh Jehanpore, a distance of

eighteen miles. From whence Sir Charles Malet intended to deviate from the usual direct route of Seronge; by which means the course will be more westerly, and probably more interesting in a geographical point of view, it being one of his primary objects in this embassy to acquire as much information as possible in that line.

The first part of this day's journey was on a very indifferent road, passing through an uncultivated tract of country: from those wild uplands we descended into a fertile valley, watered by the Lacoondra, now a small stream flowing in a broad bed, which in the rainy season must be a river of consequence. The Lacoondra falls into the Sind at some distance from hence. About half way between Turrana and Sháh Jehanpore we descended from an eminence, to view an extraordinary piece of water, situated between two hills, called Canadraka Tellow; and presently after were obstructed by a very high bank of earth; which being thrown across the road formed a head either to prevent the water from overflowing a neighbouring vale, to which we saw the traces of its having forced a passage in the rainy season, or to carry off its redundancy in some other direction. The vale was so exceedingly stony, that the greatest exertions could alone render it fruitful, and it is but justice to remark, that no cultivators can be more industrious than its inhabitants. The country was generally pleasing, exhibiting great variety in the colour and disposition of the trees. Shah Jehanpore is a large town, about a mile from the foot of Baruse Dungur, a very lofty hill, with a single tree and Hindoo temple on the summit, seen at a great distance on all sides. The town is walled, though the works are now going to decay; the river

Cheeler or Teekum flows on its eastern side; a little below the fort is a kind of bridge without arches, intended as a dam to preserve a sufficiency of water for the town, which contains some good houses and several handsome gates, leading to the principal streets, formerly paved, but now sadly out of repair, as indeed is almost every thing in the place. The Mahomedan inhabitants complain bitterly of the Mahratta government; the dreadful oppressions of the Amul within, and the cruel depredations of the Gracias without the walls, have almost driven them to despair. Here are many splendid remains of Mogul buildings, and ruinous Mausoleums in a grand style; in some of their enclosures the Hindoos had built small places of worship, which among so bigotted a people appeared very extraordinary; in another place we saw a Mahomedan mosque inhabited by a Hindoo Gosannee.

We had this day a most violent gale of wind, accompanied by such heavy clouds of dust, that until after a short fall of rain, we could not see each other; this also alleviated the extreme heat, and in the evening the thermometer fell to 60 . A few days before I took a thermometer which stood in my tent at 100°, and carried it into a house, at about eighty yards distant, cooled by tattees sprinkled with water, where in less than an hour it fell eighteen degrees.

The nature of the country now made it necessary to discharge the carts drawn by oxen, which had hitherto carried part of our baggage, and to procure an additional number of camels for that purpose; with which, on the 17th, we proceeded to Sarungpoor, a distance of near seventeen miles from Shah Jehanpore; during which we crossed several rivulets, and at length arrived at the

Cotta Sind, which runs along the west side of the town, and is by far the fullest river we have seen since leaving the Nerbudda. The eastern bank for a mile from the town is extremely beautiful. Its lofty slopes are in reality hanging gardens, planted with cucumbers, melons, and a variety of vegetables.

Sarungpoor is surrounded by remains of Mogul mausoleums, for the most part well designed, and elegantly executed; on the south-east side is a kubberstan, or burying-ground, with five large tombs still entire, and many in a state of dilapidation. Verses of the Koran are legible on their porticos. Some appear to be under a peculiar care, the chamber under the dome clean swept, and the tombs strewed with flowers; particularly a very handsome one, erected to the memory of Baz Bahauder Patshah, king of Malwa, who was killed near Sarungpoor, during the wars of Akber. In the centre of the town is a noble musjid, with a grand and lofty entrance, surrounded by a large court, with arcades, in ruins; this mosque is turned into a government hay-loft and granary for horses. Near it is the ruined gate leading to the hummums, and many other splendid remains, which fill the mind with melancholy reflections on the downfall of the Moguls, and with them all the arts and sciences they once cherished, without the smallest prospect of a revival under the wretched government of the Mahrattas, who now, under different chieftains, possess all these provinces.

Sarungpoor is famous for a manufactory of muslins for turbans, and other cottons, which are cheaper than any we have met with. A jatterah or religious fair is occasionally kept here; at which our fellow traveller, Siad Mahomed, a particular friend of Sir Charles

Malet's, was present, on his last journey to Delhi; when several men were taken up for a most cruel method of robbery and murder, practised on travellers, by a tribe called *phanseegurs*, or stranglers, who join passengers frequenting the fair, in bye-roads, or at other seasons convenient for their purpose: under the pretence of travelling the same way, they enter into conversation with the strangers, share their sweetmeats, and pay them other little attentions, until an opportunity offers of suddenly throwing a rope round their necks with a slip knot, by which they dexterously contrive to strangle them on the spot.

Sarungpore is a part of the allotment of the *Powar* family; the fine province of Malwa, having, after the Mahratta conquest, been chiefly divided between the great families of *Sindia*, *Holcar*, and *Powar*, with certain territorial and feudal reservations to the peshwa, as head of the Mahratta government.

On the 18th of April we travelled from Sarungpore to Koojneer, a large village in Holcar's districts, having in the last stage made the deviation, already mentioned, from the usual route. The road was excellent; the country beautiful, populous, and well cultivated, with hills in the distance. Koojneer is surrounded by regular groves of mangos, so contrasted by irregular forest trees, as to form a charming variety in form and colour: not more so than the crops in the intervening fields, where sugar canes, oil plants, flowers for dying, pulse and vegetables, present a rich scene of mingled hues. Large herds of cattle were grazing in the pastures, and the general appearance of industry among the peasants, afforded unusual delight. How truly happy might these people be under the wholesome regulations of a mild and fostering government, to secure the property which would then accumulate in such an enviable situation!

The commencement of the next day's journey was a continuation of the same delightful scenery; which, after a few miles, assumed a sterile stony aspect. This savage country increased so much as we approached Rajeghur, where it was intended to halt, that we anticipated a dreary encampment; and were agreeably surprised, after riding twenty miles, to find our tents pitched on the banks of the Nuaje, a broad river, with shady banks, and a plentiful stream of water. Rejeghur at a little distance appears to be built on a plain, but a nearer approach discovers the houses to stand in a straggling manner, on the sides of gullies, which form the streets. The fort, on an eminence, contains several good houses, and a tolerable bazar. The inhabitants of Rajeghur spin a great deal of cotton thread for the coarser manufactures, and express a quantity of oil from the seeds of those poppy heads which have already produced the annual supply of opium; this is the most common lamp oil used in this part of the country.

Ameer Sing, the rajah of Rajeghur, having been prepared for our arrival by a previous correspondence with Sir Charles Malet, behaved with great civility; and in addition to the usual supply of fuel, hay, milk and vegetables, sent a present of sweetmeats, tastefully prepared: among them was a plate of sugar-candy on strings, highly flavoured with roses. The rajah's cavalry made a respectable appearance in point of number and discipline.

In the evening Dewjee Goleh, a Mahratta general, in command of three thousand men, who arrived at Oojen before we left it, encamped near us at Rajeghur: and announcing his intention of paying his respects to Sir Charles, soon afterwards arrived at our encampment. He earnestly solicited Sir Charles to remain a few days at Rajeghur, to further some views he had of enforcing the collection of an arrear of tribute due to his master Mhadajee Sindia, from the rajah Ameer Sihng; adding that the report of our marching with him from thence to Ragoghur, would be equally essential to the success of his demands on that rajah also. Nor did he seem pleased when Sir Charles pointed out the impropriety of his interfering in any disputes between the native princes, and especially with any evil intentions against a rajah who had received him with friendship, and behaved with the greatest kindness and hospitality. These considerations induced him to decline any interference, and at an early hour he intended setting off for Ragoghur; on this answer, accompanied by a handsome present, he took his leave.

Dewjee Goleh, this Mahratta chief, now marching in great style at the head of three thousand cavalry, was a man of low extraction in the herdsman tribe. In order to keep clear of his troublesome encampments in future, Sir Charles resolved to make only three stages to Ragoghur, instead of four, at the usual divisions; we therefore travelled twelve miles the next morning by torch-light, which prevents a description of the country; by that light it appeared to be generally a wild forest, and a most intolerable road. At day-break we reached Polycote, the customary halting-place, a pleasant village situated near five distinct banian-trees, spreading their venerable branches to a great extent; here were also some fine mango groves profusely covered with fruit. We left Polycote with some reluctance, that we might keep the start of the Mahratta general and his cavalry.

From thence the road led through a stony uninteresting country, intersected by dry water-courses, but no running stream. We had been for some time on high ground, and now descending into a valley, we experienced that kind of pleasure which arises from variety. The scene had neither beauty nor fertility; but it differed from the monotonous stony plains over which we had so long laboured: the valley was about two miles broad, and extended several miles to a high hill, which there seemed its boundary; in the centre ran a small river, called the Parul, on whose banks we found the small village of Jellolpore, which we made choice of for our encampment. It is an excellent spot for the accommodation of a caravan, or a moderate army, a large plain, two commanding hills, plenty of water, and several deep ravines, but the extreme poverty of the village affords no supply of grain either for travellers or cattle.

The next morning we proceeded for three hours by torch-light over a barren country and a bad road. Day-break not only brought its own welcome delight, but introduced us to a fairer prospect, and we continued traversing a well cultivated plain until we reached a village called Kuchonder, near a hill-fort, where we found the inhabitants, who are subject to the rajah of Ragoghur, drawn up in battle array, at all the approaches; armed with match-locks, scimetars, spears, bows and arrows; their grain, collected in stacks, was strongly guarded, the cattle driven to a place of safety, and every possible disposition made for the defence of their property; being in hourly expectation of an attack by Dewjee's detachment, for which they had mistaken us. On finding no reason for the alarm, they allowed us to pass their village with the greatest civility. On leaving Kuchonder, we ascended some barren hills, which led to a fertile champaign, surrounding a village called Petounda, where we found our tents pitched near a well of excellent water, while the horses and camels drank at a rivulet shaded by trees.

The following day we marched upwards of twenty miles to Ragoghur; the first part as usual by massaul-light. About half way we came to the river Parbuttee, and descending its steep banks, passed near two hundred yards over its stony bed, to an island; which having crossed, we reached the stream of water, and ascended the opposite banks; the whole pass occupying half a mile. We soon came within view of a high range of hills, with a large fort in front, which our guides informed us was Rogoghur; two hours afterwards we found ourselves between two lofty hills, approaching the foot of the central range. On that to the left stood the fort, very much concealed by trees and contiguous buildings. Here we were met by a chopdar, with a request from the rajah that we would not enter the town, but turn out of the road we were then on, which led to its gates, and ascend the middle hill. Not willing to give umbrage, we complied with the request, and by this means had a leisure view of one face of the town, which appears similar to Baroche, but considerably higher: the walls seem of a weak construction, and the numerous towers mount no cannon; on this quarter it appears quite inaccessible, and on the road side for a great extent were newly-made intrenchments, and lines running from it to the fort. On gaining the summit of the hill the road took a northern direction, and we discovered the east angle with three towers; stretching to the north-west, it joined the west front, in the form of a triangle. From the ground allotted for our encampment we commanded a romantic view of woods, gullies, temples, houses, towers and rocks, strangely jumbled together, intermingled with cultivation, cattle, and large stacks of corn.

From the great extent of the walls and towers, erected at an immense expense, it is imagined the rajah intended Ragoghur as a place of safety, in case of necessity, for the whole of his subjects; yet from its situation it is exposed to so many disadvantages as must render the whole fruitless, being in a measure commanded from several places, and subject to a dangerous attack from two hills within three hundred yards of the out-works. Bulwant Sihng, the present rajah, is at war with Mhadajee Sindia, and having defeated a considerable force sent against him, is now carrying on further operations in person against a place about twelve coss off, his son, not more than fifteen years old, being in charge of the capital. The two powers have long been at variance, from a cause thus related to us from authentic intelligence.

Several years ago Ramchunder, a Mahratta chief, marching against the father of Bulwant Sihng, attacked the fortress of Jercoon; but relinquishing that attempt, he carried his force against Ragoghur, his capital, where the rajah endeavoured to purchase its safety. The sum demanded was a lac and sixty thousand rupees, which being unable to furnish he had recourse to the friendship of the Holcar family; who, on a mortgage of three villages, advanced the sum. These villages were farmed by Tookajee Holcar to a person named Tormuckjee, and on his death to his son Amujee. After his father's death the present rajah contrived to pay off the mortgage, and the representative of Holcar's family sent an order to Amujee to give up the villages. Amujee, who had now entered into Sindia's service, refused to comply, in which he was supported by Sindia. In consequence Bulwant Sihng attacked them by force, and having already taken two, and defeated a considerable detachment of Sindia's troops, is now going on successfully against the third.

I have abridged as much as possible Dr. Cruso's account of these transactions, and have generally avoided introducing disputes between the native princes of India, seldom interesting to an European reader; I insert this solely with the view of introducing the subject of a letter from Bulwant Sihng, rajah of Ragoghur, to Mhadajee Sindia, which tends to illustrate the high military spirit of the rajepoots, so often mentioned in these volumes.

The letter commenced with the intimation that Bulwant Sihng had heard of Mhadajee Sindia's intention to send a detachment from his army to attack him: he desired no paltry force might be ordered on an occasion, where he should be proud to see him in person: that so, if he proved successful, he might have the honour of repulsing a great man; if the fortune of war should be unfavourable, it might then be said that Bulwant Sihng, the rajepoot, had fought honourably to the last drop of his blood, in defending the liberty of himself and his subjects; but at length, overcome by superior strength, and overpowered by numbers, he had laid his head at the foot of the elephant of the renowned Sindia.

On the 24th of April we travelled sixteen miles, passing through an open cultivated country; about half way we crossed the river Choper, and entering a valley between two woody hills, followed its course for some distance. After riding through a thick jungle for three miles, we suddenly came in view of Jercoon, a large fort belonging to Bulwant Sihng, situated on a hill in the midst of a plain, which seemed an entire rock: the towers were of no great strength, and the face we passed bore the marks of a siege. From thence an indifferent road through a hilly country brought us to Maulpoor, the termination of the Ragoghur rajahship. The surrounding country was wild and romantic, the hills abounding with game. Here we saw a number of deer, and four large sabirs, or samboos, one considerably bigger than an ox, with hares, peacocks, and partridges in incredible numbers. We pursued the game for several hours in this irregular tract, in a heat from ninety to a hundred degrees of Fahrenheit's thermometer, without the least prejudice to our health.

The following day's march of nineteen miles, through a fruitful well-cultivated country, belonging to the peshwa, produced nothing remarkable. On the 26th we travelled eighteen miles to Boora Doongre, generally over a dreary plain, on which we saw only two villages, no river, and a few pools of stagnant water. About five miles from Boora Doongre we passed the ruins of a small village, called Durdeh, where Mhadajee Sindia was encamped, when so completely surprised by colonel Camac, from

Colarees, five years before. Colonel Camac's celebrated action, with the successful and gallant enterprize of major Popham at Gwalier, gave the highest credit to the British arms in this part of India; their names are familiar to all the inhabitants, who mention their exploits with mingled terror and admiration.

On this day's march we passed a great number of men, women, and children, on their way to their respective villages in the north, from whence they had been driven by famine, which had prevailed there during the last two years. The fertile and well-watered province of Malwa had been the resort of numerous emigrants from the neighbouring countries labouring under this dreadful affliction.

The next day we travelled seventeen miles to Sasye Seroy, through an open cultivated plain, where we passed Colarees, a large fortified town, with the remains of tanks, and a bouree, or large well, of very superior architecture. Its situation is rendered extremely beautiful by a rich surrounding grove, which forms a striking feature in the landscape long before we reach it. Sayse Seroy, where we now halted, is a large village, built entirely of stone, not excepting even the roofs of the houses, which are composed of large slabs, some a yard and a half square, laid on in so rude a manner, as to give a miserable unfinished appearance to the whole. It takes the additional name of Seroy, or Serai, from a royal serai, commonly called a caravansary in Europe. It is one of those buildings erected for the accommodation of travellers, at moderate distances, on all the padshah, or royal roads, during the flourishing state of the Mogul empire. Here the weary pilgrim, and poor itinerant, as well as the opulent merchant, found an asylum, and was supplied with some necessaries gratis. Most of these buildings are now in a state of dilapidation; those kept in repair by the Mahrattas are chiefly for the purpose of securing forage for the cavalry, as was the case at present. One gate of the serai leads to a musjid, composed of open arches supporting a dome; near it are the remains of a tank and fountain, with a well of excellent water in good repair.

The town is populous, and contains a number of houses, all constructed with the materials beforementioned. The adjacent country abounds with a kind of rugged flat stone, with which the houses are covered, irregular in thickness, size, and shape, supported by others erected perpendicularly, and the intervening spaces filled up with a light coloured soft stone, without cement, or at best but loosely laid in mud. Notwithstanding these contemptible habitations, the culley, or general grain yard, abounded with all sorts of excellent grain. The town is surrounded by a wall of loose stones, nine feet high, with the usual gates. At a quarter of a mile distance are the ruins of several Hindoo temples; two of them, and a pillar adjoining, extremely well executed: the figures, in the style of those at the Elephanta, apparently by superior artists, are grouped in great variety, but partaking of a common defect in Indian statuary, which totally fails in the delineation of joints or muscle.

To the north of Sayse, which belongs to the Mahratta family of Yaddoo, or Jaddow, runs the river Bhaw Gunga, having plenty of water; it falls into the Sind. On the 28th of April we passed Seepree, about eight miles from Sasye; this town is the residence of the managers of the Jaddoo family possessions in this country, originally amounting to three lacs of rupees annual revenue, but now greatly reduced. At this place Sir Charles Malet quitted the great Nerwar road, influenced by his former motive of proceeding by the nearest and most unknown routes, for the purpose of improving our Indian geography.

The following day we arrived at Dowlah Gaum, or Ghurr, a fortified village, about four miles beyond the river Ummir, now a dry bed, which we crossed where there was not the smallest stream. The surrounding country not only abounded with stones, but formed in some places an entire plain of stone, encompassed by immense rocks; no tract for sixteen miles together, (which was the extent of this day's journey) can exhibit more wildness, sterility, and want of comfort; we saw only two small villages, and very few inhabitants. On halting at Dowlah Gaum, one of our horse-keepers complained of a pain and swelling in the skin, and soon after found a difficulty in articulation. I very soon attended him, and found his jaw totally locked; ung. Elemi. was plentifully rubbed into his jaw, mixed with opium. He was put into a warm bath as soon as possible, and tinct. Thebaic. mixed with a small quantity of water, being forced down, he got better within twenty-four hours, and at length perfectly recovered.

For two days we travelled through those stony regions, but on the first of May we left the steril rocky plain, and gradually ascended a lofty hill: the former contained a few villages, nearly depopulated; partly from the effects of a two year's famine, and still more from an oppressive government. On the side of this hill, we passed a large fortified town, called Dooa, or Deway, where we understood were iron mines, and works for the fabrication of that metal, of great importance: had we wanted confirmation of this report from our guides, the large masses of ferruginous matter we saw on approaching the hills would have been a sufficient evidence. On attaining the summit we opened on a prospect of an amazing extent of mountains or hills, though not one was entirely detached from another; we found ourselves afterwards suddenly descend to a great depth by one of the most perpendicular roads I ever passed, partly over loose stones, but more over smooth rocks, slippery as glass, on which our horses might literally be said to slide down, in a very dangerous manner. This brought us into a valley with a little verdure, which was soon succeeded by rocky hills and immense masses of solid rock; the whole forming the bed of a river, which in a few places afforded stagnant water, to which we eagerly hastened, that our exhausted cattle might refresh themselves: we found it so strongly impregnated with iron as to be scarcely drinkable. All the surrounding rocks contained ore, of which we carried off several specimens, as the produce of the iron rocks in the Gwalier purgunna. In the midst of these unfrequented wilds I discovered a hole in one of the rocks: thinking it might lead to an excavation of sculptured rocks like the Elephanta, and possibly throw some light on the scene, I ascended a rugged and steep height, and to my great disappointment found only a wretched hole, just large enough for its inhabitant, a poor half-starved fakeer, passing his life in solitude and penance.

Proceeding from thence we ascended another rocky eminence, and beheld a pleasant valley, in which stood the large walled town of Berye, with its ghurry or citadel, the ruins of some old pagodas, and the shining domes of new temples, interspersed among verdant scenery, altogether presenting a scene to which we had not lately been accustomed. Here we encamped after a fatiguing journey of seventeen miles; although the heat was intense, and the thermometer in my palanquin at 102°, at two in the afternoon, I walked out out to view the place, and gain what intelligence I could respecting the iron works, which I knew would be deserted later in the evening. The scattered ruins were all of Hindoo architecture; one was a large circle, containing a smaller one, surrounded by a gallery covered with neat domes. The outer circle of buildings had most probably been allotted for the accommodation of travellers, but were now inhabited by a few half-starved wretches, covered with dirt and tatters. From thence going round the fort, which had a few towers of a conical form, I came to one of those dark-looking banks near the entrance of the town, where I entered a blacksmith's house, who received me with great civility, and in the course of our conversation, I found I had made a mistake in supposing that the rocks and hills of a ferruginous appearance furnished a quantity of iron ore; on the contrary it was extracted from another kind of earth, called *lohaka mittee*, or iron earth, which was only to be procured at one hill, seven miles distant. It was purchased on the spot by traders in that article, and brought for sale to Berye, Dewoy, Mohuna, Gwalier, and Nerwar, where the ore was extracted, and the metal worked by the smiths for sale far and near, at least as far as the want of an inland navigation would admit of. My host further informed me, that the greatest number of smiths, and those of superior ability, lived at a place called Maggeronee, four miles from Nerwar; that this iron-earth was sold at the mines for two pice, or one penny for a bullock-load, and was delivered to the smiths at Baroy, seven miles from the spot, at the rate of two rupees and a half for a hundred maunds, or about six shillings for nearly three thousand pounds weight of earth. Each bullock-load of earth, purchased at the mines for two pice, produced on an average twenty-five seers of iron, certainly above twenty pounds English weight.

This very low price of earth, and the great proportion of metal it contains, renders the value of iron extremely cheap; yet not so much so, as from these circumstances might be expected: this is accounted for from the great scarcity of charcoal, without which nothing can be done; none can be procured nearer than twelve miles, and there it sells for half a rupee the bullock load. The smith whom I first visited conducted me to several other forges; the process was the same in all, and the same weight of metal was generally extracted from the same quantity of iron earth. He also procured a guide to attend us to the mines, as soon as the moon arose the next morning. We then set off about two o'clock, and leaving the Gwalier road on the left, traversed a cultivated plain for three miles, until we reached a village called Naigow, where we found a number of smiths working at this early hour. Our guide expressing some doubts respecting the road to the mines, they readily supplied us with another, who leaving all regular paths led us over a wild scene of hills and dales until about five miles further we reached the mines just as the day dawned, time enough to see several loads of iron earth drawn up by torch light. I have not language to convey an adequate idea of the scene.

The darkness of the morning, the gloomy lights in the deep shafts of the mines, the black dirty miners, the shouts of the drivers, and noise of the bullocks, with the savage aspect of the surrounding hills, altogether produced an extraordinary spectacle.

I questioned the miners, here called *doharrees* or loharrees, on many points respecting the mines, and obtained the following information. The person who has the chief management of these mines, is the amull of *Santow*, in whose district is another town called *Cherowray;* each of these places is about two miles distant, in different directions from the spot we now visited. The mines therefore are indiscriminately called the *Santoo* mines, and the *Cherowray* mines; although in fact there are none at either of those places, but being under the same amuldhar, they are so named. Most of the hills in the adjacent country bearing a great similarity in external appearance to those where the iron earth is found, it is natural to suppose it would be found in many others; but it is not so, for in these hills only, and not in all of them, is this valuable earth to be met with, and chiefly in the hollow top of a certain hill, in the centre of many others, extending near two miles on every side of it. The earth which produces the iron ore is found in the hollow of this central hill, and not in the sides; there none is to be seen. There are now seven mines at work; the remains of many more which have fallen in, and the traces of others that have been attempted without success: the whole space does not appear to exceed four or five hundred square yards.

The entrance to each mine, and its descent to the bottom, form a kind of cylinder large enough to admit of the miners descending and ascending, in the manner adopted by the English chimney-sweepers, that of setting their back against one side, and their feet against the other; the rope to which the basket containing the earth is attached, being given into their hands as an assistance and security; although this rope is not affixed to any thing above, but held fast by one of the miners standing firmly on it near the precipice.

In searching for the earth they seldom go lower than twenty feet, at which depth if they do not succeed, they abandon the spot and try another; when successful, they work to the depth of thirty feet, and then proceed laterally. On being repeatedly asked, they all persisted in affirming that a mine seldom stood longer than three months; and numbers were destroyed by their falling in sooner. The Vanjarrees are the principal merchants who purchase the earth, but others of various castes occasionally deal in it. It is so abundant, that (contrary to the information given by the smiths) we found it sold on the spot at two pice, or one penny, for eight maunds of twenty-eight pounds each. The loading of each bullock was one pice. About twelve seer of iron was extracted from a maund of earth. None of the earth is kept ready dug for sale, either within or without the mines; it is only worked out when demanded: there are seven mines, and about fifty bullocks on an average are daily loaded. The workmen are not regularly in the pay of government, but are hired at the mines, and are paid for lading the bullocks by the merchants; a person appointed by government constantly attends to receive the price of the earth from the merchants.

Taking off my clothes, I descended into the largest mine, not more than thirty feet deep, but extending in four different shafts, about seventeen paces in length, through which I walked upright, after an entrance of some difficulty: but so dismal were these subterraneous regions that I was glad to make my exit at the first extremity I reached; their coolness was the only compensation for a visit. The supporters are large and substantial; the whole interior of the mine is of a deep purple colour, not easily distinguished from black by the light of a single torch, which was all we had for our guidance. The whole substance is so extremely soft, seemingly from moisture, that I broke off a handful with great facility; and a man with one of the working tools filled a basket in an instant. The ore does not run in any particular vein, but is contained in all the earth: here and there are seen small lines of a white greasy matter; and now and then a flake of that kind of stone of which the hills about this country are formed.

From the above account it will be found, that, labour excepted, a maund of iron may be made at Berye for about three rupees. One hundred maunds of iron earth cost two rupees delivered into the forge, and the charcoal fifty rupees per hundred maunds, admitting two parts of the latter to be necessary for working one of the former. So powerful was the effect of the iron in the environs of Berye, that the compass varied nearly three points.

From thence we proceeded, on the 2d of May, towards Gwalier, a name celebrated in the military annals of India, for the gallant and successful enterprize of captain Popham, in taking this fortress in the year 1780. The road from the mines thither was pleasant, but hilly; crossing the river Ummer, we reached Cherowray, a town already mentioned, situated on a hill between two vallies, commanding an extensive view. The more direct road to

Gwalier, which is seen from Cherowry, is through Nowgong; but on descending the hills we saw no more of that lofty fortress until we arrived within two miles of it.

Gwalier stands on a high hill in a circular valley, remarkable for the unusual regularity of its summit, extending about a mile from north to south. The town is situated below; great part of it now in a ruinous state, and the remainder very thinly inhabited, occasioned by a dreadful famine, with which this part of the country has been lately visited, in addition to the wars and revolutions that had previously desolated it. Gwalier stands pleasantly between the circuit of the hill, and a river flowing in its front. The fort is said to have existed for eighteen hundred years, being first built by Rajah Surej Sihng; from that time it underwent many alterations and improvements by different sovereigns, who erected several palaces, still conspicuous on the eastern face. The most elegant was built three hundred years ago, by a rajah named Maun Sihng, whence it is called Maun Mhunder; it is beautified with enamel of various colours, still bright and vivid. Gwalier was taken from him by the grandfather of Akber, and has since been in the possession of too many conquerors to enumerate.

We arrived at Gwalier on the 2d of May, and remained two days, to recruit our attendants and cattle after our late marches through the most rugged country that had occurred in our whole journey at this hottest season of the year. This place is still very interesting. Amidst a variety of ruined buildings, is a handsome serai; some parts of it are kept in tolerable repair, to answer the benevolent purpose for which it was erected; where a number of people, chiefly women, called Metrahnees, take up their abode to attend strangers on their arrival in the city. The poorest traveller is immediately furnished with a bed, some wheat bread, and cool water, for the humble pittance of two pice, or one penny. This in some measure proves the truth of Thomas Coriat's assertion, in a letter to his mother, that during his travels through Hindostan, he could live for two-pence a day.

The most perfect building is an elegant mosque, erected by Ahmed Khan, who held a distinguished post under the emperor Aurungzebe. The gate leading to it from the bazar is very grand, and two lofty minarets, seen at a considerable distance from the town, have a striking effect. Near the south-gate are the remains of a magnificent bowree, or large well, built by the same person; from which pipes extended, in different directions, to the several houses in the city which he meant to supply with water, a frequent mark of the benevolence of the wealthy in Hindostan, where all great works spring from the munificence of the prince or of rich individuals.

One of the most magnificent structures without the walls, is the Roza shrine, or mausoleum of Huzzret Shah Mahomed Gose, a celebrated peer, or Mahomedan saint. It stands within a large enclosure, consecrated by Akber as a repository for the remains of himself and family; time and religious influence have rendered it the sepulchre of many hundreds besides. The mausoleum itself contains the bodies of three of Akber's sons, and the tutor of the eldest prince. Shah Abdalla, the emperor's eldest son, raised this edifice, by the order and at the expense of his father. The royal remains are deposited under a handsome tomb of white marble, exquisitely wrought, covered by a silken pall, decorated with peacock's feathers. On a stool by the head, on the right hand, is the Koran wrapt up in a napkin. On the left, near the monument of Akber, is that of his eldest son; the other imperial princes repose at a greater distance. It is altogether a stupendous fabric, with an immense door in the centre, and twelve smaller in different apertures. The design is grand, the execution in a superior style, and the preservation wonderful, considering it has been erected two hundred and thirty-six years.

Under a neat marble tomb, near the peer, are deposited the remains of *Tanseine*, the Orpheus of Hindostan, he being the first who brought the art of singing to perfection in this part of the world. By the Mahomedan accounts he was a brahmin boy, converted to Islamism by Shah Mahomed Gose; who, struck with the sweetness of his voice, patronized him very early in life, and taking great pains in cultivating his talents, laid the foundation of that celebrity which he afterwards attained. He lived many years at the court of Akber, high in favour with the emperor, and the admiration of his subjects. Dying at Lahore, while attending his sovereign, Akber, out of affection and respect to his memory and talents, had his corpse conveyed from thence to Gwalier, at a great expense, that it might be deposited near the remains of his friend and early benefactor, Shah Mahomed Gose. Even to this hour the memory of Tanseine is so celebrated, that the musical amateurs of Hindostan, hold it in the highest veneration, and many travel from a great distance to do homage at his shrine. His tomb was formerly shaded by a spreading tamarind-tree, which has been so often stripped of its leaves, bark, and tender branches, by these musical votaries, that it is now almost a sapless trunk, in the last stage of decay. A chief reason for this spoil is the prevailing idea that a decoction from the bark, leaves, and wood of this tree, gives a clearness and melody to the voice.

Many stories are told of Tanseine, nearly as surprising as those related of Orpheus, Amphion, and other celebrated musicians of antiquity. Tanseine composed verses, as well as sang with such superiority, that when Akber, who was extremely luxurious and magnificent in his entertainments, invited strangers, and resolved to give an extraordinary zest to the royal banquet, Tanseine had his allotted share in the feast. When the company assembled in the dusk of evening to enjoy the gentle breeze, and taste the perfumes of the gardens, percolated and cooled by the numerous fountains playing round the shrubberies, darkness was gradually permitted to approach; but lamps of various colours, intended for a general illumination, were notwithstanding properly arranged, though ordered not to be lighted until a private signal was given by the emperor to Tanseine, who then suddenly burst forth into a strain so astonishingly harmonious, that the whole scene became illuminated by the magic of his voice!

There are numerous gardens about a mile from the town, laid out in a bad taste; straight narrow walks, formal trees crowded together, and flowers closely planted in small beds, like a carpet. They seem very little attended to; nor is there any thing else in the once celebrated town of Gwalier deserving the traveller's attention.

I do not enter into Mr. Cruso's detail of Captain Popham's enterprize against the fortress of Gwalier, which is already well known. It then belonged to the Mahratta government, with whom the English were at war. We kept it for ten months, and then made it over to our ally, the ranah of Gohud; he remained in possession of it near two years, when Mhadajee Sindia, who meditated the ranah's destruction for his attachment to the English interest, commenced a siege, which, having continued seven months with very little effect, he contrived to tamper with Mootee Mul, a man who had been useful to Captain Popham, and at his recommendation promoted by the rajah to a post of distinction. He was at that time of so much consequence in Gwalier, (the ranah being absent) as to share equally in the administration with the ranee, or queen, and a nephew of the ranah. Mhadajee Sindia, by bribery and intrigue, having gained over this man, contrived to have several interviews with the traitor, which were not so secretly managed as to prevent the intelligence reaching the ranah. The indignant prince immediately wrote to the ranee, who constantly resided in the fort, to take measures for Mootee Mull being cut off. This letter being intercepted fell into his hands, and instead of answering the intended purpose, only accelerated the completion of his perfidy. He communicated the discovery to Mhadajee Sindia, urging him not to lose a moment in assisting his treacherous designs. Two battalions instantly marched from his camp to that of the works commanded by the traitor, and entered the garrison without losing a man; these were followed by the main body of the army. Two thousand of the garrison went over to Mootee Mull, three thousand more, seized with a panic at this sudden turn of affairs, either fled or laid down their arms; six hundred only remained firmly attached to the ranee, who shewed the greatest magnanimity and firmness on the occasion. At length five hundred and fifty of these brave fellows being cut to pieces, the other fifty rallied round the heroine and performed prodigies of valour. All proving of no avail, the ranee retired into an inner apartment of the palace with her attendants, where having locked the door, she set fire to the building, and perished in the flames. Sindia, now master of Gwalier, marched to attack the ranah in his capital of Gohud, from whence he fled for refuge to the rajah of Caroulee, at a considerable distance. He afterwards unfortunately fell into the power of his enemy, and loaded with chains, drags on a miserable existence in the fort of Gwalier.

We left Gwalier before day-break on the 5th of May, and proceeded towards Agra, through a country so completely depopulated, that in passing near several large ruined villages, we only now and then saw a poor half-starved being peeping through a wretched hovel, hardly able to screen them from the intense heat. A good road soon brought us to Nourabad, where is the handsomest bridge I have yet seen in India, a large serai, well paved, and beautified by several small domes and minarets; also the tomb of Cunnah Begum, wife of that notorious delinquent and fugitive Ghazyul-din Khan, who died on the road, and was buried under a tree not far from the town, until her mother sent a thousand rupees to have her body removed, and interred in a manner more suitable to her former rank. It is now deposited under the mausoleum of one of the ancient kings in the centre of a garden.

The river Saunk runs by Nourabad, in a broad and full stream. About four miles further we crossed another considerable river, called Afsan, and halted at Choonda, a small village on the opposite side, where we pitched our tents for the night, and the next morning marched sixteen miles to the village Keytree, on the banks of the Chumbel, by far the broadest of any river we have yet seen, except the Nerbudda, though the stream was at this season narrow and shallow. The road was generally good, the country very little cultivated, and as we approached the river often cleft into deep ravines and immense hollows. We saw a few tolerable villages, and overtook a large caravan of oxen, laden with grain for Sindia's army, a detachment of which we found encamped near our ground. The banks of the Chumbel, intersected by immense gullies, with the general inequality of the ground, gives the landscape a wild and singular appearance. In a short excursion from our camp we saw several wolves, deer, and hares, and on our march overtook six fine brass field-pieces on their way to Sindia, said to have been cast at Gwalier; and met several larger guns proceeding with a considerable force from Sindia's army against the Ragoghur rajah.

On the 7th we marched thirteen miles. Proceeding at dawn of day through a broken country and a heavy sandy road, we reached Dolepoor, the residence of Mahomed Beg Humdannee, a jaghiredar under Sindia, and a principal actor in the commotions which caused the present change of affairs in the Mogul empire. The town is large, has many public and private edifices of great beauty, and is delightfully situated amidst groves and gardens laid out with taste. From thence we travelled through a country capable of all the advantages of cultivation, to Munnea, another town under his former government, and there passed the remainder of the day under a pavilion in the centre of a pleasant garden, not far from a handsome mausoleum without an inscription.

The next day we crossed the bed of the Gumbeer, a very broad river, now without water, which, when full, is passed by a bridge of larger dimensions, but not executed with so much taste as the bridge at Nourabad. This, like all the others we have yet seen, has not the smallest rise in the centre, but is carried on in a straight surface. It consists of twenty arches, each upwards of five yards wide, and the intermediate space of equal breadth; it is well paved and adorned with two minarets at each end. On the north bank of the Gumbeer stands the town of Jajew, where is a serai built by order of Sha Jehan, beyond comparison the most elegant we have yet seen. The entrances are uncommonly grand, each consisting of two minarets, tastefully decorated, with the gate and appropriate ornaments in the centre. On the left is a musjeed, not more remarkable for general beauty than for the delicacy of the stone with which it is built. It is of a pale reddish hue, inlaid with ornaments of light yellow, and white marble.

Soon after leaving the Gumbeer we passed a less considerable river, called the Karra Nuddy, or salt-river, which we were told has its source in a salt lake in the neighbourhood of Jaypoor; but other information attributes the spring to another spot: the water was brackish and disagreeable. From thence we proceeded to Oakwalla, our halting-place for the day, which, to avoid the extreme heat, we passed under the dome of a Mahomedan mausoleum. Near it were two Hindoo tombs; on one of them was sculptured a tiger, on the other a deer. We could gain no intelligence concerning these singular monuments, which were the first of the kind we had met with. From this spot we could discern, by the assistance of a telescope, the most conspicuous buildings and lofty minarets in the far-famed city of Agra. Thither we marched very early the next morning, and arrived there at day-break on the ninth of May, after a journey of six hundred and thirty-six miles from Surat, performed entirely on horseback, in fifty-five days including halts, at the hottest season of the year. As Sir Charles Malet preferred riding, we followed his example, though we had the option of using his elephants or our own palanquins.

The country through which we travelled for several days past has presented a melancholy picture, occasioned by a dreadful famine, which had sadly diminished population, and left the survivors in a state of misery. At Gwalier the whole suburbs were strewed with skeletons; from thence to Agra the villages were generally uninhabited, and the land become a wilderness from want of cultivation, but our arrival at Agra presented a scene lamentable beyond conception.

The gloom of the morning veiled the suburbs in a great measure from our observation, and we entered the gates of Agra, or Akber-abad, with the early dawn; and proceeding through the quarter called Momtazabad, beheld on all sides the most melancholy objects of fallen grandeur: mosques, palaces, gardens, caravansaries, and mausoleums, mingled in one general ruin. Agra had been the frequent subject of our conversation, we had anticipated much novelty, and expected every comfort at the close of our fatiguing journey. These considerations added to the poignancy of disappointment—instead of the spacious squares and frequented streets of a great capital, it was with difficulty and danger we kept our horses on their feet amidst the magnificent, but terrible mass of ruin. Few persons can have an idea of the painful sensations excited by such a view of this once celebrated city, for few have the opportunity of contemplating an object so deplorable! In the midst of this chaotic heap of desolation, our attention was suddenly roused by a stupendous fabric bursting on our view, in complete repair and resplendent beauty—a splendid structure, with domes and minarets of the purest white, surmounting the dark umbrage of rich surrounding groves, produced in such a situation a most extraordinary effect.

Previous to our arrival, Sir Charles Malet had corresponded with Mr. James Anderson, the British resident at Sindia's durbar, and his last letter mentioned that the Taje Mahal had been appropriated by the Mahratta chief for our accommodation at Agra. This was the edifice which had now excited our astonishment, and thither we were immediately conducted. On alighting at the grand entrance, built of a light red stone, inlaid with white marble, we walked into a large court, with apartments on three sides like those of the serais. To the right and left of this square, a gate of similar construction opened into the street; near each of those gates is an enclosure containing a beautiful dome of white marble, sacred to the memory of eminent persons; opposite to these mausolea is a spacious serai. Magnificent as was the first entrance, the one fronting it on the opposite side of the square was still more so; the roof being ornamented with two rows of small domes above the entablature, each row containing eleven of those elegant white cupolas with gilded spires. This superb portal, which indeed forms a spacious apartment, is ascended by a noble flight of steps;

a similar descent on the other side leads to an extensive garden, enriched with groves of cypress and other trees. In the centre is a noble avenue, with a canal and fountains, leading to a large marble reservoïr, with a beautiful jette d'eau. On each side of the garden is a respondent structure of elegant architecture; one a musjid, or place of worship, the other apparently intended for the accommodation of the great officers of the imperial court. Between those buildings, at the termination of the garden, on the banks of the river Jumna, stands the mausoleum of the empress Momtaz Mahal, deservedly the wonder of the eastern world.

This magnificent mausoleum, slightly introduced from Sir Charles Malet's manuscript in my account of Ahmedabad, is now considerably illustrated from the same valuable source, several sheets of Mr. Cruso's journal being lost after mentioning the arrival of the embassy at Agra.

Taje Mahal, standing due north and south on the southern bank of the river Jumna, was built by the command of the emperor Shah Jehan, for the interment of his favourite sultana, *Momtaz Mahal*, pre-eminent, or most honoured of the seraglio; or *Momtaz al Zumani*, superior of the age; both having been the titles of the empress. This mausoleum is commonly called *Taje Gunse*, or *Taje Mahal*, meaning the repository, or the abode of the diadem, alluding allegorically to her as the most brilliant gem of the seraglio. The word *seraglio* being an Italianization of *serah*, or *mohl serah*, signifying the female apartments held sacred amongst the Mahomedans. The posthumous title of the empress was *Mehd Aalea*, which means " Reposing in Heaven."

The emperor Shah Jehan intended erecting a similar mausoleum for himself on the opposite side of the river, and connecting the two magnificent structures by a bridge; but succeeding events having prevented the completion of this great design, his remains were, by order of his son and successor, Aurungzebe, also deposited in this beautiful edifice, which, in point of design and execution, is one of the most extraordinary works anywhere extant. The admirable art and nicety of the masonry has hitherto withstood the effect of time; nor have successive barbarous and predatory conquerors yet violated its sanctity and beauty. Two great squares or areas contain the principal buildings; those of the outer one seem intended for the convenience of travellers, distant visitors, and the inferior officers and dependents of the roza, a name for the mausoleum, but implying something saintly or sanctified. The inner square, which is entered through a stupendous dome, with brass gates, most elaborately and exquisitely worked, is an entire garden, shaded by numerous stately trees, adorned by marble canals and a fine reservoir, studded with fountains through the middle avenue. The right and left boundaries of the garden are formed by magnificent buildings for recreation and devotion.

At the extremity of the garden, opposite the grand entrance, and overlooking the river, stands pre-eminent, and alone, elevated on a very extensive platform, having a lofty minaret at each corner, composed entirely of beautifully white marble, the imperial roza; in which, under the grand centre dome, rest the ashes of the emperor and his consort in separate tombs. My inquiries respecting the quarries whence this marble was procured were not satisfactorily answered. I have been told such marble is produced in the province of Marwar, but this requires confirmation.

The beautiful inlaid work, in imitation of flowers in their natural colour, all of precious stones, forming borders and other ornaments in the white marble and alabaster of the interior, has been already mentioned at Ahmedabad, together with several other interesting particulars of this wonderful fabric.

CHAPTER XXXVIII.

CONTINUATION OF THE JOURNEY FROM SURAT TO CALCUTTA; CONTAINING THE TRANSACTIONS IN THE CAMP OF MHADAJEE SINDIA NEAR AGRA; A PUBLIC AUDIENCE WITH THE EMPEROR SHAH AALUM; AND A DESCRIPTION OF THE CITY OF DELHI.

1785.

"And yet, perhaps, if countries we compare,
And estimate the blessings which they share,
Though patriots flatter, still shall wisdom find
An equal portion dealt to all mankind,
As different good, by Art or Nature given
To different nations, make their blessing even.
—— The naked savage, panting at the line,
Boasts of his golden sands, and palmy wine;
Basks in the glare, or stems the tepid wave,
And thanks his gods for all the good they gave."

GOLDSMITH.

CONTENTS.

at Delhi—gardens at Delhi—fruit and flowers—palace appropriated for the embassy described—zenana—Surd Conna—jumma musjid—mausoleums—tomb of Khan Khanna—palaces on the banks of the Jumma—that river described—return to Sindia's camp—arrangements for the embassy's journey for Cawnpore—departure from the encampment and Agra for Cawnpore and Calcutta.

CHAPTER XXXVIII.

On Sir Charles Warre Malet's arrival at Agra, some difficulties arose, with respect to his meeting with Mahdajee Sindia, who was then encamped at Muttra, about twenty-eight miles from the city, with Shah Aalum, the degraded emperor of Delhi. The purport of this intended meeting was to concert with Mhadajee Sindia the best mode of completing the establishment of the embassy to the court of Poonah, in the manner most compatible with the interests of the English and the views of this great chieftain, through whom those interests had been for some time conducted with the peshwa, the supreme head of the Mahratta empire. This predicament, certainly of considerable delicacy, was soon cleared of its obstacles by the address of Mr. James Anderson, then resident minister from the government-general of India, with Mhadajee Sindia; and who, by the suavity of his manners, excellent understanding, perfect knowledge of the Persian and Hindostan languages, and peculiar fitness for his important situation, had established a considerable influence in the personal regard of this Mahratta chief.

On the 13th of May Sir Charles Malet received a letter from Mr. Anderson, dated at Sindia's camp, informing him that Baborao Duan and Appajee Tattea, two Mahratta chiefs of rank and consequence, were deputed to wait upon him, and conduct the embassy to the camp near Muttra. The same evening Appajee arrived at Agra with a party of cavalry, and presented himself at Taje Mahal, having left his colleague with a much larger escort at Gou Ghaut, twelve miles from Agra. In consequence of this arrangement, and the cattle and attendants being well refreshed, the baggage was ordered to proceed on the following day; and on the 16th they left the terrestrial paradise surrounding the Taje-Mahal, and commenced their journey towards Sindia's camp. A melancholy scene of ruin and desolation, similar to that already described, marked the first part of their progress from the royal gardens, through the suburbs and environs of Agra.

About half-way from thence to Gou Ghaut, or Ox-ford, they came to Secundra, celebrated for the mausoleum of Akber, situated within a large enclosure, resembling a park, shaded by noble trees, and entered by four handsome gates, leading to the roza, in the centre, which is a magnificent structure, inlaid with different coloured marble, agates, and precious stones, extremely rich and costly, but rather in a heavy style; the part most ornamented is on the uppermost terrace, and having no cover is entirely exposed to the weather; it is exquisitely finished, and the platform of black and white marble. The tomb itself is of plain white marble. The interior of the arch at the principal entrance is adorned with verses, expressive of the founder's extensive fame, and numerous victories, with moral reflections on the instability of human greatness.

The road from thence to Gou Ghaut was extremely pleasant:

Sir Charles was met there by Mhadajee's Sindia's duan, with a large party of horse to escort him to camp; he also received a letter from Mr. Anderson to express Sindia's wish that he would proceed as fast as convenient, being very desirous to have a personal interview. They arrived there the next morning, and found the Mahratta camp greatly enlarged by that of the emperor Shâh Aalum; who had appointed Mhadajee Sindia his vackeel ul mulluck, an office in the Mogul empire superior to the vizier Aazim. Mr. Anderson was also encamped near Muttra as English minister with the Mahratta chief, and was invested with powers to treat and negotiate with the last aged monarch of the imperial house of Timur. Mr. Anderson's suite consisted of a surgeon and a British officer in command of the two companies of sepoys which composed his guard.

The preliminaries of the ceremonial of the first meeting being arranged, the morning of the 20th was appointed for Sir Charles Malet's introduction to Mhadajee Sindia. Sir Charles and Mr. Anderson were mounted on the same elephant, and the gentlemen of their suite on others, or in palanquins. Mr. Anderson was escorted by a party of horse, appointed as a standing guard by the Mahratta chief; Sir Charles was attended by his own escort of horse and foot. They were met by Mhadajee Sindia some hundred yards from his tent, attended by his principal chiefs, a party of sepoys, a body of cavalry, and several elephants: he there alighted from his elephant, and, being extremely lame, was supported by two persons as he approached to embrace Sir Charles Malet, and the other gentlemen, in the order they were introduced by Mr. Anderson. He then preceded them to the durbar tent, where Sir Charles delivered Sindia a letter from the governor of Bombay. General conversation ensued, in which the Mahratta chief took a principal part, and in the course of it a gun of his own making was handed round for approbation, which was very liberally, and not undeservedly bestowed, if it really was of his own construction. But although he certainly has a turn for mechanics, the gun was rather supposed to have been the production of the artificers whom he employs than of his own hands.

After the presents had been distributed, and the usual formalities performed, the English gentlemen proceeded to their tents. On examining the khelauts, or presents, from the great Maha rajah Madajee Sindia, the serpeych (an ornament for the turban) presented to Sir Charles Malet was found to be composed of false stones; the horse and other articles of mean quality. The presents to the gentlemen of his family were two pieces of coarse chintz, a pair of very common shawls, an ordinary turban, and a piece of the cheapest keemcab.

Mr. Cruso's journal then proceeds. We rode the next morning to Muttra, or Mutturah, a large town on the banks of the river Jumma, much celebrated by the Hindoos. Several parts of it are in good repair, but much more in a state of ruin; there are still some good houses, the remains of a handsome serai, and two large musjids, one with four minarets and abundance of ornaments; the other more simple and more elegant.

On the 22d Sindia returned Sir Charles Malet's visit, and brought with him the favourite gun, to receive a second set of compliments. On the 24th the nabob Rujutt Coolee Khan, a man of great distinction and consequence, arrived in Sindia's camp, on business of importance. The first interview took place the following day; they met at a settled spot, rather nearer to the tents of the nabob than the Mahratta chief; there they alighted and embraced, and then proceeded together to Sindia's durbar tent. The interview was of considerable length, and many guns were fired as a compliment on both sides.

The following morning the nabob sent an invitation to the two English ministers, and the gentlemen accompanying them, to dine at his tents. We went there at three o'clock, and found about thirty dancing-girls collected for our entertainment. When the first civilities were over they began dancing, and continued for an hour; dinner being then announced, we adjourned to another tent, and found a table set out in the nicest order, profusely covered with a variety of dishes in the European and Mogul style. At seven we took leave, much against the wish of the nabob, who pressed us to stay a few hours longer.

On the 26th we went to Bhindera Bhund, a town about seven miles from Muttra, in high estimation with the Hindoos, and particularly celebrated as the birth-place of Crishna, the Apollo of India, in the brahmin mythology. The town is rather large, pleasantly situated on the banks of the Jumna, on which also, for near a mile in length, extends a range of small buildings called Dieuisthans, little Altars or Temples, with steps down to the water from each, for the convenience of the inhabitants, and religious pilgrims who resort thither to perform their ablutions. They are very neat, and form a pretty crescent of buildings, as the river takes that form in its course under them. In the centre is an elegant house on a small scale, lately built by the Jaypoor rajah. The exterior is decorated by a profusion of carved work, which does credit to the artist, and indicates some traces still remaining of that ingenuity which so eminently distinguishes the more ancient buildings in India. Here, seated on a cot in the uppermost apartment, we saw a gosaing, to whom the people who conducted us paid the greatest veneration, and related a number of improbabilities, and not a few impossibilities of this respectable personage. Among others, that he had been cast into a fire without being burnt, and could tread on the surface of the waters without wetting his feet. On questioning the brahmins whether they believed the stories they were now relating, they shrewdly replied, that as the gosaing was in high estimation with Himmut Bahaudur, and other chiefs of consequence, how could they discredit them?

The introduction of Sir Charles Malet to Shah Allum, "*King of the World*," the present Mogul emperor of Hindostan, or rather the shadow of the former Mogul emperors, has been hitherto deferred on account of his grand-daughter's death in the camp, which prevents his majesty from appearing in public; meanwhile we pass our time pleasantly, are well supplied with exceeding fine mutton and other excellent provisions from the Mahratta camp, and good beef from the Mogul bazar; vegetables are scarce, but we have plenty of melons, oranges, grapes, and mangos.

For some days past the weather has been extremely windy, with frequent andees, or whirlwinds, violent and disagreeable forerunners of the much-wished-for rainy season, or as Europeans call it, monsoon. The most severe took place yesterday afternoon, which overwhelming us in hot dust for half an hour, terminated in a refreshing shower of rain. Several of our people have been seized with tertian fevers, which in only one instance proved fatal; the patient having neglected his application for assistance until too late. There is a great deal of sickness in Sindia's camp.

On the 5th of June at six o'clock in the morning, we paid our visit, under Mr. James Anderson's introduction, to the king, whose encampment was not far from Sindia's head-quarters. On approaching the extensive inclosure of kinnauts, or canvas walls, which surrounded the imperial tents, we descended from our elephants, and got into palanquins. An amazing crowd of people filled the avenue, who were so intermingled and confused with the guard, that it was difficult to distinguish them. Before we entered the line, we were met by some officers of state to adjust the number of our attendants; it was settled that each gentleman of the suite should take only one servant. We then advanced towards the durbar tent, which was about fifty paces distant, where we discovered his imperial majesty seated on a silver throne ready to receive us. Three of his sons were standing on his right hand, and three on his left; and at the foot of the throne stood a favourite daughter about seven years old, having a turban on her head instead of a veil; his majesty was also attended by the few nobles who still adhered to the fallen monarch, and by an host of gold and silver stick-bearers. At this distance from the throne we were instructed to make the *tusleem*, or obeisance, three times. This ceremony consists in touching the ground with the right hand, and then carrying it to the head. We now advanced to the foot of the throne, where without speaking we presented our nuzzars, or offerings. Those of Sir Charles consisted of gold mohurs, each of the value of about two pounds sterling, rich shawls, keemcabs, and cloths of various kinds; with several curiosities in agates, cut-glass, and silver fillagree caskets, which his majesty seemed to admire; though the expression of any sensation is generally held incompatible with Mogul dignity on such occasions. A few gold mohurs were presented to each of the princes; my offering was five gold mohurs to his majesty only. The offering of a soldier is his sword, and the acceptance of it is signified by touching it.

Mr. Anderson and his suite having gone through the various ceremonies of introduction at the imperial durbar, a repetition was not expected. His majesty and the imperial princes having graciously accepted of our several tokens of respect, we returned to the place of obeisance, and thrice repeated the compliment, having received an intimation from one of the ushers to take the greatest care in retiring, not to turn our backs on the throne. We now took our stand with the rest of the gentlemen on the left of his majesty, with our hands placed one upon the other, laid across upon the waist. The emperor then entered into conversation relative to the country we had passed through in our long journey. In a short time we were informed that our *kullats* (honorary dresses) were prepared in a place allotted for our investiture. In our way thither we had to stop at the salaming spot, and perform the *tusleem* a third time. From thence being conducted into a pavilion open to numerous spectators, we were invested with a Mogul robe over our coat. We then for the fourth time paid our respects at the usual spot, and advanced to the foot of the throne, to shew ourselves in our new habiliments. His majesty then condescended to tie with his own hands a serpeych on Sir Charles's hat, and caused a bridle, as the symbol of a horse, and an aunkus, the symbol of an elephant, to be delivered to him. The aunkus is the instrument by which the elephant is driven and controlled; its handle is generally of wood, having an iron point to goad forward, and a hook to restrain or keep back. These additional marks of favour caused a repetition of Sir Charles's retrograde steps to the place of obeisance, from whence he returned to his station among the courtiers. Having thus paid his respects for this high distinction, the emperor conferred upon him a still higher honour by a phirmaun of Mogùl nobility, as an ameer of the empire. After waiting for some time longer in the demure attitude abovementioned, without a word being uttered by any person, the *King of the World* descended from his throne, and we moved once more to perform our obeisance. During this etiquette at the Mogul durbar, if his majesty asks any person present after his health, he must immediately make the retrograde motions and perform the tusleem. This was now practised by Mr. Anderson, who received that condescending mark of royal distinction.

On our return to the tents we found a horse and an elephant, the addition to Sir Charles's kullat. The royal gifts of a horse, an elephant, a princely dress, and a tiara of jewels, sound very grand, and as a part of the formula of the introduction of eminent visitors at the Mogul court, were not to be despised; but on examination, the diamond and emerald serpeych was found to be composed of green glass and false stones; the horse was worn out, and in the last stage of existence; and the elephant, on taking off his trappings, discovered a long ulcerated wound on the back, from the shoulder to the tail. The whole was emblematical of the fallen state of the unfortunate monarch, or rather the shadow of a prince, by whom they were presented. But for the honour of the imperial dignity it should be added, that Mhadajee Sindia, who had recently assumed the high office of Vackeel ul Mulluck, or absolute minister, supplied every thing on this occasion, even to the minutest article.

This unfortunate representative of the Timurean race, was about sixty years of age, of the common stature, and of a countenance bespeaking a placid and benignant mind; with an air and deportment of habitual dignity tempered by much affability. Three years after this interview he fell into the hands of Gulam Kaudir Khán, a rebellious chieftain, who caused the aged monarch to be blinded in a most barbarous manner. As the particulars of this cruel transaction are not inserted in Mr. Cruso's journal, nor transmitted me by Sir Charles Malet, it may be satisfactory, and will render the narrative more complete, to relate them briefly from an authentic account printed at Bengal soon after the perpetration of this horrid crime.

Gulam Kaudir Khán was the son of Zabda Khán: his father disinherited him and drove him from his presence on account of his vices and crimes. Shah Aalum, the emperor of Delhi, took him under his protection, treated him as his own son, and conferred on him the first title in the kingdom, Omeel ul Omraow; he lived with the emperor, and raised a body of about eight thousand troops of his own countrymen, the Moguls, which he commanded. Gulam Kaudir was of a passionate temper, haughty, cruel, ungrateful, and debauched.

In the latter end of the year 1788, the emperor had formed suspicions that some of the neighbouring rajahs would make an attempt to plunder and destroy his territories: these suspicions were verified by the approach of a considerable army towards his capital, commanded by Ismael Beg Khan, and assisted by Dowlut Row Sindia. Gulam Kaudir told the emperor on this, that he had nothing to fear, he having an army sufficiently strong to oppose the enemy; and that all the emperor had to do, was to march out with his troops, give them a supply of cash, and he would stake his head on the enemy's being overcome. To this the emperor replied, that he had no money to carry on the contest. Gulam Kaudir said this should be no objection, as he would advance the necessary supply of cash, and that all his majesty had to do was to head the army. "This," said he, "will animate and give them courage, as the presence of a monarch is above half the battle." The emperor agreed in appearance, and requested Gulam Kaudir to assemble the army, pay their arrears, and inform them of his intentions. Gulam Kaudir retired contented, but great was his astonishment when he intercepted, the next day, a letter from the emperor to Sindia, desiring him to make all possible haste and destroy Gulam Kaudir; "for," as the letter expresses it, "Gulam Kaudir desires me to act contrary to my wishes, and oppose you."

On this discovery Gulam Kaudir marched out with his Moguls, crossed the Jumna, and encamped on the other side, opposite to the fort of Delhi. He then sent the emperor the intercepted letter, and asked him if his conduct did not deserve to be punished by the loss of his throne? He began to besiege the fort, and carried it in a few days; he entered the palace in arms, flew to his majesty's chamber, treated the aged monarch in the most barbarous manner, knocked him down, and kneeling on his breast, took out one of his eyes, and ordered a servant of the emperor to take out the other.

After this he gave the place up to pillage, and went to the royal zenana, where he insulted the ladies, tore the jewels from their noses and ears, and cut off their arms and legs. As he had lived with the emperor, he was well acquainted with the places where the royal treasures were concealed; he dug up the stone of the emperor's own bed-chamber, and found there two chests, containing in specie an hundred and twenty thousand gold mohurs, about two hundred thousand pounds sterling; this he carried off, with other considerable sums. To get at the hidden jewels of the women, he practised one of the most villainous schemes ever thought of; the third day after these horrid cruelties, he ordered that all the emperor's ladies and daughters should come and pay their respects to him, and promised to set free those who should please him by their appearance and dress. The innocent unthinking women brought out their jewels, and adorned themselves in their richest attire to please this savage. Gulam Kaudir commanded them to be conveyed to a hall, where he had prepared common dresses for them. These dresses he made them put on by the assistance of eunuchs; and taking possession of their rich dresses and jewels, he sent the women home to the palace to lament their loss and curse his treachery. Gulam Kaudir did not stop even here, but insulted the princesses by making them dance and sing. The most beautiful of the emperor's daughters, Mobarouk ul Moulk, was brought to the tyrant to gratify his lust; but she resisted, and is said to have stabbed herself to avoid force.

Sindia soon after this came to the assistance of the emperor, or rather to make him his prey. Gulam Kaudir fled, and took refuge in the fort of Agra. Sindia's troops besieged him there. Perceiving at last that he must be taken if he remained in the fort, he took advantage of a dark night, stuffed his saddle with a large quantity of precious stones, took a few followers, and fled from the fort towards Persia. Unluckily for him, he fell off his horse the second night after his flight, and by this means a party of horse, which had been sent in pursuit of him, came up and took him prisoner. He was brought to Sindia; who after exposing him for some time in irons, and some time in a cage, ordered his ears, nose, hands and feet to be cut off, and his eyes taken out, in which state he was allowed to expire.

No immediate object presenting to occupy the attention of Sir Charles Malet after his conferences with Mhadajee Sindia and Shah Aalum, he adopted the plan of visiting Delhi, the ancient and far-famed capital of Hindostan; and having obtained the emperor's permission, and a party of horse from Mhadajee Sindia, the embassy proceeded thither on the 7th of June 1785, and reached it on the 10th.

The journey from Muttra to Delhi was not very interesting; the country entirely flat, with the Mewat hills in the distance, was no doubt fertile and pleasant in the flourishing state of the capital, but now, almost depopulated by famine, and the oppressions of the late changeable and rapacious occupants, it presented a melancholy aspect. In consequence of its uncultivated state, rats had multiplied in the fields in a most extraordinary manner, and wolves had become formidably numerous.

At the different stages on this road there are in general good serais, and large towns and villages, mostly on eminences, which, as the country is entirely a plain, were most probably formed by the succession of buildings and ruins for ages past, on the same spot. The road is infested by tribes of banditti called googurs and mewatties; but a light escort of fifty cavalry was a sufficient protection from insult. The infantry and heavy baggage were left at the encampment near Muttra. The soil between Agra and Delhi is uniformly sandy, entirely covered with a wild shrub called conkra, bearing a flower resembling the ranunculus, succeeded by a pod, which opening when ripe, scatters abroad a kind of silky cotton, containing the seed, which overruns the country. The lactaceous juice of the whole plant is used externally by the natives, as a remedy against bruises and sprains. What is thought remarkable in this part of Hindostan, and would hardly be credited by an inhabitant of Guzerat, is, that the whole of this sandy plain, when in a state of culture, produced abundant crops of excellent wheat.

Handsome brick minarets of a considerable height, instead of stones, as in Europe, mark the distance from Agra to Delhi, many of them in very good repair; but the road having in course of time, and by the prostration of property, been much altered, they are in many places a great way from the present road. They seem to be regulated by the jereeby measurement, of twenty-five guz to one jereeb, and two hundred jereebs to one coss. The rismi coss, which is the general rule of computing distance, falls considerably short of this measure. The distance from Sindia's encampment to Delhi is fifty-eight rismi coss; about eighty-seven English miles.

The ruins of serais, mosques, mausoleums, and other magnificent structures, commenced about three or four miles before the entrance of the present city. Amidst the melancholy heaps, the tomb of the emperor Humaioon, still in perfect preservation, stands conspicuous; the obelisk of Cutbal Deen is equally so, at a distance on the left. About a mile and a half from the gate of the new city of Shah Jehanabad is the old fort, standing in the midst of the ruins of the old city of Delhi; it is a most ponderous structure, and of great antiquity; but the excellence of its masonry, notwithstanding its being totally neglected, has in general withstood the ravages of time. From some circumstances, particularly the appearance of the only gate toward the river Jumna, it seems to have been originally visited by its stream, though the channel is now at least half a mile from it. The new city called Shah Jehan-abad, from its founder Shah Jehan, is about sixteen miles in circuit, and now occupies the space between the old city and the river, on whose bank it stands. Its citadel is the imperial palace; the streets are broad and level, mostly paved with brick, but the houses are low and mean. An aqueduct occupies the centre of the principal streets, built by the Ameer Ally Murdaen Khan, by which he brought water from Kurnal to Delhi, a distance of seventy miles; the greater part is now in ruins.

The ameers' palaces, though extremely spacious and elegantly disposed within, make no figure from without, being all excluded from observation by walls, and a dewry, or gateway, in which there is room for an ample guard; and over it for the nobut-konna, or band of music, which is one of the appendages of certain ranks of nobility. It was usual for all the Mogul ameers to have mansions in the capital. Their magnitude in general, on account of their immense establishments, exceeded any of the palaces belonging to the nobility in Europe. Not only the palaces above mentioned, but in fact every habitable house is in Shah Jehan-abad. The old city of Delhi is an entire scene of desolation; not a human being to be seen in the ancient metropolis of this vast empire.

From Mr. Cruso's Journal.

I was driven for shelter from a shower into the old fort, which is still thinly peopled by herdsmen, gardeners, and labourers. On approaching the new city we passed several extensive gardens; but the owners not being able to afford gardeners, have built up the gate-ways, to prevent the entrance of cattle and destruction of the pleasure-houses; the walls being very high, we could not see the interior. At length we reached a garden belonging to an omrah still in power; this being open and well taken care of, I had the curiosity to alight, and was highly gratified with the view of a large square, laid out with some degree of taste in beds of flowers, surrounded by a number of dwarf pomegranate trees, bending under a weight of fruit of the largest size and richest colour. From thence we descended by many steps into another garden of similar dimensions, with an arched walk on one side shaded by grape-vines, entirely covered with large bunches of fruit in the most tempting profusion; but although now near the middle of June, they were still unripe; whereas when we left Surat two months before the grape season was over. This second square is thickly planted with fruit trees in great variety; among them a number of peaches, the first I have seen in India, not yet ripe; neither were the pempelnoos, or shadocks, which were equally abundant. Figs, which were nearly over at Surat, were still unripe at Delhi, so were the small oranges, (called at Bombay the Aurungabad oranges) which we have purchased at most of the principal towns since leaving Oojen. We have in this latitude one great advantage over the southern provinces of Hindostan, in a journey at this season, when the day breaks at four in the morning, and it is not dark until eight in the evening.

We entered the new city at the Delhi gate, leading to a long street of a miserable appearance, containing one very handsome musjid, with gilded domes; from thence we were conducted along one face of the fort, to the house, or rather palace allotted for our accommodation. It was a spacious edifice, or rather a multiplication of courts and edifices, built by Sufder Jung; still belonging to his descendant Asuph ul Dowlah, and lately occupied by his vackeel, the eunuch Lutafut, a man of great consequence at this period. Here we found convenient quarters for all our party, totally distinct from each other; also for our cattle and attendants.

In the evening, on taking a more complete view of this Mogul mansion, we were surprised to find the apartments just mentioned formed only a very small part of this immense pile, which occupies six squares, corresponding with that in which we immediately reside. Each of them comprising an elegant mansion, capable of accommodating, in a magnificent style, half a dozen numerous families, while the various ranges of inferior rooms, lodges, and out-offices of every description, were amply sufficient to cover, at the least, five thousand troops; there were also stables for five hundred horses.

The hall, which we converted into a dining room, was a square of sixty-three feet, opening in front to a pretty garden, and backwards to a large tank, paved with marble, for cold bathing. Two rows of handsome pillars in front gave it an elegant appearance; the roof of carved wood was beautifully painted. On each side of the hall was a central large room, and two smaller, the former with a cove roof, the latter under a dome. The pannels, walls, and ceilings of these rooms were all carved and painted with taste, the concave roofs ornamented with borders and compartments of chain-work, painted white, and the interstices filled with looking-glass. The windows were of a composition like isinglass, which only the nicest examination, or the touch could distinguish from glass. They had a peculiar light and airy appearance, disposed in a pretty tracery. The small recesses, which in most Indian buildings are formed in the walls, and generally produce a disagreeable effect, are in these rooms rendered ornamental by the well-adapted expedient of introducing fruit and flowers, painted in a brilliant style.

Some smaller apartments in a different quarter, which formed part of the haram, were entirely lined with looking-glass, and the octagonal columns around them covered with the same material. This range, when illuminated in the former profuse fashion of the Moguls, must have made a brilliant appearance. Belonging to this part of the zenana, I had, for the first time, an opportunity of seeing another species of eastern luxury, in the apartment called surd conna, or teh konna, which signifies in Persian, cool place, or below-ground place. To this we descended by a long flight of steps, and found it consisted of a subterraneous gallery, divided into three distinct rooms; the whole occupied a space seventy-eight feet long, by twenty-seven broad. The side divisions were raised two steps above the centre, which was entered through two arches, formed by marble pillars, exquisitely wrought; in front was a low elegant railing; and between the side rooms, within these marble arches, were three fountains, to cool the atmosphere, when the ladies were there assembled, such places being generally appropriated to the pleasures of the voluptuous Mogul, and his favourites in the haram. The whole of this singular apartment, the walls, pavement, and pillars are of delicate white marble; the concave domes which form the roof are richly painted, in such a manner as to produce the effect of blue and silver. The light is admitted by three lattices, so constructed as to prevent the rays of the sun.

The morning after our arrival we visited the jumma musjid, a noble building which does honour to the magnificent taste of its founder, the emperor Shah Jehan, who erected this superb edifice five years after the completion of the Taje Mahal at Agra. The entrances are all extremely grand, the lofty minars elegantly fluted, and the whole in good preservation. Besides the jumma musjid, are many smaller mosques; some with gilded domes make a dazzling appearance, the majority are of plainer materials, and many falling to decay.

Our limited stay at Delhi prevented us from seeing more of the city than came within the compass of this morning's ride. On leaving the jumma musjid, we proceeded through several streets, despicably poor, and thinly inhabited. Two or three of a larger size seemed more populous, were of considerable breadth, and occupied by the aqueduct already mentioned in the centre, now in a state of dilapidation.

The fort of Delhi has more the appearance of an ornamented wall, constructed round a royal residence, than a fortification against an enemy. To such an extreme has this expensive taste been carried, that all the towers, erected at stated distances along the walls of the fortress, are covered with domes of white marble, richly ornamented with gold.

The following morning we rode through the suburbs, to view the celebrated mausoleums. That of Humaioon is truly magnificent, and occupies a large space; the centre dome is uncommonly bold, and admirably formed, the lower part divided into numerous sepulchral chambers, each containing the tomb of some relation of the royal line, whose body is deposited beneath the platform. These chambers, connected with each other, penetrate the whole extent, and were individually appropriated to a descendant of the house of Timur. These are too numerous to particularise; but among them is the chamber of Allum Geer Saunee, father of Shah Aalum the present emperor; another containing the remains of his eldest son; a third of his sister. The tombs placed over the bodies are all of plain white marble chunam, the exterior sepulchres of white marble.

The mausoleum of Khan Khannah, or Lord of Lords, the vizier of Humaioon, stands near the sepulchre of his royal master. This edifice is said to be characteristic of its founder, constructed at a great expense without taste or elegance, and such was the extraordinary dissipation and extravagance of Khan Khannah as to have become proverbial. He was originally a slave named Phaheem, Khan Khannah being his honorary title, which gave occasion to this proverb, peculiarly expressive in the Persian language; " what Khan Khannah amasses, Phaheem squanders." The stories related of his boundless profusion are not less numerous than wonderful.

Within the compass of half a mile are several other large structures, sacred to the memory of Mogul ameers or nobles, and peers, or holy men, some of elegant proportion. That which most attracted our attention was a mausoleum, beautiful in appearance, and delightful in situation, at three miles distance, containing the remains of Munsure Ally Khan, grandfather of Asuph ul Dowlah; this is executed with great taste. On my return I missed the Delhi-gate, and wandered among the ruins, until I arrived at a portal into the city, on that side which is washed by the Jumna, which gave me an opportunity of seeing much the prettiest part of this ancient capital. On this face are a number of beauiful palaces and pavilions, situated in the midst of verdant groves; their gilded domes, and varied style of architecture, reflected in the clear stream gliding gently below the walls, fully compensated for my lengthened journey. The Jumna at Delhi is so extremely narrow, and the stream of so little depth, that I saw the washermen cross it in many places not higher than their middle. The opposite country is so extremely low, that in the rainy season it must be entirely under water.

The next evening (13th of June) we set off on our return to

Sindia's camp, and instead of a magnificent palace, passed the night in a miserable roofless hut. The next evening brought us to our former pleasant quarters at Ooral, and on the third day we arrived at Sindia's camp. Sir Charles having finished his public business with Mhadajee Sindia, through Mr. James Anderson, so far as related to personal communication, we remained there only two days, and then returned to our royal apartments at the Taje Mahal at Agra, where we arrived on the 18th.

The object of Sir Charles Malet's mission to Mhadajee Sindia having been accomplished by the conciliation of that chieftain to the establishment of his embassy at the court of Poonah, Sir Charles received orders early in July to proceed to Calcutta, there to receive the requisite powers and instructions from the Governor-General, Sir John Macpherson, who had succeeded Mr. Hastings since the commencement of the embassy, for carrying the negociations into effect. In consequence of these orders the escort of regular sepoys and native cavalry, also the elephants, horses, camels, and attendants which had hitherto been necessary, but would now become an encumbrance, were put under the care of Mirza Syed Mahomed, with orders to proceed to Gwalier, there to await the junction of such other camels and followers, as it might be necessary and practicable to return from Caunpore, from whence Sir Charles Malet and suite intended to embark on the Ganges, and proceed by water to Calcutta. On the arrival of the party from Caunpore, Mirza Syed was to conduct the whole from Gwalier to Surat.

Having thus completed every requisite previous arrangement,

the embassy, with its reduced equipment, left Agra on the 21st of July, to cross the *Doaub*, the Mesopotamia of India, for Caunpore, the nearest military station belonging to the East India Company under the Bengal government. From Surat to Agra, Sir Charles and his party had travelled entirely on horseback; from hence to Caunpore they intended proceeding in palanquins.

CHAPTER XXXIX.

CONCLUSION OF THE JOURNEY FROM SURAT TO CALCUTTA, CONTAINING AN ACCOUNT OF THE COUNTRY CALLED THE DOUAB, FROM AGRA TO CAWNPORE: WITH A DESCRIPTION OF ALLAHABAD, BENARES, AND THE PRINCIPAL PLACES ON THE BANKS OF THE GANGES FROM CAWNPORE TO CALCUTTA.

1785.

"Thrice happy, blest Britannia's bounded kings!
"To clothe the naked, feed the hungry, wipe
"The guiltless tear from lone Affliction's eye;
"To raise hid Merit, set the alluring light
"Of Virtue high to view; to nourish Arts,
"Direct the thunder of an injur'd state,
"Make a whole glorious people sing for joy,
"Bless human kind, and through the downward depth
"Of future times to spread that better sun
"Which lights up British soul: for deeds like these,
"The dazzling fair career unbounded lies;
"While (still superior bliss) the dark abrupt
"Is kindly barr'd, the precipice of ill.
"O luxury divine! O poor to this
"Ye giddy glories of *despotic thrones!*
"By this, by this indeed, is imag'd Heaven,
"The boundless Good, without the pow'r of Ill."

THOMSON.

CONTENTS.

ment to his memory—Cotgong—Peer Payntee, or Saint's town—Sickligullie—Fall of Pearls—Rajemahl—Jumma Musjid—Ooda-nulla—Bhaugretty river—Cossimbazar—Moorsheabad—Lake of pearls—palace—curious dwarf horses—sya-goos—tame fish—Duperah, a Hindoo festival—manner of celebrating it on the Ganges—singular boats—Plassey—Plassey-house and grove—variety of game—quantity destroyed on a shooting party—Baugretty and Jellinghy rivers—drowning of dying Hindoos—funeral dirges—dandies or boatmen on the Ganges—their mode of life—Chinsura, Chandernagore, Serampore,—arrival at Calcutta.

CHAPTER XXXIX.

SIR Charles Malet, as already mentioned, having made every arrangement necessary for our journey to Caunpore, we left Agra in the afternoon of the 21st of July, and made our first stage to Hemetpore, six coss distant. The country was neither interesting nor well cultivated; about half-way we crossed a deep narrow river, provided with a ferry-boat at the pass, and on arriving at Hemetpore, put up for the night under a large dome in the centre of a tank, and found it a comfortable accommodation.

The rainy season in this part of Hindostan commenced the beginning of June. So much had fallen when we left Delhi as to render our journey from thence to Agra extremely delightful, and clothe the country with fresh verdure. Having made arrangements to travel chiefly in palanquins, and proceed a morning and evening stage each day during the remainder of the journey, we set off at four the next morning for Ferozabad, where we arrived at nine, and halted until evening in a small mosque, about five hundred yards from the town, near a large pleasant garden. Ferozabad, seven coss from Hemetpore, is a large populous town, belonging to Hemet Bahauder, miserably infested by religious beggars.

When the sun declined we commenced our second stage of five

coss to Shakuabad; something more than half way we came to Muckenpore, the commencement of the territory belonging to Asuph-ul-Dowlah, nabob of Oude. The road was generally through a flat marshy country, abounding with water-fowl, except near the entrance of Shakuabad, where a gentle rise of hills diversified the prospect. We passed the night within the serai, and found the town noisy, populous, and full of prostitutes.

The next morning at day-break we left our disagreeable lodging, and travelling through a marshy country, and heavy rain, stopped a short time at a village to rest the bearers; but finding only wretched accommodation we were under the necessity of proceeding to Jesswant-Nugghur, fourteen coss from Shakuabad. It is a spacious town, well inhabited, but overrun with Fakeers and other mendicants, who might be usefully employed in cleaning the streets, which are filthy to the last degree. The general aspect of the district this day, though flat, was beautifully wooded, and abounded with antelopes.

On the 24th we left Jesswant-Nugghur before sun-rise, and travelling six coss through a beautiful country, and a good road, we reached Attowe, or Ettaya, at eight o'clock. Here we were accommodated with a large house in the midst of a garden, profusely stocked with roses, jasmin, tuberoses, and other flowers, varied by fruit-trees. The rain continuing very heavy, we passed the remainder of the day in this delightful situation, and at three the next morning proceeded to Buckeur, a small village at seven coss distance. The road was good, and the country beautiful; we stopped there eight hours, and then went on another stage of five coss to Adjut-Mhel, a large populous town, remarkably neat and clean, with a good serai, and a pretty mosque in its centre. Here we passed the night, and early on the following morning continued our journey through a country richly adorned with groves of mangos and tamarinds. After travelling seven coss we reached Auriah, a neat and populous town, with a comfortable serai; but preferring a mango tope without the town, we unfortunately attracted the attention of two sets of dancing-girls, who annoyed us a long time; the more so, as they possessed neither beauty, grace, nor harmony. We left the grove and its sirens soon after three o'clock, and before sun-set arrived at Secundra, five coss from Auriah. The road was excellent and the country uncommonly beautiful, especially between Cojepore and Secundra; the former is remarkable for the ruins of a grand serai, and a noble tank, in a sad state of dilapidation. Secundra is surrounded by beautiful groves. We passed the night among some majestic ruins, on the margin of a large tank without the town, which contains nothing remarkable.

Soon after three o'clock on the next morning, we proceeded through a wild country to Tunwapore, a wretched village, almost depopulated, and affording no convenience for a traveller, except a shady clump of trees, where we halted six or seven hours, and then renewed our journey to Akberpore, which we reached at sunset. The greater part of the road was through a country intersected by deep gullies, particularly near the river Singore, where we found a ferry-boat at the pass. After crossing it, we re-entered the ravines and gullies, at this season covered with jungle, or underwood, in full verdure. This irregular scenery differs widely from the rest of the country called the *Dooab*. Emerging from these gullies about two miles from Akberpore, we entered a lovely plain, and reached the town by an excellent road. It is not easy to fancy a more delightful spot for the accommodation of an oriental traveller. The buildings are spacious, the groves shady and varied, and the prospects no less singular than magnificent. In our front was an ancient edifice, on the margin of an extensive lake, with a picturesque island in the centre; a building of modern architecture, never finished, adorned the brow of a hill half a mile further, near a large tank, environed by pagodas, mosques, minars, and other decorations, each deserving a particular description.

We left this delightful situation before three o'clock the following morning, and at seven reached Chechindee, seven coss from Akberpore: it is a large town, situated in a pleasant country, in a much better state of cultivation than any we have been lately accustomed to. The next stage brought us to Caunpore, a large cantonment belonging to the East India Company, on the west bank of the Ganges, situated in the *Douab*, literally *two-waters*, being that tract of country lying between the Jumna and the Ganges, over which we had now travelled from Agra to Caunpore, a distance of one hundred and seventy miles.

The whole road from Agra, on the banks of the Jumna, to Caunpore on the Ganges, being across the Douab, is through a flat country and a light soil, apparently fertile, and richly wooded, with beautiful mango groves, and other umbrageous trees. The inhabitants in general, both Hindoo and Mahomedan, are tall and handsome, with a peculiar neatness, I could almost say elegance, of form and feature. They are also reckoned remarkably brave and high-spirited. The villages have commonly little mud forts attached to them, which on the late reduction of the country by the vizier, frequently made a gallant defence, even against our regular troops acting with him: those forts are now mostly dismantled. As we left the Jumna and approached the Ganges, we found the country more populous, better cultivated, and abundant in cattle, the late famine having raged with much less violence in this part of the Douab. I wish also to impute it in some measure to the better government of our ally the vizier, under British influence.

Caunpore is the Company's most remote northerly military station, except Futty-Ghur. It does not seem to be judiciously chosen; for, if with a view to protect the Douab, Etaya appears to be preferable: if to support the vizier's government in Lucknow, the opposite side of the river seems to claim the preference. The brigade stationed at Caunpore, consists of about ten thousand men, including infantry, cavalry, and artillery; from which I understand the force at Futty-Ghur is a detachment.

Thus, from Mr. Cruso's journal, contained in about five hundred folio manuscript pages, and the valuable communications from Sir Charles Malet, I have conducted the embassy from the Taptee to the Ganges; a journey exceeding eight hundred miles, chiefly through a country hitherto but little known. It is not my intention to enter into military details at the different cantonments in the Bengal provinces, nor to particularize the manners, customs, amusements, and local habits in the British character, which are fully discussed throughout the remainder of the journal. The journey from Surat to Caunpore had been entirely among the natives, and I selected only what I thought would furnish novelty, interest, and entertainment. The narrative, exclusive of more valuable information, has given life and spirit to a set of unconnected memoranda, collected from the information of Gosaings, Vanjarras, and other travellers at Dhuboy, which were reserved for a separate chapter, as not being derived from my own knowledge. In the sequel I shall sedulously confine myself to the general aspect of the provinces, the remains of the once-splendid cities, and the native inhabitants of a country, which, like Guzerat, was formerly dignified with that expressive title, the PARADISE of NATIONS.

> "Scenes, where the gorgeous East with richest hand
> Shower'd on her kings barbaric pearl and gold:
> Where goodliest trees, laden with fairest fruit,
> Blossoms and fruits at once of golden hue
> Appear'd, with gay enamell'd colours mix'd:
> On which the sun more glad impress'd his beams,
> Than in fair evening cloud, or humid bow,
> When God hath shower'd the earth: so lovely seem'd
> That landscape—a land where gentle gales,
> Fanning their odoriferous wings, dispense
> Native perfumes, and whisper whence they stole
> Those balmy spoils." MILTON.

The journal dwells with grateful delight on the warm reception of Sir Charles Malet and his party at Caunpore, particularly under the hospitable roof of their friendly host Mr. Munro; and the successive entertainments provided for them by the commandant Colonel Ironside, and the officers on that station, amounting to about three hundred. Friendship and hospitality so universally mark the British character in India that I shall suppose it always understood.

Among the various amusements at Caunpore were abundance of *Nautches*, or exhibitions by the dancing-girls of the country, which, however pleasing, were far exceeded by a set of young girls lately arrived from Cachemire, of such surpassing beauty, grace, and elegant accomplishments, that, not venturing on the detail, I shall proceed to the distressing circumstances attendant on the nightly visits of the numerous wolves by which the cantonment and its vicinity had been for some time infested. These savage animals were it seems first attracted thither in such numbers, during the late dreadful famine, by the dead bodies of the poor wretches, who, crawling for relief, perished through weakness before they could obtain it; and filled up every avenue to the cantonment with their sad remains. Long accustomed to human food, they would not leave their haunts, and were now grown so fierce, that they not only frequently carried off children, but actually attacked the sentries on their posts, who had in consequence been doubled. The first night the embassy arrived at Caunpore, Sir Charles Malet ordered his cot, or bed, to be placed in the garden, and was surprised in the morning to hear that a goat had been carried off from very near the place where he slept.

Three of these monsters, as Mr. Cruso was credibly assured, had attacked a sentinel, who after shooting one, and dispatching another with his bayonet, was overpowered by the third, and killed at his post. While the embassy was there, a man, his wife, and child, sleeping in their hut, the former at a little distance, the mother was awakened by the struggles and shrieks of the child locked in her arms, which a prowling wolf had seized by the leg, and was dragging from her bosom. She grasped the infant, and exerted all her strength to preserve it from the foe, but in vain; the ravenous animal tore it from her maternal embrace, and instantly devoured it.

After a few delightful days at Caunpore, on the 10th of August we reluctantly entered the budgerows, or boats, provided for our voyage to Calcutta, consisting of one for each gentleman, a kitchen-boat, and others for the clerks and servants of the embassy. We dropped down with the stream to Nudjuf Ghur, at eighteen miles distance, where we were hospitably entertained for some days by Colonel Ironside, commandant of the station.

On the 15th we reimbarked, and keeping close along the banks of the Ganges, covered at this season by the most luxuriant vegetation, we had a distinct view of a varied scenery, consisting of pagodas, fortresses, and villages, in various stages of prosperity and decay; with dark groves and rich pastures, abounding with flocks and herds; which, uniting with the irregularity of the shore, afforded a constant succession of delightful objects.

We arrived on the 18th at Allahabad, an imperial fortress built by Akber, Jehanghire, and Shah Jehan, (three succeeding princes on the throne of Delhi) on the site of the ancient and holy Hindoo city Praag, proudly situated at the confluence of the Ganges and Jumna: one face of the fortifications extends along the banks of each of these celebrated rivers. The outward appearance of the walls resembles that of Agra and Delhi, though less magnificent. The expensive gates and other costly workmanship, rather indicate the elegant enclosure of a palace than a strong and judicious fortification. In the first is a pillar inscribed in Persian characters with the names of the imperial descendants of Timur; the expenses of the building are engraved in the Hindoo language. The second court forms an oblong square, surrounded by a range of handsome apartments, covered with domes, formerly occupied by the royal household. The third square contains the famous subterranean Hindoo temple, erected over the pepel tree, from whence the city takes its name. This celebrated tree is said to have resisted every attempt made by the Mahomedan invaders to destroy it, and many are the stories told to that purpose. In consequence of these vain efforts, the Mahomedans themselves are said to have called the spot Allahabad, or the ABODE OF GOD.

The temple being perfectly dark, we descended by torch-light to a square supported by numerous pillars, extremely damp, and pervious to the water from the surface, which drops down in many places, and makes the floor wet and dirty: The sides are filled with niches, containing a variety of Hindoo deities of a similar character, and much the same kind of sculpture, as many in the excavations at the Elephanta. On the side facing the sea is the celebrated pepel tree, (ficus religiosa, Lin.) preserved by miracle, and surrounded by a low circular wall, like most consecrated trees of the Hindoos.

The inner square contains the palace; situated in the centre, it overlooks twelve other squares, in which were the habitations of the royal concubines, where the voluptuous monarch could receive the homage of the whole without moving from his apartments. The palace is heavy, incommodious, and ill executed. It forms a square, with a fountain and cascade on each front. The zenana indicates nothing remarkable in its structure, but the side overlooking the Jumna is very pleasant, above a large court, where the emperor, seated in an upper pavilion, received the prostrations of his subjects.

The grand mosque going fast to decay, is debased to a grain-market. It has been extremely beautiful, and its situation at the immediate confluence of the two rivers, is truly fine. The Hindoo bathing-place is at the bottom of the fort; a flight of indifferent steps leads to the Ganges, where the brahmins make the sacred marks on the face after performing their ablutions. There are three remarkable trees opposite Poppamow, called by the natives Valattee-Emlee, or Europe tamarind, the Adansonia of Linnæus; the centre one measures thirty-two feet six inches round the trunk, the tree on the left nearly an inch more, and the other not quite thirty feet. They grow within fifty yards of the Ganges; and about three hundred yards distance is another of still larger circumference. The branches of these celebrated trees rise from the trunks by a large base, disproportioned to their general bulk. The first was extremely small when I saw it, and covered with a down of light green like velvet; it ripens in February, the fruit is then the size of a cocoa-nut, containing a white pulp, abounding with red seeds. The brahmins spoke highly of this fruit, thinking it extremely delicious, and the acid peculiarly grateful.

The mausoleum of Kusroe, the son of Jehanghire, and brother of Shah Jehan, said to have been assassinated by his connivance, stands at the extremity of Allahabad, without the walls, near the tombs of his mother and sister. The tomb of Kusroe is of plain white marble; the dome which covers it, and all the rest of the whole structure is free-stone. The garden shews the remains of walks, canals, and fountains; the buildings are appropriated to a battalion of sepoys stationed here by the vizier. The town in general is populous, the streets long and straggling, the houses mean, and such of the women as fell under our notice, remarkably plain.

In respect to the junction of the Ganges and Jumna, the velocity with which the latter rushes into the former is worthy of remark. It occasions a visible rise across the stream, and turned round the boat in which we attempted crossing, with an inconceivable rapidity.

From Allahabad we went down the Ganges on the 21st to Chunar, called by the natives Chundal-Ghur. This fort is strongly situated on a hill, with a disadvantage of being commanded by one still higher. The commandant's house is a fine building, and the staff officers have an excellent suite of apartments. The mausoleums of Shah Cossim Soolimanee, and Shah Wassub, are singularly beautiful; and the stone railings which enclose these shrines, are curiously wrought in open mosaic patterns. The quarries at Chunar furnish abundantly a light-coloured stone, resembling Portland stone, which is easily worked, and well adapted for public buildings of the natives, on which they lavish a variety of ornamental sculpture. The city of Calcutta is supplied with this useful article from the quarries at Chunar, easily transported by water.

We next stopped a short time at Ramnaghur, where a heavy pile of building forms a fortified palace on the brink of the river;

behind it is the town of Ramnaghur, from whence a road is carried for about a mile through fields of roses and mogrees, to the new pagoda, tank, and gardens, left unfinished by the famous ex-rajah Cheyte Sihng. The garden and tank are each two hundred yards square. The pagoda is erected on an eminence about fifty yards from the steps by which the Hindoos descend to the water at their ablutions. This building is of that heavy style so common in the Hindoo temples; but some sculpture from their mythology on the exterior is better than usual; the attitudes easy and graceful, especially the musicians, playing before the divinities, assembled in groups. The interior sculpture, which I did not see, is reckoned still more beautiful.

The following evening, 26th, we crossed over to Benares, which is nearly opposite, and spent some days there and at Sercole, in a very pleasant society, during which we visited all the curiosities in the celebrated city of Benares, which is extensive and populous, but the streets narrow and dirty, the houses mean, and the women neither so cleanly or delicate as the Hindoos in general. A great nuisance here is the number of yogees, senassees, and nanghas, or religious mendicants, who go about entirely naked; we occasionally meet a few of these people at other pl ces, but at Benares they abound. The three most remarkable things here are the pagodas, the observatory, and the Jumma Musjid. The lofty minars of the latter are conspicuous at a great distance; from the gallery on one of them we had a complete view of the city, which, from the narrow streets and crowded population, presents a scene of great confusion. There are some large houses which appear to little advantage in their close situation; those on the banks of the Ganges have greatly the advantage, and seen from the river make a good appearance.

The three principal pagodas are sacred to Andepora, Gunga, and Vississore. These owe their celebrity more to their reputed sanctity, and the immense concourse of pilgrims from all parts of Hindostan, than to any superiority in architecture or sculpture. They are small, heavy, and confusedly crowded with ornaments ill executed, excepting the figure of Sureje, the Sun, seated on a car drawn by a horse with seven heads, driven by a furious charioteer. It is to be remarked, that most probably these are allegorical representations of the days of the week; and Sir Charles Malet thinks the months, hours, and other component parts of the designation or division of time are introduced into this piece of curious sculpture. Near these temples I was disgusted with seeing fifty or sixty of those naked mendicants, employed in rolling small balls of sacred mud, on each of which they stuck a single grain of rice, and arranged them in great order along the front of the verandas, for the Hindoo devotees to offer as a sacrifice to the Ganges.

From thence we proceeded to the observatory, so renowned throughout India, and the subject of much discussion in Europe. We ascended by a flight of steps to an open terrace, where several astronomical instruments, formed of stone, are in perfect preservation. The principal object is a large semicircle graduated, seemingly intended for a dial.

I pass over Mr. Cruso's further remarks on the observatory at Benares, which so far from ascribing to remote antiquity, he did not consider to have been erected more than a century. The following remark in the Edinburgh Review on Mr. Bentley's treatise on the Hindoo systems of astronomy should not be omitted. That "the consideration of the facts ascertained therein, and of many more which it would be easy to produce, ought to keep our curiosity alive to the remains of science in the east. Their extent and accuracy are so considerable—their origin and genealogy so completely unknown—they are united with so much extravagance and superstition, and so totally separated from any general stock of knowledge, that we cannot but consider them as forming altogether the most enigmatical monument of antiquity that is to be found on the face of the earth. A great degree of scepticism on this subject ought most carefully to be preserved, until the industry and learning of the Asiatic Society, to which we have already so great obligations, shall furnish us with a more complete catalogue and description of the remains of oriental science. We may then decide, whether the east has only borrowed from the west, or whether it be true, as Lucian says, that it was in India that philosophy first alighted on the earth."

We left Benares and our hospitable friends there on the 1st of September, and on the 3d arrived at Buxar, a neat little fortress erected on an eminence, commanding a great extent of flat country, adorned with rich groves and plantations. The lines are extensive, intended principally as shelter for the ryots in case of an attack; the whole is uncommonly neat, and in excellent order. After viewing the field of battle where General Munro gained the victory over Serajah Dowlah, we dined with the commanding officer, and, resisting the most pressing solicitations for a longer stay, slept in our budgerows. On the 4th we passed the long straggling towns of Chuprah and Cherun, where pastures abounding with herds and flocks, varied by rich groves, afforded a beautiful scene. Here the sight of a few palmyra trees, after a long absence from those objects, unexpectedly rising above the mango topes and banian trees, produced a delightful sensation; which, tracing to its source, proceeded from a recollection of the pleasant diversified island of Bombay; a little spot abundantly occupied by the cocoa-nut and palmeto, and drawing a thousand associated ideas from the tablet of memory sacred to friendship and affection. At Chuprah is a factory of saltpetre and opium; all the latter produced in Berah is collected at this place. A variety of nullahs, or brooks, which intersect the neighbouring plains, pour their streams into the Ganges near Chuprah. Here also are a number of wide-spreading banian trees, many of them walled round and consecrated; those overhanging the river with their drooping branches, dispose the mind to solemn musing.

So great is the rise and overflow of the Ganges this season, that the eye cannot discover the extent; and the villages are so entirely surrounded that they appear to be floating. Indeed the lower part of most of the houses are under water, and the inhabitants betake themselves to stages erected for the purpose. From thence we reached Dinapore on the 4th, and dined with some friends we had formerly known with General Goddard's detachment at Surat, in the elegant and extensive cantonments which are said to have cost the Company twenty-five lacks of rupees. They form a large and small square, and each suite of apartments consists of a hall or sitting-room, and a bed-chamber on each side; the field-officers' quarters are excellent; those belonging to the commanding officer form an elegant and spacious building. The kitchens and offices are at a proper distance. The area of the principal square is a grass-plot, divided by gravel walks into four equal parts, regularly planted with beautiful nym or lym-trees. During our stay we took the advantage of two fair days to go to Monheer, celebrated for a mosque and tank of singular beauty; in them we were disappointed, but the neighbouring country afforded us excellent sport in hunting the wild hog.

After a reluctant parting with our friendly hosts at Dinapore, we proceeded, Sept. 21, to Banguepore, a few miles from Patna, and the residence of the civil servants on that station. On landing, we met with the usual kind reception; and among other things saw the gola, a building intended for a public granary, or a deposit of grain to be provided, as are similar ones at other stations, against the future ravages of famine. Its external appearance is that of an immense dome, covering one of rather smaller dimensions, within which the grain is deposited.

The following morning we rode from Banquepore to Patna, to view the monument erected in commemoration of the massacre in the year 1763, ordered by Cossim Ally Khan, and executed by Samnoo. By this inhuman mandate upwards of two hundred civilians, military officers and soldiers, prisoners with Cossim Ally, were deliberately murdered. The monument stands near the house where the cruel deed was committed; it is surrounded by an enclosure which forms the English burying-ground. The column is in a good style, but has neither an inscription, nor any device explanatory of the purpose for which it was erected. Patna is a large populous trading city, and from the river makes a good appearance. There we found a number of vessels employed in its commerce, and the bazar well stocked with merchandize, particularly abounding with coppersmiths, cooks, and confectioners. A large space was allotted to the bird-sellers, who daily frequent it with a variety of birds, from the voracious hawk to the innocent dove: the most abundant were the languishing love-sick bulbuls; for so these nightingales are described in the zenanas, whither they and the doves are generally destined.

The morning we left Patna the snowy mountains were distinctly visible in the N. E. quarter. Our next landing was at Mongheer, where we arrived on the 27th, but apprehensive of the usual hospitable reception and friendly detention, we concealed our arrival, and walked immediately to *Seeta Coond*, a celebrated hot-well at some distance from the town. It is secured by masonry, and a centinel is placed over it to prevent nuisances. The water is extremely hot, so that could not bear my finger in it a single moment. It smokes and bubbles violently, and is perfectly clear and tasteless. Near it is another well, called *Ram Koond*, where the water is only tepid: that in the Seeta Coond is of such purity, as not only to be preferred to any other by the natives, but is procured by those who can afford it, on the voyage from India to Europe, as it never putrefies, nor becomes in the least offensive. *Ram* and *Seeta* are as eminent in the Hindoo mythology as Jupiter and Juno in the Grecian.

The fortifications of Mongheer appear extensive but ruinous. The commanding officers' quarters, situated on an eminence, command a fine view over a pleasant diversified country; many parts of it are covered with a high grass, or reed, with bunches of seed-vessels on the top, so white and singulâr in their growth as to give the fields the appearance of feeding numerous flocks of sheep, for which I at first took them. Intending to proceed on the 28th, we were prevented by a furious tempest, and forced to take shelter under the river bank, where we passed the night with great danger, and the loss of two men drowned.

Violent gales and heavy rains delayed our reaching Bhaughulpore, on an interior branch of the great river, until the 1st of October. The English chief's house is a large beautiful building on the Italian model, finely placed at the top of a lawn, sloping down to the river, planted with flowering shrubs, and near it is a paddock with elks and some curious deer. Bhaugulpore, now a flourishing place, is indebted for all its beauties and improvements to the late chief, Mr. Cleveland, whose good name stands infinitely beyond any panegyric I can bestow, being established on the most permanent basis, the universal praise of a grateful people, liberated from perpetual invaders by his exertions, and enjoying security and protection under his fostering care.

When Mr. Cleveland took charge of the chiefship of Bhaugulpore, the jurisdiction of which extends to the distance of a hundred and twenty miles, the country was in many places a perfect waste, and cultivation in general relaxed and deficient, arising chiefly from a scanty population, in consequence of the insecurity of property from the depredations of a savage race who inhabited the neighbouring hills; and not only robbed, burnt, and destroyed the villages, but to devastation frequently added cruelty and murder. A military force became necessary to repel these invaders, which was not effected without much bloodshed. On Mr. Cleveland's appointment to this station, he projected a plan, which admirably included the protection of the inhabitants, the conciliation of the robbers, the increase of population, and the encouragement of agriculture. Such was the ability and perseverance with which he furthered its execution, that in a few years the desert became a scene of fertility, conducted by the very people who had formerly struck the country with terror, and rendered it uninhabitable. The ancient ryots of the plains, who had fled from the mountaineers as their murderers, now mingled with them in friendship; and, certain parts of the land remaining yet untilled, were distributed to the invalids of the Company's native troops, who were invited by advantageous terms to spend the remainder of their lives in the vale of peace, and the salutary employments of husbandry.

INSCRIPTION ON A MARBLE MONUMENT AT BHAUGULPORE, ERECTED BY THE GOVERNOR GENERAL AND COUNCIL OF BENGAL, TO THE MEMORY OF AUGUSTUS CLEVELAND, ESQ.

To the memory of Augustus Cleveland, Esq.
Late collector of the districts of Bhaugulpore and Rajamahal;
Who, without bloodshed, or the terror of authority,
Employing only the means of conciliation, confidence, and benevolence,
attempted and accomplished the entire subjugation
of the lawless and savage inhabitants of the Jungleterry of Rajamahall,
who had long infested the neighbouring lands

by their predatory incursions,
inspired them with a taste for the arts of civilized life;
and attached them to the British Government,
by a conquest over their minds;
the most permanent, as the most rational dominion.

The Governor and Council of Bengal,
in honour of his character, and for an example to others,
have ordered this monument to be erected.
He departed this life
on the 13th day of January, 1784, aged 29.

Having taken leave of our hospitable friends at Bhaugulpore on the 8th, we proceeded down the river, and in the evening went on shore at Colgong. On ascending a hill, where Mr. Cleveland had erected a bungalo, we commanded an extensive view over a country which had been lately overflowed; much of it appears to be a jungle, or forest land. About fifty yards from the shore is a most singular island, which appears to be composed of numberless distinct rocks, intergrown with a variety of trees; on the top is a *dirgah*, or shrine, having a hermitage devoted to religious retirement, at present inhabited by a celebrated derveish, or Mahomedan saint.

On leaving Colgong we passed on the right a long succession of hills: the land between them and the river seemed to have been lately overflowed, and produced only the reed, so generally used throughout this part of India for thatching the houses. We found the main river (which we now re-entered) extremely wide, but affording nothing particularly interesting, until we approached a remarkable point of land, called *Peer Payntee*, or Saint's-town, whereon was a Mahomedan dirgah, or musjid, in a good style of architecture. We soon after saw a hill with a fort, and a few houses called Taliaghurry, the residence of a rajah so entitled. We next passed Sickligullee, and soon after saw a grand cascade called Mootee-jernah, or the "*Fall of Pearls.*" In the afternoon a very hard gale impeded our progress for many hours. The next day we proceeded by the branch of the river leading to Rajemahl, from whence we viewed this celebrated place. The Jumma-musjid is of great antiquity, and superior architecture; it is now a noble ruin, doubly picturesque by many large trees growing out of the dilapidated walls, and curiously mingling with the massy fragments. The lofty minars are still in good preservation. The steps in each lead to the upper gallery, from whence you enter eight rooms on either side, covered with separate domes, surrounding the magnificent cupola in the centre. The seventeen domes forming the roof are nearly perfect, and seen among the trees produce a fine effect. In front is a spacious area, with a tank, and the remains of a fountain.

The principal buildings at Rajemahl front the nullah; some appear to have been extremely grand, but now displayed only an extensive scene of ruins, which we left for [illegible]danullah, the scene of a British victory over the troops of Cossim A[illegible] Khan. Advancing up the nullah, we viewed the bridge built over it by that nabob; it consists of a single arch, the masonry ornamented with small minars and domes. Two hundred yards in front of this nullah are the lines of Cossim Ally, still in good order, with a deep fosse twenty yards wide, extending from the Ganges across a swamp to the opposite hills.

On the 11th of October, taking a final leave of the main stream of the Ganges, we entered the Bhaughretty, or Cossimbazar branch. The country on the right banks appeared higher than that we had lately passed, and was consequently more dry and comfortable for the inhabitants; yet much of this is low, and the waters had just subsided. Pelicans, cranes, and a variety of aquatic fowl frequent the nullahs, which also abound with fish. The next day we passed Jungepore, famous for its silk manufactory. The houses in this town and all the neighbouring villages have roofs which in shape resemble a hog's back. Much of the country, especially on the rignt banks, was covered with woods and forests. In the afternoon we arrived at Moorshedabad, the Mogul capital of the province of Bengal; where, having procured bearers, we set off in our palanquins to see a celebrated piece of water, called Mootee-jil, or the "*Lake of Pearls.*" Taking the figure of a horse-shoe, it nearly insulates a considerable space of ground, formerly a beautiful garden, adorning a large palace, now in ruins, and removing for the purpose of building an elegant house for the English resident at the durbar. The Jumma musjid and public buildings at the adjoining city of Cossimbazar resemble those in other large oriental cities. In the nabob's stable was a collection of curious small horses, several not exceeding three feet in height; and one, a most extraordinary dwarf, under that size, had the head, chest, and body of a full-grown horse. We also visited the

Cheetah-connah, the place where the nabob's panthers and other animals for hunting are kept. Here were some fine cheetahs, and a beautiful sya-goos, in much esteem for chasing the antelope and other deer. One of the gardens contained a large pellucid tank, stored with tame fish which were taught to repair daily to the steps for food, and perform certain evolutions. We regaled them with sweetmeats from the bazar, and were much amused by their docility.

This being the desserah, a great Hindoo festival, annually celebrated not only on shore but on the Ganges or Gunga, and all the tributary streams, which more or less partake of its sanctity, we resolved to delay our departure, and see some part of the ceremonies. At five P. M. the boats began to be in motion; they are of a singular construction, particularly those called Moor-Punkees, or peacock-boats, which are made as much as possible to resemble the peacock; others are decorated with the head and neck of a horse, and different devices: one sort in particular, which proceeds with the greatest velocity with oars, is extremely long and narrow, and on that account called a snake. In the most commodious part of these boats are laid carpets, cushions, and pillows, covered with silk, satin, or keemcobs, fringed and embroidered with gold and silver: especially those which contain the images and religious ornaments; these are placed before the apartment just mentioned, where the wealthy Hindoos are seated: while on a platform near the deities a man dances, sings, and beats time to the oars of the rowers, ornamented with bells. A number of these boats, all in swift motion, the company in their best attire, the images gaudily decked, and enwreathed with flowers, the songs and dances of the choristers, uniting with the stroke of the oars and paddles, gave a lively interest to the scene. Some of these boats are rowed by forty paddles, each with its bells. The attitudes of the dancers before the images were frequently not only indelicate but disgusting. At night the illuminations commenced, but being only in the usual style, we left the festive scene; and passing the factory at Cossimbazar (which by the artificial lights appeared to be a very extensive building) we proceeded to Burhanpore, and the next day dined at the cantonments, which are more convenient, though less elegant, than those already described; but so unusually high have been the inundations of the present year, that the cantonments at Burnanpore are entirely insulated, and the road to Cossimbazar impracticable.

On the 16th we reached Plassey, which gives the title of Baron to Lord Clive, in honour of the victory he obtained on the adjoining plains, over the troops of Serajah Dowlah in 1757. We visited that memorable spot, with the hunting-seat called Plassey-house, and the immense tope, or mango grove, which will long identify the place which gave such a happy turn to the English arms and interest in India.

The surrounding country abounds with beasts of prey, and game of every description. A gentleman lately engaged on a shooting-party in the wilds of Plassey, gave us an account of their success in one month, from August the 15th to September the 14th, in which space they killed one royal tiger, six wild buffaloes, one hundred and eighty-six hog-deer, twenty-five wild hogs, eleven antelopes, three foxes, thirty-five hares, one hundred and fifty brace of partridges and floricans, with quails, ducks, snipes, and smaller birds in abundance.

On the evening of the 17th we reached the confluence of the Bhaugretty and Jellinghy rivers; the former bounding the island of Cossimbazar on the west, the latter on the east. The junction of those streams forms the Hooghly river, which we now entered. On taking leave of the Bhaugretty I must mention the *moorda* or *chuttries* placed on different parts of the bank. These are small chuprahs, or huts, in which a Hindoo when given over by his physicians, is deposited, and left alone to expire and be carried off by the sacred flood. We fastened our boats opposite the town of Nuddeah, where the songs and dances throughout the whole night, for the festival of the desserah, and some funeral dirges at the Hindoo cremations on another part of the bank, engaged our attention until day-break, when we dropped down to Culnah, a large village; and soon after entered a nullah, which brought us to Ballyghurra, where the waters having entirely subsided, we were gratified with a view of ploughs, harrows, and the various implements of husbandry at work on the arable plains, now ready to receive the seed.

During the last few days, sailing with a light wind has given some respite to the labours of the *dandies*, or boatmen, who pass their lives in great exertion on these rivers; in coming down the Ganges they are obliged to row, and in going up against the stream, are constantly tracking with the rope. As few conditions are without their relative comforts, so the dandies have theirs. During the evening meal and nightly halt, the toil of the day is forgotten; they generally contrive to bring their boats to some convenient station, where numerous fires blaze on the banks, a good supper is dressed, and mirth and festivity unite with the adventures of the day, to beguile the time till their meal is finished, and all lie down to repose. No fires are permitted in the burdjerows; those who wish for hot meals have them dressed in separate boats.

On quitting the nullah we re-entered the Hooghly river, and at noon reached Sook Saughur, an elegant house of European architecture, highly finished, and the grounds disposed with great taste. The next morning we had a fine view of the Dutch settlement at Chinsura; and immediately after of the French establishment at Chandernagore: they both make a very respectable appearance from the river; especially the house belonging to the French chief, at a little distance from the town. We next passed the Danish settlement of Serampore, where the Danes have long enjoyed themselves in undisturbed tranquillity, and a flourishing commerce. Four large ships were at anchor before the town, where the neatness of the houses and gardens, the goodness of the roads, and the stir of business, indicated peace and comfort.

A short distance brought us within view of the forest of masts before the magnificent buildings at Calcutta, where we landed in the evening of the 18th of October, after a voyage of much interest and variety.

"No man," saith Lipsius, in an epistle to Lanoius, "can be such a stock, or a stone, whom that pleasant speculation of countries, cities, towns, rivers, will not affect."—"Peregrination charms our senses with such unspeakable and sweet variety, that some count him unhappy that never travelled, and pity his case, that from his cradle to his old age beholds the same still; still, still the same, the same."—BURTON'S *Anatomy of Melancholy, in* 1621.

CHAPTER XL.

VOYAGE FROM BOMBAY TO GOA, AND TELLICHERRY; INCLUDING THE SIEGE OF ONORE, AND ENSUING BLOCKADE, BY THE ARMY OF TIPPOO SULTAUN. 1784.

" Quis fuit, horrendos primus qui protulit enses?
 Quam ferus, et verè ferrens ille fuit!
Tunc cœdes hominum generi, tunc prælia nata;
 Tunc brevior diræ mortis aperta via est.
At nihil ille miser meruit; nos ad mala nostra
 Vertimus, in sævas quod dedit ille feras.
Divitis hoc vitium est auri: nec bella fuerunt,
 Faginus adstabat dum scyphus ante dapes.
Non arces, non vallus erat; somnumque petebat
 Securus saturas dux gregis inter oves. TIBUL. EL. 11.

" Who was the first that forg'd the deadly blade?
Of rugged steel his savage soul was made;
By him, his bloody flag Ambition wav'd,
And grisly Carnage through the battle rav'd.
Yet wherefore blame him? We're ourselves to blame;
Arms first were forg'd to kill the savage game;
Death-dealing battles were unknown of old,
Death-dealing battles took their rise from gold:
When beechen bowls on oaken tables stood,
When temperate acorns were our fathers' food,
The swain slept peaceful with his flocks around,
No trench was open'd, and no fortress frown'd."

CONTENTS.

fort—letter to general M'Leod—the garrison attacked by the scurvy, means adopted for the restoration of health—Fortified Island treacherously taken by the enemy—evasive conduct of Maw Mirza—letter from the Madras cammissioners—peace with Tippoo Sultaun—consequences at Onore—general orders—visits between the commandant of Onore and Maw Mirza—entertainment by the latter—orders for evacuating Onore—difficulties attending the safety of some brahmins under the English protection—evacuation of the fort, and embarkation of the troops—the fleet sails for Bombay—public testimonies of the brave and gallant defence of the fortress of Onore, the good conduct of the troops; and the promotion of captain Torriano, as a reward for his gallant services.

CHAPTER XL.

On the eighteenth day of January 1784, I embarked with my family connexions, and several valuable friends, who had taken their passage for Europe, in the General Elliot East Indiaman; many others accompanied us on board, from whom we parted with sincere regret. We sailed immediately for the Malabar coast, where we were to complete our cargo of pepper, at Goa and Tellicherry; a fair wind carried us clear of the harbour, and in a few hours we lost sight of all the endeared and interesting objects on Bombay.

In two days we arrived at Goa, and spent a fortnight there with Mr. Crommelin, the English resident; a respectable and venerable gentleman, who had been governor of Bombay twenty years before, but, by a reverse of fortune, then held that inferior station in the Company's service. He resided at Panjeem, a pleasant spot on the banks of the river, some miles from the city of Goa, not far from the governor's country seat.

While the ship was receiving her cargo, we passed our time very pleasantly, under the hospitable roof of Mr. Crommelin, and made several excursions into the adjacent country; sometimes sailing up the river, we visited the desolate city of Goa, formerly described, which now presented a still more melancholy picture of wretchedness and ruin. The churches, monasteries, prisons, and inquisition were kept in repair; but the streets in general exhibited only mouldering palaces and falling houses, depopulated and silent! The governor, Don Frederic, no longer styled *viceroy*, but captain general of India, was a nobleman of amiable manners, and an accomplished gentleman: he entertained us in a princely style at his palace, and formed in every respect a striking contrast to the courtiers by whom he was surrounded.

Alternate land and sea breezes wafted us pleasantly from Goa to Tellicherry. The diversified scenery in that part of the coast has been described. In giving an account of a former voyage from Bombay to Anjengo, I have inadvertently mentioned that, after leaving Mirzee and Barcelore, there was nothing worthy of observation until we reached Fortified Island, a little to the northward of Onore. Sir James Sibbald, for many years the English resident at Onore, informs me that Mirzee (the Musiris of the ancient Greeks) is situated twenty-two miles to the northward of Onore. At spring tides large ships can sail over the bar, at the entrance of the river, and remain in safety during the monsoon. The Bombay-Merchant, a ship laden with military stores for the nabob Hyder Ally, by the government of Bombay, was in the month of May 1764, on her passage from thence to Mangulore, when the south-west moonsoon suddenly set in much earlier than usual, with a most tremendous gale; had not the commander determined, at all hazards, to run over Mirzee bar, his vessel must have been lost. The East India company for seventy years, had a large banksaul, or warehouse, at Mirzee, for the reception of the pepper and sandal-wood purchased in the dominions of the Mysore rajah, afterwards usurped by Hyder Ally, who allowed the company the same privilege.

Barcelore, the Baracé of the Greeks, and now frequently called Cundapore, is twenty-five miles to the southward of Onore, being a sea-port in a direct line with Bednure, which Hyder Ally, on conquering the Canaree dominions, named after himself, *Hyder-naggur*. Sir James Sibbald was at Barcelore on the company's business, in the month of April 1763, when Hyder Ally came there, immediately after the conquest of Bednure, at the head of sixty thousand cavalry and infantry; and three hundred state elephants: he had also a body of French troops, and a great many French officers in his army.

I described Onore in the voyage to Anjengo; it was now in possession of the English, who took the fortress from the sultaun of Mysore at the commencement of the unfortunate expedition under general Mathews. Onore fort was at this time defended by captain (now major) Torriano, an officer in the Bombay artillery, frequently mentioned for his gallant behaviour when acting as brigade major to the British troops employed in Guzerat, for the assistance of Ragonauth Row. This enterprising officer acquired additional honours in his defence of Onore against the force and treachery of Tippoo Sultaun, during a siege of three months, and a blockade of much longer continuance. Captain Torriano was my intimate friend, as also of several other passengers on board the General Elliot. We knew his arduous situation, we knew him resolutely determined to maintain his post until a peace, although in want of ammunition, stores, and provision for the garrison, and destitute of almost every comfort and necessary of life; what then must have been our feelings when we were obliged to pass within view of the blockaded fortress, without affording relief to himself and his brave comrades!

Among the deceased Mr. Cruso's papers, at present in my possession, is a very interesting account of the siege of Onore, by Tippoo Sultaun's army, and the sufferings of the garrison, which he was fully competent to describe, from his situation as chief surgeon of the hospital in that fortress, at this memorable period. He was afterwards intrusted with a packet of materials, for the purpose of drawing up a history of the campaign under the command of General Mathews, when ordered to make a diversion in favour of the British operations in the Carnatic, by an attack on the nabob's settlements on the Malabar coast. These documents were too imperfect for such a history; but from the writer's personal knowledge of the perseverance and sufferings of the Onore garrison, he was enabled, from those documents and the papers furnished by major Torriano, to frame a faithful and connected detail of that memorable siege. It contains an excellent account of Asiatic operations, as well as some peculiar traits of oriental military character, differing from any in the preceding pages. I have selected the most interesting passages from those munuscripts, as a valuable acquisition, which I could not otherwise have obtained. The courage and conduct displayed by the commanding officer and his gallant comrades, throughout this eventful period, are their best panegyric; and in Mr. Cruso's full detail, he modestly hopes he may not have obscured, what it was out of his power to brighten.

The English batteries under the command of captain Torriano, opened against the fort of Onore on the first day of January 1783. It was taken by storm on the sixth: several of the besieged fell in the fury of the assault; the rest, in number about two thousand, received quarter, and were soon after set at liberty, except the killidar, (or commander of the fort), the buxey (paymaster), and a few principal officers. The confusion from the storm having subsided, the following day was dedicated to the burial of the dead, and collecting the wounded of the enemy, upwards of a hundred of whom, together with all the sick and wounded of the Company's troops, were placed under the care of the army surgeons, in the house which had formerly been the English factory; this being a large and commodious building, was now appropriated for the general hospital. Several prisoners remained there more than three months, where they experienced every kind attention, and when discharged the commanding officer gave each of them money to enable them to reach home.

Captain Torriano being disabled by a wound received in the batteries from proceeding with the army to invade the enemy's country, was appointed to the command of the fort of Onore and its dependencies. On the 12th of January General Mathews constituted this fortress the grand magazine of the British forces, and in his instructions to captain Torriano, mentioned it as a trust of the highest importance to the welfare of the army, and requiring his utmost vigilance.

The night before the departure of Shaik Muckdum, (the nabob's late killidar of the fort), captain Torriano privately delivered to him the jewels belonging to his family; which at the commencement of the storm by the English had been secreted under some ruins. Captain Torriano was informed of this circumstance at midnight, by a confidential servant of Shaik Muckdum, who intended them as a present to the captain, in return for his kind attentions while a prisoner in the fort; he was consequently overwhelmed with gratitude when the jewels were thus restored to him. Similar was the conduct of the commandant on receiving information of some valuable articles concealed in the woods near Govind-ghurry. He sent trusty persons in boats to search the spot alluded to; who returned with several bales of cloth, jars of sandal-oil, and ottar of roses. They were immediately placed under a guard, and a publication issued throughout the country, that they would be gratuitously restored to such persons as could prove a title to them. The following week they were claimed by a merchant, who jointly with his father had been the company's brokers at Onore factory. He proved the articles to have been secreted by his father and himself when the English forces landed on the coast, from an apprehension (afterwards realized) of their being ordered by Ayauz Saheb to Bednore, where his father was cruelly put to death, and the son escaped with the greatest difficulty. These facts, as also the humanity shewn to the prisoners taken from Tippoo Sultaun, are thus particularized, in contradiction to some unfounded assertions, of a contrary tendency, which appeared in the historical records of the Annual Register at that period.

About this time the former inhabitants of the town of Onore, who had fled from their habitations on the arrival of the British troops, won by the humanity shewn to the wounded of their enemy, and the liberty granted to the other prisoners, began to return home with their families and effects.

On the 23d Fortified Island, a post belonging to Tippoo Sultaun, situated a little to the northern entrance of Onore river, capitulated to captain Torriano. The month of February was ushered in by the important intelligence that general Mathews had forced the formidable pass of Hussen-ghurry, and that the English colours were then flying on the ramparts of Bednure. But, alas! this glorious news was of short duration; for, on the second of March, a cavalry officer, with a small party of horse, arrived at Onore, bringing the afflicting intelligence that on the preceding afternoon the Sultaun's troops had carried Hyder-nuggur ghaut, or pass, by storm; and that before day-break the next morning they forced the small party posted at Ciddapore river. To this was added the disgraceful report, that in consequence of the arrival of the fugitives from Hyder-nuggur, a council of war had been called at Cundapore, (or Barcelore) the members of which had unanimously declared their post to be untenable; and when the cornet's party left the place, measures were actually taking to abandon it, though not a man of the enemy had appeared. The circumstance of Cundapore being deserted by the English troops was confirmed a few hours afterwards by an officer, with the melancholy addition that many guns were spiked, a quantity of stores burnt, and ammunition destroyed; the whole garrison proceeding in a straggling manner towards Onore.

Alarmed for the glory of the British arms, and animated by a zeal for the good of the service, to which a fatal blow would be given by the loss of its grand magazine, which had been removed to Cundapore, and all communication being now cut off with general Mathews, captain Torriano conceived a design of saving Cundapore, as no enemy had been seen when the last fugitives left the place. But it was soon rendered fruitless by still later intelligence, that the enemy were in possesion of it. This being the case, boats and canoes were in constant attendance on the south side of Onore river, to bring over such of the fugitives from Cundapore as escaped the villagers, who every where turned out against them: fortunately many arrived safe. The commanding officer, to alleviate their situation, and encourage a more soldier-like behaviour, made each European a present of a little money, to procure the necessaries they stood so much in need of.

Early on the 21st six Europeans appearing on the south bank of the river, a boat was sent to bring them over. These with a larger party, under the command of cornet Rowland, had escaped in one of the boats originally dispatched by captain Torriano with a view to the repossession of Cundapore, which proving leaky, obliged them to land the preceding evening, some miles below Onore, whither they were now on their march. Boats were immediately sent over for their accommodation, and in a few hours they appeared marching in regular order to the water side; with Missauber, a subahdar, at their head. The cornet being ill, the subahdar had procured him a litter, in which he accompanied the detachment. This circumstance is particularly mentioned, because, at this critical period, it was a happy demonstration that the contagion from our loss of Hyder-nuggur, which had already infected the country, had there been checked.

The exertions of the Onore garrison, which had been ever

active, were now increased in proportion to the superior importance it derived from our loss and disgrace in other quarters; and to that necessity of defending the fortress against a triumphant enemy, whose near approach was announced by the reports received from the neighbouring districts. The attentions and precautions now rendered necessary by a reverse of fortune already mentioned were not confined to Onore. Effectual means were immediately adopted, after the loss of Cundapore, to prevent the ships daily expected with reinforcements and stores from Bombay, from putting into that port. Night signals were constantly made, and pattamar-boats cruised in their track, to give timely notice. Nor was this vigilance useless; a fleet being then on its passage from Bombay, conveying a reinforcement for the army, as also a committee of gentlemen appointed by the governor and council for the civil government of Bednore. This fleet parted company in a gale of wind, and many of the vessels standing in for Cundapore, were thus prevented from entering a hostile port.

On the 30th captain Nugent, commanding the first battalion of Bombay sepoys, arrived at Onore with a letter from the Bednore committee to the commandant of Onore; an extract from whose answer, dated May 2d, will explain its purport. "Should I admit the propriety of obeying your orders to destroy and evacuate Onore fort, so directly contrary to those I have received from the commander in chief of the army, I am still of opinion, the executing them at this period would be injurious to the welfare of the present service, having a quantity of powder, stores, and rice, belonging to the army in this depot. The enemy, now encamped on the opposite side of Onore river, threaten the destruction of every inhabitant who has shewn the least attachment to the British government; should the fort be evacuated, they will obtain possession of all the grain in the Onore district, which I am now purchasing, and laying up in store for the army; which from the quantity sent to Bombay from Mangulore, and lost at Cundapore and other posts abandoned to the enemy, may stand greatly in need of that necessary article before the next harvest. I am not at all apprehensive respecting the safety of Onore; which I will defend with fifty regulars, and the recruits, while we have an army in the field; but desirous of adopting any measure for the interest of the service, I could wish, gentlemen, that, if possible, all orders from you may come through the commander in chief of the British army, or the officer commanding the troops on this side the Ghauts, which shall be immediately obeyed."

On the 12th of May captain Torriano received intelligence, that LUTOPH ALLY BEG, a veteran Persian officer in the nabob's service, was on his march to besiege Onore with ten thousand men. In order to give some confidence to a small garrison, the greater part composed of raw recruits, and fugitives from the posts abandoned by the English, they were immediately encamped near the glacis without the fort, and the remains of the cavalry furnished with such arms and furniture as our situation would admit of. On discovering the enemy, captain Torriano, with a party of sepoys, the cavalry, and a one pounder field-piece, advanced towards the hills, while small parties of sepoys were detached to different quarters of the village, where some of their horse were perceived; those on the hill approached, but were soon dispersed by a few shot from the field-piece. The next morning the enemy appeared in much greater force.

On the arrival of Lutoph Ally's army, between two and three thousand inhabitants of the town of Onore who had fled from their habitations during the siege by the English, and returned home under the protection of the company's government, once more forsaking their shops and houses, flocked in terror to the out-works of the fortress, and implored protection. There being no alternative between granting their supplications, or abandoning them to certain death from a cruel despot, they were instantly permitted to enter.

The same day a letter was sent to captain Torriano from Lutoph Ally, informing him the nabob had reconquered Bednore, and represented the impossibility of defending Onore, now that the former important post, with the flower of the British army, had fallen into his master's possession; at the same time observing, that no culpability could attach to the commandant for giving up the fort of Onore, when a large force was marching to besiege it. To this a polite answer was returned. Shortly afterwards a reconnoitring party of the Onore cavalry, commanded by captain Torriano, came suddenly upon the enemy's advanced post at the village, consisting of a small detachment of horse and foot, who fled precipitately on the first charge. We took eleven prisoners, two of whom proved to be deserters from our cavalry at Bednore. They confirmed the distressing report of the loss of that place, and the imprisonment of the army commanded by general Mathews.

On the 17th of May parties of the enemy were moving in different directions on the opposite banks, and a second letter was sent from Lutoph Ally, repeating the contents of the former; and urging, as an additional motive to a surrender of the fort, that the batteries would be finished and mounted with heavy cannon in two days; to this no answer was returned. The next day brought intelligence from undoubted authority of the capture of Bednore, and the loss of the British army.

Early in the morning of the 10th of June the enemy opened his battery, and kept it up the next day from seven pieces of cannon, twelve and eighteen pounders. As they constantly drew the guns within the merlons after firing, the fort was cautious in its firing slowly, from such guns only as played directly into their embrazures. This was renewed for four hours the day following, when the guns were better served than usual, and no longer withdrawn. As the stock of eighteen pound shot in the garrison was small, the fire from it was deliberately and carefully managed; and its aim confined to disabling the enemy's guns. The fortress now began to suffer greatly from the weakness of its defences. The rampart was narrow and bad; the high walls not more than three feet thick, generally more a mass of mud than of masonry, and through which an eighteen-pound shot easily passed. Against these and the cavalier tower, the enemy had hitherto principally directed his fire. The engineer, lieutenant Blachford, an active and spirited young man, and all the officers, laboured indefatigably to remedy these defects by field works. An embrazure was opened to the right of the cavalier, to effect a more direct fire on their eighteen pounder, and the palisading of the covert-way was carried on with great diligence. The commanding officer judging a sally expedient, with a view of spiking the enemy's guns, and destroying the factory-house, the principal part of the garrison intended for that service were paraded in the evening, and a small party of sepoys ordered to attack a picket on the left shoulder of their battery, near the river side; they were also to cover the sallying party. The commandant followed with the cavalry and a party of sepoys.

The enemy were completely surprised, and a few minutes put us in possession of their whole range of batteries; seven guns then mounted were spiked, and the factory house set on fire. The only annoyance our people met with in the battery, was from the desultory fire of a contiguous post. In the retreat two Europeans, a subahdar, havaldar, and two sepoys were wounded; the havaldar not being missed, was left on the ground. The enemy's batteries were found to be very strong, with thick breast-works, and several traverses behind each other.

On the 14th of June a sepoy, formerly of the eleventh battalion, deserted from the enemy; who kept up large fires behind their merlons throughout the day, from which we supposed they were endeavouring to soften the guns, in hopes of unspiking them. Lutoph Ally, much to his honour, having no skilful surgeon, sent in the wounded havaldar, who had been left on the ground, with both his thighs broken by a shot. The commanding officer rewarded the people who brought in the wounded man, and sent a genteel present to Lutoph Ally, in testimony of his humanity and politeness.

The same afternoon our picket of six men, posted in front of the half-moon battery, was attacked. The commandant hastening to the out-works, ordered a party of sepoys to advance to its support, and a larger force to follow, in hopes of beating back the enemy into their works; but our expectations were too sanguine, for on reaching the village, the sepoys halted, and neither the example, menaces, nor encouragement of their officers, could make them advance. The enemy, alarmed by the fire of the musketry, collected from all quarters; and, rushing down in a formidable body, completed the panick of our sepoys, who made a precipitate and confused retreat, leaving their officers in the rear. The commandant seeing this unfortunate affair, immediately advanced with a field-piece, and throwing himself between the fugitives and the enemy, rallied the sepoys, and beat back their pursuers. The enemy afterwards threw several rockets, and fired briskly from the batteries, by which we lost two sepoys killed, and several wounded, five of whom afterwards died. As the guns from the fortress kept up a constant fire, the enemy's loss must have been considerable.

A sepoy formerly on the Bengal establishment, who deserted from the enemy, having greatly distinguished himself on this occasion, was immediately promoted, and presented with a pair of silver bangles, or bracelets. The bangles worn by the natives, are often given by the oriental generals as a reward to men who distinguish themselves in action. The commanding officer had previously ordered a number of gold and silver bangles to be made for this purpose, inscribed with the words, MILITARY MERIT: these bracelets were kept for occasional distribution. This example is worthy of imitation, since whatever evil may arise from the abuse of donatives, it seems as necessary to excite emulation by rewarding courage, as to check cowardice, by rigorous punishment. Captain Torriano also made a present of tobacco to each European and sepoy in garrison; as that luxury, or rather necessary article to the natives, could not then be purchased for money.

On the 15th the enemy were remarkably quiet, and the garrison taking advantage of the cessation, pushed on the works with all possible expedition. A grenadier company was now selected from the sepoy corps, to be ready on all occasions; and the command given to lieutenant Reynolds, an able gallant officer. The fort continued for several days little disturbed by the enemy's fire. On the 19th a general indignation was excited by a most cruel act committed in their camp on three men, inhabitants of the neighbouring country, who had been formerly useful in the fort; and having unhappily fallen into the enemy's power, were sent to the commanding officer with their hands cut off.

Many rockets had been thrown into the fort, with little effect, until one worked itself into the wall of a powder magazine. This being observed by an European of the artillery, he ran instantly and plucked it out, at the risk of his life, by which he saved the magazine, and escaped with only a slight burn on his hand: his presence of mind and gallant enterprise were liberally rewarded.

Nothing particular happened from that time until the first of July, when the enemy recommenced a well-directed fire against the breach, and defences of the large tower. The former was enlarged, two embrazures in the latter laid open, and an eighteen-pounder in one of the embrazures disabled. When the enemy ceased firing, the repair of these damages employed the whole garrison. The exertions of officers and men, under concealment of the night, were such, that notwithstanding a hot cannonade, they had before morning not only rendered the ruined defences respectable, but added strength to the retrenchments.

The enemy recommenced their fire early the next morning, chiefly against the newly-repaired breach. It was more briskly returned, accompanied by several shells. We lost a serjeant of artillery, killed, and some sepoys wounded. They continued their fire again the whole afternoon, and damaged two of our twelve-pounders. In the act of laying one of them captain Torriano was wounded.

A disease generally called "*Mort-de-chien*" at this time raged with great violence among the native inhabitants; and carried off such numbers, that the commanding officer humanely ordered all who were attacked with it to be placed under the care of the hospital surgeons. The weather continuing extremely boisterous, accompanied by almost incessant rain, he gave all the Europeans in garrison a portion of English broad-cloth sufficient for a suit of clothes. The same evening an old woman was detected in the character of a spy: on examination she confessed her mission; said she had been already two days in the fort, and was to have paid a longer visit, to fulfil certain instructions, and make inquiries, by order of Lutoph Ally; particularly whether the commanding officer had survived the wound it was reported he had received in the breach two days before. The old woman was introduced at head quarters, and was moreover desired to request

Lutoph Ally, that should he on any future occasion send female emissaries to the fort, they might possess more youth and beauty; that they should be well received, and returned to his camp with as much safety as the antiquated duenna who was then conducted out of the garrison.

Desertion among the native troops, especially in the Malawar corps, was now very common, sixteen of their recruits went off in a body; and a few nights afterwards one of them was detected in deserting from his post as sentinel. The commanding officer, determined to prevent an evil which might otherwise eventually endanger the loss of the fort, ordered all the troops who were off duty under arms; and with the dead march beating, the deserter was conducted in front to a spot near the attacked face of the works, and blown from the mouth of an eighteen-pounder.

The day following the fort sustained a heavy and skilful fire from the enemy's grand battery, which did great execution. Three of our guns were considerably damaged, and several of the garrison wounded. Since the commencement of the siege a few non-commissioned officers and Europeans have been killed and wounded, besides several of the Bombay sepoys and native troops entertained at Onore.

The enemy's fire was now kept up briskly for several days, destroying the defences of the large tower; many of the garrison were killed and wounded. The disease before mentioned was very destructive, and great desertions prevailed among the Onore recruits. On the 19th of July, an intelligent native, employed as a spy, returned from the enemy's camp, with information that our last fire bad disabled three of their best guns, and killed and wounded several people; among them a sirdar of consequence, the chief conductor of their works. He also said they were digging across the plain, in the rear of the most distant work, intended as he supposed for a mine.

It is unnecessary further to detail the events of the siege. The enemy occasionally kept up a brisk fire, especially from their enfilading batteries, by which we lost several of our small garrison, and more by desertions among the Onore sepoys. Early on the 24th of August the enemy sent a flag of truce, with a packet containing the terms of a cessation of arms concluded on the 2d of that month between Tippoo Sultaun and the commander in chief of the British forces at Mangulore; in which were inserted the following articles respecting the garrison of Onore.

A guard shall be placed in the fort from the sultaun's troops, and one in the trenches from the fort, to observe that no operations are carried on, nor any works erected on either side.

A bazar, or market, shall be daily supplied to the fort, containing all kinds of provisions, which the troops belonging to the garrison shall be allowed to purchase.

Thirty days provision may be received monthly from Bombay, but no military stores or ammunition will be allowed to enter the fort.

During the siege a guard had been placed by Lutoph Ally at the entrance of the river and the north point of the bar. This was immediately objected to, as a violation of the articles, and Captain Torriano insisted on its being removed. Lutoph Ally pleaded ignorance, and the guard was recalled. Soon afterwards a similar party was discovered on the south point, which after much altercation he also agreed to remove, but evading his promise, he only diminished the number. This early perfidy highly incensed and embarrassed the commanding officer: to submit to it was too painful a humiliation; to counteract it might be attended with serious consequences. He therefore resolved to take the sense of the commander in chief without delay.

Jehan Khaun, second in command of the sultaun's troops before Onore, was said at this time to be at open variance with Lutoph Ally; and as he bore the character of a brave soldier, and professed the greatest respect for the gallantry of the British troops, Captain Torriano was of opinion a private correspondence with this officer might tend to the advantage of the service, and prove a source of such information as might enable him to guard against the machinations of the enemy; nor were his expectations disappointed. Through this channel he received frequent information of what passed in the enemy's camp, the state of affairs at Mangulore, and the most solemn assurances that should any thing happen likely to affect the subsisting truce, such timely notice should be given as might frustrate those villainous stratagems, to which Jehan Khaun himself observed the Moguls were so much addicted.

In consequence of the cessation of arms, the commissary's men were sent into the country to procure cattle for the garrison. In a few days they returned with the unpleasant intelligence that none could be obtained. This disappointment, and no supply of grain having been furnished either for men or horses, notwithstanding the most pressing solicitations, provoked a stronger remonstrance to Lutoph Ally than had hitherto been made, against such gross evasions of the treaty. This remonstrance being equally unsuccessful, Captain Torriano communicated once more to the commanding officer at Mangulore the painful predicament in which he was placed, and the little reason he had to expect better treatment, unless the sultaun sent him decisive orders; at the same time hinting a suspicion, that the treatment he experienced was sanctioned by Tippoo Sultaun himself.

At length the stock of cattle being nearly consumed, and the patience of the garrison almost exhausted, the commanding officer communicated to Lutoph Ally his suspicion that the letters confided to him had never been sent to Mangulore, and consequently being deprived of all hope of redress from his commander in chief, he must seek it himself. If in so doing he should adopt measures incompatible with the existing treaty, and those measures should lead to a renewal of hostilities, the blame must fall upon Lutoph Ally himself: the English had, in all respects, religiously kept their faith, while he had uniformly sported with his master's honour; and, in defiance of a sacred treaty, aimed to effect by perfidy, what by direct and open hostility he had been unable to accomplish. He was therefore informed his promises were like the wind, of which British officers would not be the sport; on the contrary every nerve should be strained to frustrate his designs; but as it was the character of the English to deal openly and honourably, he forewarned him of the consequence. In the first place, as the commandant was determined the men who had bled in defence of the fortress, should not be starved out of it, he resolved so soon as his stock of cattle was expended, to send a detachment in search of a supply, which should be paid for; but if such detachment should be molested by Lutoph Ally's troops, they would repel force by force. That having written to Bombay and Goa for refreshments, the boats which brought them, should, on their arrival be permitted to come into the river and land their cargo; if they were fired at by the party on the south side of the bar, the guns of the fort should return the fire. In the present uncertainty respecting letters intrusted to the sultaun's halcarrahs, they should no longer be sent by them, but some other mode of conveyance adopted. On these resolutions being communicated, a party of British troops was posted on the north point, to assert the command of the river, on which the cessation was founded.

In consequence of this determination, (and while waiting for Lutoph Ally's reply) the daring spy before employed was dispatched with information to the commanding officer of the British forces, and was promised that on returning with an answer, he should himself name his reward for the service performed. It may not be irrelevant to observe, that although this man had to pass through the enemy's camps before Onore and Mangulore, he effected the purpose required by entering through a hole in the wall of the latter fortress, when strictly blockaded by Tippoo Sultaun. The messenger returned with Colonel Campbell's answer, and being then desired to take whatever sum he thought proper, from a bag of venetians (or gold ducats) placed before him, he not only declined this mode of remuneration, but submitted it entirely to the generosity of the commandant; and further requested he would become his banker, declaring he would continue to serve him faithfully, and would never receive any recompence for his services until he might conceive he was suspected by the enemy, when he should avail himself of the fruit of his labours to such an extent as in his opinion he could carry off free from molestation.

This trusty messenger was a squalid meagre figure, without the smallest appearance of enterprize, but possessing great acuteness and firmness of character. It may be satisfactory to know, that this man continued faithfully attached to the British interest, and rendered many important services to the garrison of Onore for some time longer. The period at length arrived when he called upon the commandant, and informing him that he had reason to conclude himself suspected by the enemy of holding an intercourse with the fort, he must consult his safety by a precipitate and secret flight. To this no objection could fairly be made. The garrison had essentially benefited in many instances by his firmness and fidelity, and he was entitled to trace out his own line of conduct whenever it seemed most advisable. On parting, Captain Torriano was not without anxiety for his safety: he told him the fate of Onore could not long remain undecided; that should he survive until that period, it was his resolution to reward his services still further by settling on him a pension, provided he could contrive to join him in any of the Company's districts. He was then desired to remunerate himself to the fullest extent of his wishes, and ample means set before him for the purpose. He was however satisfied with little; saying, that in the event of his being seized, and much money discovered upon him, the very circumstance would prove his destruction. He then took his leave, and passed the English posts; but whether he succeeded in effecting his escape into the interior part of the country, or was taken in the attempt, and put to death, has never been known, no tidings having ever been heard of him since that period.

Many anecdotes of attached and faithful Indians similar to this recorded in Mr. Cruso's journal might be adduced. The contrivance of the native halcarrahs and spies to conceal a letter are extremely clever, and the measures they frequently adopt to elude the vigilance of an enemy are equally extraordinary. Many instances have occurred of their suffering severe torture and a cruel death rather than betray their trust. War, although replete with misery, is certainly the means of calling forth some of the noblest virtues and finest traits in the human character, from the commander in chief to the soldier in the ranks. The events of a campaign, a battle, or a siege, furnish occasions for all—but alas, by what dreadful scenes are they contrasted! Truly sings a venerable poetess in the present eventful period of Europe.

> "Bounteous in vain, with frantic man at strife,
> Glad Nature pours the means—the joys of life;
> In vain with orange-blossoms scents the gale,
> The hills with olives clothe, with corn the vale;
> Man calls to Famine, nor invokes in vain,
> Disease and Rapine follow in her train:
> The tramp of marching hosts disturbs the plough;
> The sword, not sickle, reaps the harvest now;
> And where the soldier gleans the scant supply,
> The helpless peasant but retires to die;
> No laws his hut from licens'd outrage shield,
> And War's least horror is th' ensanguin'd field!" A. L. BARBAULD, 1811

In reply to the representation made to Lutoph Ally, as beforementioned, by the commandant of Onore, he declared it was his earnest wish to preserve friendship with the garrison, and requested a suspension of hostile measures until the arrival of letters from the sultaun, which he was assured would terminate the existing difficulty. Another letter was immediately sent from Captain Torriano enforcing the former conditions, and stating to Ludoph Ally that his adherence to the treaty would best prove the friendship he professed; his conduct, not his language, was the subject of complaint; while the former continued unreformed, no credit would be given to the latter. The crafty Persian, perceiving there was no medium between a breach and compliance, prudently resolved on the latter. He sent in a polite explanatory message, accompanied by a supply of ten sheep, of which the commandant immediately expressed a proper sense; the sheep were paid for; and a seasonable supply of other refreshments were received into the garrison.

When the English captured Onore fort, there were two large vessels on the stocks, belonging to Hyder Ally. These stood in the centre of the outworks. A message was now sent from Ludoph Ally, founded on a falsehood, that as Tippoo Sultaun, in consequence of the treaty of peace concluded between him and the English, would in a few days send an order for his troops to take possession of the fort, he requested to be permitted immediately to take charge of the two ships, and build a shed in the fort, for the preservation of the sultaun's arms and military stores which had fallen into our hands, and would now be returned agreeably to the late treaty. Lutoph Ally received for answer, that as he had informed the commandant the ships and arms, together with the fort itself, were so shortly to be delivered up to the sultaun's troops, the compliance with his request was too trifling on the eve of such an important event; and that in the interim all possible care should be taken of the articles in question.

On the 27th of September, a boat was observed from the ramparts to approach Onore bar, on which two others belonging to the sultaun were sent to meet her. On coming alongside, a gentleman went from the boat newly arrived into one of them, and on landing at the batteries was conducted to Lutoph Ally. The garrison of Onore having been long cut off from all communication with their countrymen, their anxiety may be easily conceived. In this state of agitation, Captain Torriano sent his palanquin to the sultaun's grand battery, for the accommodation of the stranger, which soon after returned with Mr. Cruso, who had been appointed head surgeon of the hospital at Onore, and brought letters from Brigadier General M'Leod, commander in chief at Mangulore, and Lieutenant Colonel Campbell, lately commandant of that garrison. These letters informed Captain Torriano of General M'Leod's arrival at Mangulore on the 20th of August; and confirmed his suspicions respecting his correspondence with Colonel Campbell, who had never received one letter intrusted to the care of Lutoph Ally.

The letters from General M'Leod and Colonel Campbell bearing such honourable testimony to the conduct of Captain Torriano and his brave comrades, must not be entirely omitted. The general wrote thus:—" I give you and your brave little garrison much joy and praise for the gallant defence of Onore. I beg you to publish in your orders my hearty approbation and thanks to yourself, and all therein. Every thing here wears the appearance of peace: the sultaun seems anxious for it; and I have every reason to suppose that we shall agree to an equal one with him. Be, however, careful and vigilant. I go to Seringapatam with the sultaun, who is to give me up all the English prisoners as a preliminary, and has already released the officers taken at the Octagon.

Signed, N. M'Leod, Brigadier General, &c."

The contents of Colonel Campbell's letter were equally satisfactory.

"The gallant and spirited defence which you and the brave troops under your command have made, merit from your employers their highest encomium and approbation. It is with pain I reflect on the number of brave fellows who have fallen on that service. However, we have the satisfaction to think that a soldier killed in the execution of his duty dies happy and gloriously. Your exertions have been very great; and no doubt the fatigue both of duty and work must have been extremely severe on your small garrison, particularly on yourself. I sincerely congratulate you upon the prospect of your brother and our other friends of the Bednore army being released; the sultaun having promised to send all the British prisoners to their respective settlements upon parole, as soon as General M'Leod arrives at Seringapatam; where, at the sultaun's desire, the general accompanies him to assist in negociating the peace.

Signed, J. Campbell, Lt. Colonel, &c."

Among other communications from Mr. Cruso, he mentioned, that although the litigious and evasive disposition of the nabob, and the insolence of his people, had heretofore rendered every thing extremely disagreeable to the garrison of Mangulore, yet, before he left it, things were ameliorated; some cattle had been sent in and distributed to the troops, and a few of the officers were permitted to extend their ride beyond the works.

In hopes of preventing the continued desertions, by once more inflicting exemplary punishment, another sepoy was blown from the mouth of a cannon; and as a natural distrust of the enemy now prevailed, all the Europeans and additional gunners were ordered to sleep every night by the guns, and the sepoys off duty to lie on their arms at their respective stations; the commandant himself thenceforward sleeping every night close to the principal breach.

On the 15th of October a subahdar from the enemy's camp announced the arrival of Maw Mirza Khaun, to take the command of the sultaun's army before Onore, in the room of Lutoph Ally Beg; with a request from the new commander that a person of understanding might be sent from the fort, to communicate with him on a subject of great importance. Messaubar, the subahdar formerly employed in negociations with Lutoph Ally, was accordingly dispatched to head-quarters. After the commandant's congratulatory compliments, Mirza was informed, that presuming from his confidence with the sultaun he was intrusted with more discretionary powers than his predecessor, so the generous feeling of a gallant soldier (which was his general character) could not fail to insure a proper use of them. Hence he trusted that the treaty for a cessation of arms would, in future, be as closely adhered to as it had hitherto been scandalously neglected.

Mirza, in return, professed the highest respect for an officer and garrison who had so bravely maintained their post; lamented the little intercourse which had hitherto passed between them and the sultaun's camp, and hoped a sincere friendship would thenceforth take place, instead of the distrust and distance which had hitherto subsisted. Mirza admitted the propriety of the commandant's representations, promised the minutest attention to the treaty, and expressed his regret that a personal interview had not been desired. After many other compliments and promises, Mirza declined performing any of the latter until he should receive Capt. Torriano's answer to a request from Tippoo Sultaun himself, sent by his own vackeel (or ambassador) who accompanied the subahdar on his return to the fort. This suspension of his civilities to the garrison, Mirza was pleased to say, arose, not from any doubt of an immediate compliance with the sultaun's request, but from anxiety to acquaint his sovereign with its success, before he entered on other business.

This request proved to be a repetition of that formerly made by Lutoph Ally, respecting the two ships upon the stocks, with this difference, that whereas that officer had only desired to take charge of them, Mirza stipulated for four hundred workmen being immediately employed in repairing the injuries they had sustained during two sieges, and from the inclemency of the monsoon; at the same time intimating that much might depend upon a ready compliance. An immediate answer being requested, the vackeel was instantly returned with the following:—That the sultaun's extraordinary request could not be complied with; but as one of his declared views was to shelter the ships from the weather, it was engaged, if proper materials were sent in, they should be applied to that purpose; and as this refusal did not affect the treaty, which no where restored the marine-yard to the sultaun, Captain Torriano deemed it in full force, and insisted that the article for supplying cattle should be immediately complied with.

Shortly afterwards another messenger arrived from Mirza, to express his surprise at the little attention paid to the sultaun's request; and as he must suppose there had been some mistake in its delivery, he sent another person to state it more clearly, when he was assured of receiving a different reply; particularly if well understood that Mirza's complying with the treaty must depend in a great measure on granting as a favour what had been made the express condition of acceding to his demands.

Captain Torriano, justly incensed, desired the second emissary to acquaint his master, that conceiving the request to have been first made in obedience to the sultaun's commands, while his own mind reprobated his conduct, he had preserved great moderation in his answer, which he flattered himself would have been ascribed to its true source, a personal delicacy to Mirza. But since a repetition of the demand had been made, he deemed it an insolent puerility, so little becoming the character of Mirza, that he hoped he did not err in imputing it to the short-sighted policy and chicanery of the brahmins by whom he was surrounded. That the proper time for restoring the ships would be, when the sultaun's troops were able to take the outworks in which they stood; until that event, the commandant was determined, not only to keep possession of the vessels, but, if wood for fuel was not immediately supplied for the garrison, the ships would be broken up for that purpose. This answer was just delivered, when a boat proceeding from Onore fort to Fortified Island was prevented going out of the river. To the spirited remonstrance on this fresh insult Mirza replied, that as no anxiety had been expressed to continue on a friendly footing with him, no favours were to be expected.

As yet there had been only a war of words, affairs seemed now ripening to action; and few situations were more unpleasant than that to which the garrison was now reduced. The commandant seized the opportunity afforded by the detention of the boat, to inform Mirza, that finding him resolved on a recommencement of hostilities, he should regulate himself accordingly. If cattle were not sent in the next day, he would recall the English guard from the sultaun's trenches, and order his men out of the fort—if the boats going from Onore to Fortified Island met with any further impediment, the English galliot (an armed vessel) should be stationed at the entrance of the river, to ward off any insult, and prevent the passage of all boats belonging to the sultaun. And that although he wished not to be the aggressor, he would certainly defend himself if attacked, having every thing to hope from the bravery and attachment of his garrison; which, although considerably weakened by death and the desertion of the Malwar poltroons, was fully sufficient to resent insult; and, wearied by the mean and paltry impositions daily practised by an insidious enemy, was impatient for an opportunity of becoming their own avengers.

This line of conduct produced the same effect on Mirza as it had previously done on Lutoph Ally. He declared the severity of the sultaun had made him so strenuous respecting the ships; but as the adoption of violent measures was far from his intention, he trusted there might be an immediate accommodation. Having obtained this point, affairs went on smoothly until the 26th of October, when Captain Torriano received a letter from Colonel Campbell, dated the 13th, at Mangulore, informing him of a surprize intended on his fortress, and advising him to be on his guard. This letter was brought by the faithful spy formerly mentioned. In consequence every operation that could be conducted with secrecy, was immediately commenced. Frazes, chevaux de frize, and fascines, were prepared, trees brought into the fort, and the approach to the covert-way rendered difficult by trous de loups. Organs of various sizes made from the damaged arms, (and so formed that forty or fifty barrels be discharged at one time) to place round the fort and covert-way, and every precaution taken to meet the exigency.

The following day one of the Company's cruizers, with General M'Leod on board, anchored off the port; the general sent a letter and some provisions to the commandant, who knowing his answer would be safely received, informed the general that he was guarded against the arts as well as arms of the enemy, that every exertion would be made by his small garrison, and trusting in him for relief, they would not disgrace the British arms.

About this time Mirza having a diseased leg, requested a visit from the surgeon. Mr. Cruso accordingly repaired to head-quarters, and finding Mirza's case required attention, paid him frequent visits; establishing, on his professional abilities, a connection

highly useful to the English garrison. At the first interview Mr. Cruso discovered Mirza to be the same officer who commanded in the sultaun's trenches before Mangulore, when the British guard entered them, agreeably to the articles of cessation; and it was said his highness had been so greatly incensed at some civilities he had shewn our troops, that he removed him with a severe reprimand. This in some measure accounted for his late conduct at Onore. On all Mr. Cruso's visits Mirza professed the highest respect for the British character, and a partiality for their customs, manners, and even dress; producing a pair of silver buckles made in the sultaun's camp, after an English pattern, and wishing to procure some shoes and a pair of boots from Europe. At the next visit Mr. Cruso carried him the best supply of those articles procurable in the garrison.

Gaming having arrived at an alarming pitch in the garrison, the commanding officer published an order, purporting that as that abominable vice prevailed to so great a degree among the non-commissioned officers and privates, the first man found guilty should be punished with the greatest severity; and that any man who lost his money by this breach of the articles of war, should not be obliged to pay it. At this time intelligence was received that Captain Mathews, brother of General Mathews, and Lieutenant Wheldon, having been shipwrecked on the coast belonging to the rannee (or queen of Cannanore) were sent by her to Tippoo Sultaun, when the inhuman tyrant, with that wanton cruelty which marked his character, doomed them both to a most ignominious death.

The commanding officer observing the daily desertions from the different sepoy corps, issued a general order, in which he of-

fered a discharge to any native soldier, who, from mistaken ideas of the enemy's prowess, should be so base as to request it; promising at the same time to any non-commissioned officer or private a handsome reward who detected a coward deserting his colours; the commandant being determined to punish such an act by every degree of severity, and in the most ignominious manner. It being suspected the sultaun's people were employed in seducing the sepoys from their allegiance, and encouraging them to enter into the enemy's service, Mr. Cruso represented these suspicions to Mirza, adding, that even if they were unjust, the deserters must either be entertained by him, or suffered to pass through his camp: therefore if he did not in future return them, the commanding officer, for his own preservation, must put a stop to all communication between the fort and the sultaun's trenches. To this Mirza solemnly declared he had himself taken no measures to induce the British troops to desert, nor did he know of such practice in others. He confessed that a few deserters had been brought before him, who so far from being fit persons to entertain as soldiers, were miserable spectacles, famished with hunger, and sinking under disease. They laid their little all at his feet, and declared they only fled for the preservation of life, which they implored his leave to seek in a more healthy atmosphere. To these wretched beings he had granted a passage through his camp; but that in future these, and deserters of every description, should be restored; and his officers prohibited, by the strictest orders, from suffering the smallest intercourse between the sultaun's troops and the garrison of Onore.

Desertions and death at length became so frequent, that it ap-

pears necessary to relate them a little more particularly, to form a judgment of the state of the garrison, and the anxiety of the commanding officer. On the 11th of January three veteran sepoys, two recruits, six artificers, with many inhabitants deserted, and six sepoys died. On the following day nearly as many more followed their example. A Malawar recruit being taken in the act, was condemned to death, and a proclamation issued through the corps, that if no more deserted their comrade should be pardoned; but the sentence would most certainly be executed on the first desertion. This compassionate intention was frustrated the very night the gibbet was erected, by the escape of two regulars, three of the Onore corps, and another Malwar, who carried off the sentry with them. The strong ties of caste and consanguinity were thus dissolved by general misery, and all social considerations gave way to self-preservation. Disease was now so prevalent, that hardly one man in the fort remained untainted; eight or ten died daily, and so soon became offensive, that a number of graves were constantly kept in readiness; but the dogs, savage with hunger, generally tore up the dead bodies at night, and strewed the outworks with their mangled remains.

Two days afterwards a jemautdar deserted with two regulars from the sepoy corps, followed by four officers and three privates of the Malwars. The fate of their comrade, confined under sentence of execution, had been hitherto suspended from motives of clemency. Stern necessity now dictated the severe example. In such a trying situation, that discipline, whose perfection lies equally distant from wanton cruelty, and more destructive compassion, compelled the unfortunate wretch to be hanged in front of the Malwar battery, attended by a jemautdar's party from each sepoy corps. Notwithstanding his ignominious exit, another desertion followed the same evening.

One of Tippoo Sultaun's battalions employed against Onore was commanded by Ramchunder, who had formerly been an officer in the Company's service. Captain Torriano had frequently received presents of fruit and vegetables, with other kind attentions, from this subahdar, and an officer named Jehan Caun; which, although trifling in themselves, were very refreshing, and doubly acceptable from being the result of gratitude. They prove that benevolent actions even to an enemy seldom go unrewarded; for Jehan Caun and Ramchunder both acknowledged their friendship arose from a just sense of the tender treatment shewn the sultaun's subjects on the defeat of Saduk Caun at Tellicherry, and at the capture of Onore. The commandant receiving intelligence that Ramchunder would that night pass Onore in his way to Ancola, sent a trusty messenger to request a conference: this was not deemed prudent by Ramchunder; but by the same messenger he returned a friendly farewell, with much cautionary advice; intimating that the native officers who had deserted the British colours, had given Mirza full information of the distressed and reduced state of the garrison, and especially of those hours when the works were most practicable. Although Ramchunder did not absolutely say treachery was intended, he proceeded so far as to advise the strictest vigilance, particularly at the hours of three and six in the morning.

At day-break some ships appearing in the offing, application was made to Mirza for permission to send off a person, should they lay to: this he peremptorily refused; alleging it was positively prohibited by the sultaun; but he promised to send one of his own people on board, with an open letter from Captain Torriano, if he thought proper. He accordingly prepared two letters, interlined with lime juice, and sent them to Mirza. The contents written with ink were calculated by their ambiguity to perplex Mirza's European interpreters, and by exciting curiosity for the answer, might impel them to be sent off in hopes of obtaining further intelligence. The part written with lime-juice pointed out the distresses of the garrison, and the urgent necessity of relief. One letter was from Captain Torriano to the commander in chief, the other from Mr. Cruso to the ship's surgeon. While anxiously waiting the success of these epistles, the garrison ramparts had the mortification to see the ships bear away and steer to the southward. The letters, after being first copied, and sent by an express to the sultaun, were returned to the fort.

On the 21st a Naique and nine sepoys deserted, followed by several more within a few days. One night five regular sepoys, six of the Onore corps, and six volunteers, went off with their family connexions, amounting to thirty persons. Their example was soon followed by a Havaldar, with some other officers and privates, one of whom was shot in the attempt. So great was the distress of the garrison, that the commandant resolved once more to adopt the plan of sending private intelligence through an open intercourse with Mangulore, by the sultaun's halcarrahs; the secret information being interlined with lime-juice. But all these schemes were frustrated by the infamous conduct of a British ensign, who on the 24th of January deserted his colours, went over to the enemy, and communicated to Mirza every intelligence he could desire. This was the severest blow yet sustained!

It being reported to the commanding officer, that a sepoy on the preceding day had been guilty of some mutinous expressions, he immediately rode to the parade with pistols, and assuring the whole corps he would no more appear without them, threatened with instant death the very next man who should utter one word of a similar tendency.

On the second of February 1784, a confidential messenger from Mirza, brought Captain Torriano the intelligence that Mangulore had capitulated to Tippoo Sultaun; at the same time informing him he had received an order from his master to summon the fort of Onore to surrender, accompanied by some other papers from his highness, which Mirza wishing the commandant to be acquainted with, desired Mr. Cruso might immediately be sent to head-quarters for that purpose. On his arrival he found one of the papers really contained the articles of capitulation at Mangulore, and was shewn another, written in the Mahratta language, said to be the sultaun's purwannah; which, at Mirza's desire, Mr. Cruso carried to the fort. The purwannah contained the following particulars:

Translation of the Purwannah from Tippoo Sultaun, accompanying the Articles of Capitulation at Mangulore, enclosed to his Officer Mirza, in command of the forces before Onore.

"MANGULORE is surrendered; the killidar applied to me, acquainting me he was desirous to give up the fort, with liberty to retire. I observed in reply, that as the treaty of peace drew near to a conclusion, and the gentlemen employed in the negociation were hourly expected, he had better wait four or five days, in which time they would certainly arrive. He informed me he had so often heard of their coming, and had so long expected them, that his patience was exhausted; and therefore should he wait any longer he might possibly die in the vain expectation. He was therefore determined not to remain within the walls an hour longer. 'You will therefore,' says he, 'please to take the fort, and give me a receipt for it, and all such things in it as were formerly your property.' I complied with this request, and granted him such an acknowledgment. After which he proposed to me some certain articles, in number twelve, soliciting my accession to them as a particular favour. To these I agreed also; in consequence the fort was delivered up, boats were furnished, agreeably to the stipulation, and the garrison went away. When Colonel Campbell embarked, he informed me that if I forwarded a copy of the articles to the killidar of Onore, he would capitulate on similar conditions. You will therefore submit what I now transmit to you, to the killidar's consideration; and if he is desirous to surrender, you will offer him the same terms, and provide for him accordingly. Should he in that case be in want of provisions for his people, you will supply him properly."

Mirza having sent many fruitless requests to surrender the fort, Mr. Cruso went by appointment to his durbar on the 4th of February, when he apologized for the trouble he had given him, assuring him he had been induced to send these messages entirely from friendship to Captain Torriano, and his good wishes for the garrison in general.

Being unable to procure cattle from the neighbouring country, and no fresh provision being supplied from Mirza, the commanding officer and gentlemen in the garrison caused the few bullocks they had reserved for their own occasions to be killed, and distributed in equal proportions among themselves and the private Europeans. Such of the garrison as ate flesh, had now lived for some time upon salted buffalo and horse flesh, of which there was constantly a dish at the commandant's table. Roasted rats were esteemed a dainty; and, upon the report of a cavalry horse being at the point of death, his throat was cut, and the flesh given to the Mahomedan sepoys and lascars, (native artillerymen) who flocked greedily to receive it. Notwithstanding tobacco had been purchased at an extravagant price by the commanding officer, and occasionally given to the European and native troops, several who had cautiously saved this necessary article, sold it to those who had been less provident for its weight in silver.

About this period the fortress exhibited a dreadful scene; the hospitals overflowed with patients in every stage of the horrid disorder already mentioned; such of the remaining inhabitants as could possibly be attended, were placed under care of the surgeons in their own hovels; many, from necessity, were left to more casual assistance at the village in the out-works. The bodies of the diseased were for the most part so distended by putrid air, as scarcely to leave a trace of the human frame; and it was with difficulty a feature could be distinguished in the countenance; while their laborious breathing indicated every appearance of strangulation. The ear could nowhere escape the groans of the dying, nor the eye avoid these shocking spectacles; but why should language attempt to describe distress, which the conduct of the sufferers paints in more vivid colours? These poor wretches, formerly subjects of a sovereign whose soul never knew mercy, nor felt for human woe when the victorious flag of Britain first waved on the ramparts of Onore, fled to it as an asylum from the sultaun's oppressions, and received protection: yet now did these devoted beings, snatching a transient degree of strength from despair, crawl into the public road, and waiting there until the commanding officer went his evening rounds, prostrated themselves at his feet, imploring permission to quit this dreadful scene, and, as a lighter evil, meet the vengeance of an incensed tyrant. Their prayer was granted, and the same principle of national honour, which originally insured them protection, was now extended for their safety. Proper persons were appointed to see them go out in small parties, after it was dark, hoping by this precaution, that such as were not too much exhausted to reach the enemy's lines unperceived, might from their deplorable condition excite the commiseration of the centinels at the out-posts, and ultimately reach the distant villages.

The following morning presented a dreadful spectacle. On the preceding evening eighty-eight of the inhabitants, men, women, and children, had been permitted to leave the fort; but were so entirely exhausted, that their route to the sultaun's trenches was traced by a line of dead bodies, with the more aggravated spectacle of living infants sucking the breasts of their dead mothers. A venerable Portugueze priest, who had for many years been vicar of the Roman Catholic church at Onore, being dangerously ill of the same distemper, now desired permission to leave the fort. Captain Torriano immediately accommodated him with his palanquin, wrote a suitable letter to Maw Mirza, and sent him properly attended to the saultaun's army; where, to the honour of Mirza, he was kindly received and treated with great humanity, until in a few days death happily released him from his sufferings.

On the 18th of February, the moody, or native commissary, who had been sent into the enemy's camp, returned with a complimentary messsage to the commanding officer from the rajah of Zeremullee mentioning his illness, and requesting Mr. Cruso might visit him in camp. This Hindoo rajah was one of the tributary princes dependent on Tippoo Sultaun; he then commanded a thousand men in that army, and was much in the confidence of Maw Mirza. On Mr. Cruso's arrival he found the rajah's indisposition very slight, and more a pretence to procure an interview, than any real disorder. He accordingly desired him to remonstrate in his name with captain Torriano, on the folly of not accepting the terms of capitulation now offered, as the garrison must from necessity fall in a very short time; and the sultaun, being minutely informed of their wretched situation, had directed Mirza no more to summon the fort to surrender, nor to recommence hostilities; but when the English chose to evacuate it, to suffer them to do so unmolested. The rajah further added, that the commissioners expected from Madras to settle the terms of peace had not yet descended the ghauts; and the hostages, wearied by their irksome delay, had requested the sultaun's leave to proceed to Tellicherry, which would be granted in a few days. Mr. Cruso thanked the rajah for his friendly communication; assuring him that he had been authorised by captain Torriano, should such a conversation take place, to inform him his sentiments on that subject remained the same as expressed in his answer to the sultaun's first summons; nor would he surrender the fort while a man adhered to his colours, unless by command of his superiors.

A few days afterwards a havaldar from the sepoy guard posted in the enemy's trenches reported to captain Torriano a rumour that the fort was to be stormed on the 22d, about four o'clock in the morning. This information was not to be entirely slighted, especially as it was soon after confirmed by Jehan Caun's halcarra, who came with a similar message to that sent by the rajah of Zeremullee, and received the same answer. The breach in the fort, being cleared and scarped, with a thick and formidable abbatis in its front, it was not supposed they would have the temerity to attack it; especially as the native troops are not expert at general assaults; but in the reduced state of the garrison every prudent measure was to be adopted, and the commissary's men, with their stores, were all ordered within the walls.

By the fort adjutant's report, the whole number of Europeans, sepoys, and recruits at this time in the garrison, including black officers, and the sick and wounded in the hospital, amounted only to two hundred and fifteen. Many desertions had lately taken place among the native troops of every description; during the preceding night, although a sepoy was shot in the attempt, five others deserted before morning; one of them, a havaldar and orderly to an English officer, carried off with him the gentleman's sword, silver plates, and other articles. Every hour's experience now created fresh doubts of the fidelity of the sepoys, nor did that of the native officers in general escape suspicion. A distrust which at length gave rise to a very disagreeable circumstance.

On the 23d of February, in consequence of a horseman having imputed treachery to the subahdar Missauber, the Europeans came at night to the commanding officer, alleging the horseman could prove the subahdar to have frequently received letters from Mirza, and carried on his correspondence by the man who formerly conveyed letters from captain Torriano to colonel Gordon; adding that the subahdar was accessary to the late desertions, and particularly to those of the preceding night: all this was firmly believed by the regulars, and under this circumstance the distressed state of the garrison rendered it difficult on what measures to resolve. If only a private and delicate investigation took place, the complainants might attribute it to an ill-founded confidence, and be apprehensive of falling a sacrifice. If, on the contrary, a public inquiry was adopted, they might lose the attachment of an officer, whose great exertions and general good character had given him much weight in the garrison, and particular influence over the sepoys. Engineer Blachford was also informed, that two sepoys of the sultaun's guard had just been with the quarter-master serjeant, and informed him of a concerted plot for assassinating the officers and seizing the fort: the attack was to commence at head-quarters.

A fresh difficulty now arose, in consequence of two sepoys being ordered for execution in the evening. The Europeans employed to execute the last criminal, having been stigmatized by their companions as hangmen, were averse to a repetition of that disagreeable duty, and modestly represented their objection to the commanding officer; who informed them the duty must be done, and he would be present at the execution. This representation having been respectfully made, no notice was then taken of it: at the appointed hour captain Torriano, accompanied by three other gentlemen attended the party. The place of execution was between the enemy's batteries and the fort: while on their way thither they were interrupted by the hasty arrival of a person who had been employed to gain information; after a private conversation with the captain he retired, and the party proceeded. While the criminals stood under the gallows with halters about their necks, the quarter-master serjeant, hitherto distinguished for exemplary conduct, with a countenance expressive of every humane sensation, dropped upon his knees; and, in the name of all the Europeans supplicated for a pardon to the deserters. The commandant immediately replied, that both himself and his brave comrades must be sensible it was his first wish to oblige them in every reasonable request, but in the present instance a paramount duty to his employers, himself, and every man under his command, precluded all possibility of compliance. This he was assured they would readily credit, when at a proper time they were informed of the reasons for this resolution. The execution was then ordered; but on the appearance of some reluctance, captain Torriano took a pistol from the holster, and threatening to shoot the first man who refused obedience, the criminals were launched into eternity.

On leaving this distressing scene, captain Torriano hastened to the fort, where an alarming occurrence required immediate attention. The person who so hastily addressed him, when proceeding to the place of execution, gave information that all the sepoys posted in the outworks, headed by their jemautdar, had agreed to desert to the enemy the following night. The guards were directly withdrawn from the outworks, and the guns brought into the fort. The jemautdar, suspected to be the ringleader, was put in irons, and sent into close confinement; where, conscious of his guilt, he committed suicide.

In the mean time Mr. Cruso repaired to Mirza's durbar, to complain of his not having relieved the sultaun's guard stationed at Onore, and to inform him, if not immediately done, twenty of his men would be ordered out of the fort. Mirza sent an apology with the necessary order, which had only been prevented by a multiplicity of business. In the evening the sepoy who communicated the intended assassination of the European officers, underwent an examination, in which it appeared he was addicted to drinking, and his story proved altogether absurd and improbable; the garrison were nevertheless so strongly impressed with the idea, that at night when the commanding officer retired to his couch near the breach, he found himself attended by a guard of Europeans, with fixed bayonets. On the sultaun's guard being relieved, agreeably to the stipulation, two field-pieces, loaded with grape-shot, were placed under a proper guard, with lighted matches, immediately opposite the station; where they remained until the evacuation of Onore. It is almost unnecessary to remark, that this step was taken for the sole purpose of dissipating the prejudices of the Europeans, which no argument could subdue. When it is considered that these prejudices originated entirely from fidelity and attachment to their officers, they will be found more deserving of applause than reprehension.

The commander in chief being daily expected in a vessel off Onore, captain Torriano prepared the following letter to be ready on his arrival, which affords a statement of affairs on the 28th of February, 1784.

" It is with the greatest surprise and regret, I find the repeated representations I have made of the distress, and alarming situation of the Onore garrison, totally unattended to; and my frequent and ardent request that some vessel of force, for various reasons, should lay off this port, not complied with. Regardless of my own fate, I cannot but acutely feel the sufferings of my brave comrades, who although now greatly reduced in number, a prey to disease, surrounded by death, and deceived by fruitless promises of relief, still adhere to me. To enumerate their sufferings would swell this letter beyond a prudent size for its conveyance; I shall therefore only mention, that within the short period of six weeks five hundred persons, soldiers and natives, have fallen victims to a cruel pestilence which rages within these walls. Desertion nearly keeps pace with death: so serious and so incredible is the former, that among the number lately gone over to the enemy is a British officer. The effect of such conduct on the mind of the now almost desponding garrison, is easier to conceive than describe. Mirza, the sultaun's commanding officer, is daily urging us in the strongest terms and most threatening manner, to capitulate; assuring us we need no longer indulge any hope of relief; and that if the terms granted by Tippoo Sultaun to the garrison of Mangulore are not now accepted, less merciful will be the portion of those, who, from famine and disease, must in a short time inevitably fall into the hands of the sultaun.

" Every means in my power shall be exerted to defend the place, while a grain of rice remains for subsistence; but I trust the British arms will not be so shamefully tarnished as to admit this fortress, unsupported, to fall into the enemy's hands. Of my few officers, death has deprived me of one, desertion of another; my garrison is reduced to sixty effective men: to preserve *them* I have been reduced to the necessity of withdrawing the guards from the outworks, the enemy having nearly succeeded in seducing the whole; for although every man taken in the act of desertion, has been put to death, still so great is the dread of the horrid disorder, which sweeps away all before it, and so little the hope of relief, that the executions have not had the intended effect. The quantity of provisions remaining in the fort is very small; and with regret I add, that great part of the rice, the only food of the sepoys, is much damaged.

" The enemy have received a strong reinforcement, and the buxey informs me they are to be increased by ten additional battalions: on their arrival we are told more hostile measures will be adopted, to bring us to a proper sense of our condition; for which purpose the sultaun has sent another officer to command the Onore army. Much of this information was intended to intimidate the garrison; and I am sorry to add it has had the desired effect on most of the sepoys.

" I hear hostilities are commenced in the Sadurhagur quarter; and from various causes I have great reason to be apprehensive for the safety of Fortified Island. I flatter myself it is needless to add anything further to evince the necessity of some step being immediately taken to relieve this fort; nor will I relinquish the hope that I shall not be left to a capitulation, even though accompanied by the best terms, and originating in the most absolute necessity. Should this be received, please to fire two guns and lower the ensign. In any future notes, my private communications will be by interlineations with lime juice, which a clear fire will bring to light."

Several officers, with every one of the non-commissioned officers, and European privates, were now, more or less, afflicted by the scurvy; on its appearance, the surgeons pronounced vegetables and exercise to be the only things from which either prevention or cure could be expected: people were accordingly employed secretly to purchase a quantity of garden-seeds in the enemy's camp; which were portioned to the Europeans and sepoys, with an earnest exhortation to cultivate them for the preservation of life. This being actively pursued for some time, the fort and outworks exhibited a scene of verdure, but from long confinement, and the indolence inseparable from scorbutic disorders, their minds lost the necessary energy, and sunk into a state of torpor inimical to exertion. In a few weeks both Europeans and sepoys gave up gardening, and the disease gaining strength, became dreadfully fatal. The gentlemen in the fort left nothing undone which even parental solicitude could have devised. They laboured with their own hands to supply the feeble Europeans with vegetables; and by example endeavoured to excite emulation. They made skittle-grounds, and gave every encouragement to the exercise, by joining in it themselves. The few remaining horses of the cavalry were ordered out to accommodate such invalids as could be lifted up and keep their seat, by the assistance of supporters. These humane exertions were frequently efficacious, and reflect the highest honour on the officers; their conduct also exhibits a striking proof of the infinite advantage which may be derived from resolutely combating a disorder which inevitably destroys those who give way to it; for while the most dreadful mortality pervaded the native inhabitants and sepoys, only five out of thirty-five Europeans fell a sacrifice.

On the 4th of March, about four o'clock in the morning, the centries were alarmed by the firing of musketry at Fortified Island, and on the officers repairing immediately to the ramparts, it became evident that fortress was attacked by the enemy; the firing continued for some time, and then ceased. At sun-rise the officers discovered by their glasses about twenty men sitting in the veranda of a house on the summit of the hill; whom they concluded to be the garrison, which amounted to that number, who were supposed to have been seized and secured by the enemy. Soon after the English colours were hoisted, either with the hope of deceiving the garrison of Onore, or to decoy the vessels expected with a supply of provisions.

The treacherous veil was now withdrawn, and the capture of Fortified Island no longer admitted a doubt in the minds of the gentlemen at Onore that the fort would be attacked. The commanding officer therefore thinking it necessary to make these suspicions publicly known, dispatched Mr. Cruso to Mirza with a remonstrance on such shameful conduct. That gentleman entertaining no doubt of his personal security, proceeded to the enemy's trenches, where he was informed the caun had rode out: he went again the next morning, and after waiting some time was received in the durbar. Mr. Cruso, in the name of his commanding officer, informed Mirza he could not sufficiently express his astonishment at the sultaun's open violation of public faith, in having assaulted and taken Fortified Island; that the present visit to his durbar was not so much to know whether the fort of Onore was to be next attacked, as to give him notice, that as he fully expected such a treacherous attempt, so was he resolutely prepared to resist it. Extraordinary as it may appear to those unacquainted with the duplicity and chicanery of the Indian character, Mirza positively denied having attacked the island; and gravely replied, that the English officer commanding there had for some time given great disgust to his sepoys, by refusing them proper provisions, whilst he luxuriously feasted upon poultry and liquors sent from time to time for the use of the gentlemen at Onore. At the time his people were thus disaffected, this imprudent officer endeavoured to seduce the wife of a Naique, who was by caste a brahmin, and at length had recourse to violence. On this outrage the husband flew to his comrades, interested them and their jemautdar in his cause, and then went in a body to the officer's quarters; where remonstrating with a freedom which he construed into insolence, they were threatened with death. The aggrieved party had immediate recourse to arms, and attacked the officer, who was supported by half his garrison. This occasioned the irregular fire heard at Onore. While these mutual hostilities were pending, one of the sultaun's boats accidentally passing Fortified Island, was hailed by the mutineers, who intreated to be taken on board. This being reported to Mirza, he sent over a messenger to the English officer to represent the folly of continuing at his post with only eleven men, recommending him to leave the island, and offering every accommodation in his camp, until an opportunity presented for proceeding to an English settlement. The officer declined quitting the island, but desired Mirza would send over a sufficient force to take charge of the fort; his request was complied with, and these were the men who had been seen from the ramparts of Onore. All this was related by Mirza in the gravest manner; and the jemautdar, the brahmin Naique and his wife, with five sepoys (tutored for the purpose, at the peril of their lives) were brought into the durbar, to corroborate Mirza's story. It is almost unnecessary to observe that the whole of this tale was a fabrication of the sultaun's officer to deceive the commandant.

To one so fertile at invention and villainous evasion as Mirza, Mr. Cruso could make no reply, except that he should repeat this extraordinary tale to the commanding officer at Onore, and took leave by observing, that as he was not a principal, it did not become him to discuss the subject; but he could not suppress an apprehension, that when he asserted at the English head-quarters, he had been told such a story by the officer in command of the sultaun's army, his own veracity would be called in question.

At this time captain Torriano received a letter from general M'Leod, dated March 7th, 1784, on board the Chesterfield Indiaman off Onore, desiring to be informed of the state of the garrison, and offering his best services. The sickness of the garrison, the late threatening combination, the debility of the Europeans, the treachery of the sultaun in the capture of Fortified Island, and beyond all, the general despondency which now prevailed, and would no doubt greatly increase when the general sailed, induced the commanding officer to wish for an honourable termination to his difficulties; he therefore resolved to profit by an opportunity so critically presented to convey a soldier's feelings, and accordingly sent a copy of the letter previously written to general M'Leod, and already inserted.

A draft of this letter having been explained to Mirza by Mr. Cruso, he assented with much apparent satisfaction to its being sent off to the Chesterfield, but he took especial care it never should be delivered to the general; or if delivered and answered, he suppressed the answer. Deceitful as had been his conduct respecting the capture of Fortified Island, his behaviour with regard to the letter sent to general M'Leod exceeded it in folly, cruelty, and duplicity. The falsehoods he permitted to be told in his durbar, by boatmen and messengers tutored for the purpose, who were supposed to have been employed in the delivery of the letter, and intrusted with a cool indifferent verbal answer, instead of a written reply to its interesting contents, were uttered before Mr. Cruso in the gravest manner possible. The stories fabricated on this occasion by Mirza and his colleagues, to answer their own wretched purpose, would astonish and disgust a generous Briton, unused to such chicanery. They occupy many pages in the journal, but the detail would now have little interest; it will suffice to say that the commandant and garrison of Onore had the mortification to see the vessel sail away with the general, without the smallest relief to their distress.

Sanguine as had been the hopes of the gentlemen upon the issue of this communication with the general, and encouraged still more by the warmth with which Mirza had appeared to adopt their views, this behaviour in full durbar became highly provoking, and occasioned Mr. Cruso to tell Mirza he was at a loss which most to admire, the ingenious tales just fabricated, or the story of the officer at Fortified Island, with the rape, the mutiny, and seasonable arrival of the boat; adding, that hitherto he had been considered as professing a respect for the Onore garrison consistent with the sentiments of a liberal enemy; but where was that liberality and respect, when forgetting they had even the common feelings and understanding of men, he insulted them with such foolish and unfounded fictions? He then declared that if any chicanery had been used with captain Torriano's letter, or any imposition practised upon the general, there was an end to every hope of the garrison leaving the fort, consistent with that sense of honour and duty by which they had been hitherto actuated; and he would take upon himself to say, the fort would never yield to the sultaun until every European was cut to pieces. To which Mirza replied with the most cutting indifference, "We are not going to cut you to pieces."

On the 9th a small party was ordered to patrol the outworks during the night, lest the enemy should take possession of them, under pretence of being entirely abandoned. At this time the subahdar of the fort-guard in the enemy's trenches, sent word that forty Malawars, and other natives of the coast, were desirous of deserting to us; an artifice too shallow to succeed.

The next morning the faithful spy, formerly mentioned, was dispatched to the enemy's camp, to procure, if possible, a secret interview with the officer taken at Fortified Island, and convey him a little money. In this he fortunately succeeded, and on the 13th returned, with a letter from the officer, apparently written with charcoal and water, and scarcely legible: it contained an account of the island having been taken by the sultaun's people. That himself with the other officers, and a private European, were confined in the same prison, after having been plundered of every thing, except the clothes on their backs; they were threatened with being sent to Seringapatam, unless they entered into the sultaun's service; and the infamous ensign, whose desertion has been already noticed, had been frequently with them, to offer, on such conditions, the restoration of their property, and a supply of every other convenience. That the sepoys, and even the officers' servants taken with them, had been compelled to enter into the sultaun's service; in which the jemautdar was promoted to the rank of subahdar, and sent back to Fortified Island. This gentleman acknowledged the receipt of the money, and declaring that no hardship should drive them to enter into the sultaun's service, entreated captain Torriano to exert himself for their release.

There had not been any communication with the enemy since Mr. Cruso's last interview with Mirza; who had since twice denied himself when that gentleman repaired to the batteries. Early in the morning of the 16th a messenger came to the fort, with a polite message from the caun, requesting to see Mr. Cruso immediately, on the contents of a very important perwanna just received from the sultaun. No time was lost in obeying the summons, and that gentleman soon returned with the joyful news of peace being concluded between the English and Tippoo Sultaun; he brought also the following letter from Messrs Sadleir, Staunton, and Huddlestone, the Madras commissioners, enclosing an extract from that part of the treaty which related to Onore.

To Captain John Samuel Torriano, commanding at Onore.

SIR,

WE have the honour to inform you that peace was yesterday concluded between the Honourable Company and the nabob Tippoo Sultaun Bahadaur. We enclose you an extract of the article of treaty which relates to Onore, Carwar, and Sadasheraguda: agreeably to which, we desire you will deliver Onore, &c. to the officer of the nabob, who shall produce this letter; and embark with the troops on the vessels now sent for that purpose.

"We enclose a letter to you from the select committee of Bombay, in which they desire you to obey our directions. Should Carwar and Sadasheraguda be included in your command, you will give orders for their evacuation and delivery, as well as Onore, and embark the garrison. We enclose the nabob's order to his officers for supplying the troops with provisions and other necessary assistance; and have the honour to be, with much esteem,

Your most obedient, humble servants,

ANTHONY SADLIER,
G. L. STAUNTON,
J. HUDDLESTON.

Camp near Mangalay,
12th March 1784.

As Mirza had intrusted Mr. Cruso with those papers, not officially, but for the private satisfaction of captain Torriano and the Onore garrison, until the duplicates arrived, Mr. Cruso returned them the next morning, when Mirza invited him to ride in the evening, and afterwards to a nautch (of dancing girls) and a supper. This entertainment was confined to a few of Mirza's select friends; when all was hilarity and good-humour he led his guest into an inner apartment, and there shewed him colonel Gordon's answer to the letter sent him by major Torriano on the 7th of February. Taking advantage of this festive season, Mr. Cruso reminded Mirza of a former promise to communicate the contents of general M'Leod's answer to captain Torriano's letter written when the general was last off the port; this also he produced, but positively refusing to part with it, Mr. Cruso read it with so great attention as to be able on his return to the fort to commit it to paper, and next morning delivered it to the commanding officer, the contents, at the time peculiarly interesting, are now unnecessary to be inserted.

On the 18th two vessels, with several boats, anchored in the offing; the largest making a signal for a boat, an open letter was, as usual, sent to Maw Mirza, who dispatched it by a special messenger. In the evening he returned with a letter from captain Scott, of the Hawke Indiaman; mentioning his arrival from Mangulore, with orders from the commissioners to evacuate Onore, and embark the garrison on the vessels then under his convoy for that purpose.

General Orders, Onore 20th of March 1784.

"Replete with the highest sense of gratitude to this garrison, the Commandant, in the warmest manner thanks the officers, heads of departments, non-commissioned officers, and privates of every corps, for their courage, toil, and conduct, during a fatiguing siege of more than three months, and a painful blockade of much longer continuance. He is assured, from a determination to do ample justice in his representations to the Honourable the Select Committee at Bombay, and to brigadier general M'Leod, commander in chief of the army, of the spirit and perseverance they have in so great a degree evinced, they will receive more flattering commendations on their arrival at the presidency, than it is in his power to bestow."

The same evening, captain Torriano, in compliance with a pressing invitation, paid his first visit to Mirza, accompanied by captain Scott, and three other gentlemen. They met, agreeably to a preconcerted plan, at the sultaun's batteries. Mirza was attended by the rajah of Zeremullee, and a numerous suwarree; the sultaun's troops forming a line from the batteries to the durbar, paid the British commandant all the European military honours as he passed their respective corps. After a plentiful supper, consisting of every dainty procurable, the company were entertained till day-light by the best dancing girls in the camp. They then returned to the fort; the road from the durbar to the batteries being, as before, lined with troops.

During the conviviality of the evening, captain Torriano asked Mirza some questions regarding the officer who had so shamefully deserted his colours during the distressing siege. Mirza answered he was a villain, or he never would have left his comrades at such a moment. But if it afforded the smallest gratification to his injured countrymen, he could assure them the ignominious culprit was then in irons for misconduct recently committed in camp, and confined within a few yards of the spot where they were then sitting.

On the 22d Mirza and the rajah of Zeremullee, attended by Mr. Cruso and an officer, went on board the Hawke Indiaman, which presented to them a scene of perfect novelty and surprise. They were much pleased with the exterior of the ship, but appeared in astonishment at the arrangements and accommodations within; which they minutely examined, and expressed the highest satisfaction. On going on board, and departing from the Hawke, they were saluted; and in every instance treated by captain Scott with the politest attention. At night Mirza prepared another supper, and entertained his guests with music and dancing girls till day-break.

On the 24th, seven bullocks, thirty sheep, a supply of dholl, ghee, tobacco, and jaggree were shipped for the use of the troops; but from a want of boats, and the dilatoriness of the sultaun's people, the embarkation went on slowly; nor could either remonstrances or persuasion accelerate it. Several small guards from Tippoo's troops being observed in different parts of the outworks, on which innovation the commandant had not been consulted, he sent a complaint to Mirza, with an inquiry why they were thus posted. He apologized for their having been posted without a proper representation, which was the fault of the messenger, but said that they were thus placed to prevent the escape of Narrain Row, a brahmin of consequence, whom the rebel Hyat, on his treaty with general Mathews, had appointed collector of the revenue; as also to hinder the flight of the former inhabitants of that country, who might then be in the fort; adding that the sultaun had given him the most positive orders not to suffer the garrison to embark unless all his people were given up.

Had the smallest doubt existed of the fate to which these unfortunate persons were devoted upon their falling into the hands of the sultaun, this order would have removed it. It therefore became the duty of humanity, as well as national honour, to shield them from the tyrant's vengeance. Captain Torriano immediately determined at all events to save them; but in the present situation of affairs he thought it most prudent to temporize; and practising a virtuous deception, he acquainted Mirza that whatever number of people under this description had remained, he must have considered as part of that garrison he had received orders to withdraw, and should consequently have insisted upon embarking them; but they were then totally out of the question; for, suspecting what would happen, they had made their escape. Mirza replied he was greatly misinformed, as he himself had taken such precautions, that it was impossible for a man to have passed the camp without his knowledge; he therefore hoped there would be no objection to his searching the fort and gallivat; observing, that although it was of little consequence to him whether Narrain Row was really taken or not, it was of the first importance for him to prove that every effort had been exerted for that purpose.

Measures having been adopted during these messages to render the search abortive, Mirza's request was readily complied with. To conceal these men in the fort was not difficult, but to convey them on board the vessels required the utmost caution. A brahmin, bigoted to his religious ceremonies, will hardly forego them even for the preservation of life. When the search in the gallivat was ended, the wretched Narrain Row, terrified almost to stupidity, was sent on board, disguised as a Lascar, and shut up in a small dark place, separated from the hold. The brahmin had not been there more than an hour, when Mirza informed captain Torriano that having in vain searched for him on shore, he must be permitted to place a guard on board the gallivat until she sailed out of the river, to prevent the brahmin obtaining admittance. The commandant having a point of consequence to carry for the Company, with Mirza, thought it prudent to grant his request. The point so material, was the embarkation of the guns and stores of the fort, together with the treasure belonging to the Company: for, strange and reprehensible as it must appear, not one of these articles, nor the destiny of the inhabitants, had been mentioned, either in the Commissioners' orders, or in the third article of peace, which they sent to the commandant. Fortunately, after a long altercation, which terminated in a handsome pecuniary gratification, this difficulty was surmounted, and the eighteen-pounder guns, field-pieces, running-shot, shells, musquet-ammunition, and a quantity of powder were shipped off, and a receipt obtained for some powder unavoidably left behind for want of a proper conveyance.

Narrain Row, whose weak frame and debilitated system rendered existence almost impossible in his close confinement in the hold of a gallivat, passed the sultaun's centinel in his disguise of a Lascar, and was once more safely lodged in the fort; there he remained until the 26th, the day destined for embarking the private baggage, the sick, unnecessary servants, women, children, and all but the men under arms; nor were the brahmins forgot. But the hopes for their safety were slender, and the general prospect discouraging. Maw Mirza, in obedience to the sultaun's orders, insisted on posting confidential persons to examine the contents of all chests and packages, and the countenance of every person who should embark; some of these inspectors had been employed in the fort, and resided in the town, so that neither sircar property, nor any inhabitant of Onore, could be clandestinely carried off. The keen vigilance of these examiners suggested the idea of making it the instrument of their own deception. The venerable vicar of the Romish church, lately deceased, had deposited in the fort, with the commandant's leave, several large chests filled with images and ornaments belonging to the Portugueze church at Onore; these were sent down to the beach with the greatest care, and particular orders given that the sultaun's people should on no account be permitted to open them, except in the commandant's presence. The extraordinary magnitude of the chests, and the affected mystery of the attendants, did not fail to excite the expected curiosity. At length captain Torriano arrived, and ordering the chests to be unlocked, instead of the expected brahmins, they turned out twelve images of the apostles, with a number of saints, all the size of life, and splendidly dressed. While the attention of the inspectors was thus engaged, the poor shivering brahmin, who had been waiting at some distance down the river, up to his chin in water, was received on board the Indiaman's pinnace, and stowed away under some bullocks. The boat having been previously examined, rowed briskly under the batteries, and to the satisfaction of the whole garrison, carried him in safety on board the Hawke.

The principal object of the sultaun's vengeance having thus found an asylum, the safety of the other brahmins required equal consideration, lest an open interference should create a rupture with Mirza. It was at length suggested, as the most feasible method, to attempt passing them among the sick. Mr. Cruso accordingly rolled a large bandage, dipped in turmeric, round the head of one, and placing him in a dooly, (a sort of palanquin), he made him swallow a strong emetic, with an intention it should operate at the time of his examination. Thus prepared, the brahmin was sent down to the hospital-boat, the commandant keeping within view to watch the success of humanity, and prevent mischief in case of failure. Fear, unfortunately, took such strong possession of the brahmin's mind as prevented all power in the emetic, and the bandage proving too flimsy a disguise for the argus-eyes of the inspectors, he was challenged by name, and instantly surrounded: beginning to be very roughly handled, the commandant rode up, and demanded who had dared to commit outrage on the sick? The sultaun's people declared it was all a deception, and growing clamorous, the commandant immediately ordered the man to be taken back to the fort, saying the surgeon should explain the business, he having the sole management of the hospital to which the patient belonged. The only remaining expedient was to clothe the brahmins in the sepoy uniform, and intermix them with the regulars of that corps, who were to embark the next day; thus arranged, the boats containing the sick, baggage, and garrison stores, dropped down to the bar, to remain at anchor until the whole embarkation was ready.

The next morning Mr. Cruso repaired to Mirza's durbar, to clear up the affair of the sick brahmin, and demand a positive answer to a request (which had been previously evaded) for a boat to carry off eleven valuable horses belonging to the commandant and other English gentlemen. When this request was first made, he promised compliance; but as often as it had been repeated, some evasion succeeded. Respecting the brahmin, Mirza behaved well; it was represented that being originally a man of low station in the brahminical tribe, he had been employed in the hospital to wait upon the invalids of his own caste; and at Mr. Cruso's earnest solicitation, on taking upon himself the responsibility of getting him away, Mirza agreed to make no further opposition. The paltry equivocations concerning a boat for conveying the horses, were now too notorious to admit a doubt of the sultaun having ordered them to be detained for his own use.

On this intimation, captain Torriano, ordering the guards from the sultaun's trenches, and the troops to be ready to embark, sent Mr. Cruso with an officer to Mirza's durbar, finally to demand the restitution of the officers and garrison treacherously captured at Fortified Island, to request a pilot to conduct the Company's gallivat over the bar, and to stipulate that a British guard should keep possession of the fort until all the rest were embarked. Further, that the sultaun's troops should not enter the fort until the last man had struck the colours and entered the boat, when the keys would be delivered to the sultaun's officer appointed to receive them. To the demand for the prisoners taken at Fortified Island, Mirza declared it could not be complied with, without an express order from Tippoo Sultaun. A pilot to conduct the gallivat was furnished, and the proposed plan of evacuation acceded to. These arrangements being concluded, the troops marched to the beach; among them were the devoted brahmins, in full uniform and accoutrements: they had been previously admonished to shew no alarm, nor be under the smallest terror from the Sultaun's people; but, in full confidence of support, to bayonet the first man who should attempt to seize them.

While the commandant was giving orders for the delivery of a few horses belonging to Tippoo's cavalry, taken at Bednore, to the persons waiting to take charge of them, he received a message from Mirza replete with affected sorrow at the Sultaun's boats not being sufficiently strong and commodious for the gentlemen's horses, to accompany the present embarkation; but promising they should be sent after their departure, so as to meet them at Sedashagger. The obvious meaning and palpable falsehood of this message rendered its insolence intolerable. The troops were therefore ordered instantly to embark, and the officers, indignant at the infamous conduct of Mirza, saw their horses shot upon the spot!

The sacrifice of these noble animals, while it excited the commiseration of their owners, struck the Sultaun's people with astonishment. But neither did that astonishment, nor the confusion occasioned by the act itself, divert their attention for one moment from their principal object, the seizure of the brahmins. Deeply versed in that cunning and artifice, the peculiar characteristic of Asiatics, they suspected a counter-plot, and turning all their attention to the embarkation of the troops, singled out, to a man, every brahmin recruit, and insisted on their being delivered up. Captain Torriano resolving steadily to adhere to those honourable and humane principles which had hitherto regulated his conduct, determined they should not be sullied by his last act on this ill-fated spot. Upon being threatened that if the brahmins were not instantly given up, the Onore garrison should be detained, he positively declared not a man should be touched while he had power to defend him; and resolutely commanding the troops and brahmins immediately to embark, his decided conduct silenced all further opposition.

The guard was now ordered to leave the fort: while they were embarking, the subahdar, Missauber, having locked the gates on the inside, at a signal made by captain Torriano, struck the British colours, and coming through a sally-port, resigned the keys to the Sultaun's officer ordered to take possession; whose detachment waited without the outworks until this ceremony had taken place. The whole being now safely embarked, captain Torriano followed with two chests of treasure belonging to the Company. Night coming on, they were obliged to anchor under the guns of the fort until day-break, when the Wolf gallivat and all the boats proceeded over the bar; the officers embarked on board the Hawke Indiaman, and the whole fleet sailed for Bombay.

During the voyage thither captain Torriano rewarded the services of the subahdar Missauber with a pair of gold bangles; promoted four of the sepoys, whose conduct had merited his approbation, and presented each of them with silver bangles. The majority of the European soldiers, for the same reason, were raised to the rank of non-commissioned officers. Their behaviour furnishes an additional proof to a remark of Marechal Saxe, that " the bravery of troops is a variable and uncertain quality of the mind," for most of these very men fled from Cundapore, and had scarcely breathed after their disgrace, when their conduct at Onore merited the highest commendation, which was never forfeited during the siege.

As public testimonies of an honourable discharge of confidential trust justly merit a degree of consideration, to which the commentaries of an individual have not an equal claim, the narrative cannot be more consistently, nor more honourably concluded than by inserting the sense the government of Bombay were pleased to express to the Court of Directors of the brave and gallant conduct of the commandant and garrison of Onore.

Bombay, 15*th April* 1784.

" WITH much pleasure we embrace this opportunity of acknowledging ourselves highly satisfied with the brave and gallant defence of the fortress of Onore, by captain Torriano, of your artillery, during the continuance of the siege; and his conduct since the cessation of hostilities took place, until he received the Commissioners' orders to surrender Onore to the nabob."

(Signed) JAMES BECK,

A TRUE COPY. Secretary.

General Orders, Bombay, 4th May, 1784.

"THE honourable the President and select committee, in testimony of the just sense they bear of the brave and spirited defence of the fortress of Onore, as well of the regular conduct of the troops, since the cessation of hostilities took place, until it was evacuated on the conclusion of the treaty of peace, return their thanks in particular to captain John Samuel Torriano, whose conduct on this command reflects on him the highest honour; and to all the officers, and men in general, who lately composed that garrison."

To these testimonies of approbation in India, the Court of Directors in England were pleased to confer a Major's brevet-commission on captain Torriano, and to express their approbation in the following paragraph of their general letter to the governor and council of Bombay.

"WE have considered of your representation in favour of captain John Samuel Torriano, the senior officer of artillery upon your establishment; and from the peculiar circumstances of his case, and as a reward for his gallant services in the defence of Onore during the late siege, we hereby direct that you grant him a Major's brevet-commission, to bear date from the 14th of September, 1784."

I now take leave of the Onore manuscripts: in a military point of view, I cannot expatiate on their merit; nor whether I have, in particular instances, too much dilated or abridged Mr. Cruso's narrative. Had it only related to the siege of Onore, however interesting that event was to the friends of the gallant officers who so bravely defended it, there might have been many desiderata to render it equally so in a distant country, and at a remote period; but the siege of Onore contains an epitome of human nature; its little history exhibits a striking contrast between national and individual character, actuated by different motives, and pursuing different means—a contrast in which the British officer stands on an exalted pedestal; encircled by courage, honour, fortitude, and humanity; opposed to an oriental tyrant, with a train of fear, distrust, chicanery, and the meaner vices. Thus, eminently favoured, I have enjoyed a peculiar pleasure in collating the preceding pages from the voluminous collection of a gentleman highly respected, who was an eye-witness of what he relates, endued with every requisite qualification for the purpose, and who had compiled a narrative expressly for publication. My own suppressed memoranda at Goa and Tellicherry are of comparatively little consequence, and are abundantly superseded by Dr. F. Buchanan's invaluable publication. But to have been the means of rescuing from oblivion this interesting episode, in the history of the Mahomedan dynasty of Mysore, affords me some satisfaction. I shall conclude the subject with a remark of Tacitus in his life of Agricola, a little altered for the present occasion; which, although the characters alluded to may differ in their respective situations in public life, the general truth of the observation is sufficiently obvious.

"To transmit to posterity the lives and characters of illustrious men, was an office frequently performed in ancient times. In the present age the same good custom has prevailed whenever a great and splendid virtue has been able to surmount those two pernicious vices, which not only infest small communities, but are likewise the bane of large and flourishing cities; I mean the vices of insensibility to merit, on the one hand, and envy on the other. With regard to the usage of antiquity, it is further observable, that, in those early seasons of virtue, men were led, by the impulse of a generous spirit, to a course of action worthy of being recorded; and, in like manner, the writer of genius undertook to perpetuate the memory of honourable deeds, without any motive of flattery, and without views of private ambition, influenced only by the conscious pleasure of doing justice to departed merit. Many have been their own historians; persuaded that in speaking of themselves they should display an honest confidence in their morals, not a spirit of arrogance or vain-glory; so true it is, that the age which is most fertile in bright examples, is the best qualified to make a fair estimate of them."

CHAPTER XLI.

TRANSACTIONS ON THE MALABAR COAST; SUFFERINGS OF THE BRITISH OFFICERS AND PRISONERS TAKEN BY TIPPOO SULTAUN; AND CONCLUDING VOYAGE FROM INDIA TO ENGLAND.

1784.

"Now swell on every side the steady sail,
The lofty masts reclining to the gale;
On full-spread wings the vessel springs away,
And far behind it foams the ocean grey:
Afar the lessening hills of India fly,
And mix their dim blue summits with the sky.

"Their foreign tale on Albion's shore to tell
Inspires each bosom with a rapturous swell;
Now through their breasts the chilly tremors glide,
To dare once more the dangers dearly tried.
Soon to the winds are these cold fears resign'd,
And all their country rushes on the mind:
How sweet to view the native land!—how sweet
The father, brother, and the friend to greet!
While listening round the hoary parent's board,
The wondering kindred glow at every word;
How sweet to tell what woes, what toils they bore,
The tribes and wonders of each various shore:
These thoughts, the traveller's lov'd reward, employ,
And swell each bosom with unutter'd joy!

CAMOENS' LUSIAD, by MICKLE.

CONTENTS.

Mahomedans for Abyssinian slaves—melancholy fate of a young lady, and friendly tribute to her memory—dispatches for the General Elliot received from Bombay—paragraph in the Governor and Council's letter—cargo completed, and final dispatch for Europe—sail for Tellicherry—pass Calicut--anecdotes of Hyder Ally and Zamorine of Calicut--end of that dynasty—anchor at Chetwa—departure for Europe—reflections on that event, and the melancholy fate of former shipmates—particulars of the voyage from the Malabar coast to St. Helena—storms off the Cape—Camoen's Spirit of the Cape—arrival at St. Helena—additional anecdotes and descriptions of that island—Sargasso, or Grass-sea—flying-fish—terrific storm—arrival in England.

CHAPTER XLI.

WE continued a fortnight at Tellicherry to complete the cargo of pepper. Mr. Church, the chief of that settlement, was one of our oldest Bombay friends; and under his hospitable roof we passed our time as pleasantly as the painful intelligence daily received from Mangulore, and other parts of Tippoo Sultaun's dominions, would allow us.

Our Tellicherry friends formed parties for us to Mahie, Durmapatam, and other places in its vicinity. The country is extremely pleasant for such excursions, and the weather at this season delightful. Indeed the climate of Tellicherry, in the latitude of 11° 47″ north, is reckoned one of the finest in India; the land winds are generally moderate, the sea breezes cool and refreshing. A constant trade during the fair season, with vessels of all descriptions from different parts of India, renders this settlement very lively; while the number of civil servants, with the garrison officers and their families, beguile the rainy months in cheerful society and domestic enjoyments.

During our stay my friends kindly procured me every possible variety in the natural history of this part of Malabar; among others a beautiful frog, richly shaded and spotted with blue, yellow, orange, white, and black; the black and white halcyon, mentioned at Fort Victoria, and some delicate specimens of the tree-frog, and flying lizard, called by naturalists draco volans. Most of the plants in the Tellicherry district are similar to those indigenous to Anjengo, already described. Many of the wild flowers are beautiful, none more so than the gloriosa-superba, which in the southern districts of Travencore is a destructive weed. The specimens brought to Tellicherry well deserved the epithet sûperba; the elegant clusters of flowers, arrayed in brilliant flame-colour, pendent in every graceful form, from this climbing plant, running over the hedges, add an uncommon richness to the foreground of the Malabar landscape. The root of the gloriosa is of a poisonous nature, and being sometimes mistaken for edible roots, occasions very deleterious effects, and sometimes death.

Every rural excursion in the neighbouring country, and every social pleasure in the fortress, was tinged with gloom from reports daily reaching us of the sad fate of our unfortunate countrymen in the dominions of Tippoo Sultaun. Some gentlemen belonging to the embassy lately sent from Madras to Mangulore to settle terms of peace with that prince, as noticed in the preceding account of Onore, brought us the most dreadful intelligence of the British prisoners in Mysore. Bednore capitulated to Tippoo Sultaun the end of April 1783, on honourable terms. On an ill-founded and frivolous pretence of an infringement of the treaty, General Mathews, and a garrison of six hundred Europeans and fifteen hundred sepoys, were treacherously made prisoners, treated in the most ignominious manner, and marched with savage cruelty to different fortresses in the Mysore dominions, where they were so closely confined, that during the commissioners' journey they could neither see nor hear from any one of them. By different channels they learned too much of their unparalleled sufferings. During the march from Bednore to their allotted prisons, the officers and men were indiscriminately tied to each other with ropes, and sometimes chained together in pairs, without any distinction; the feeble with the strong, the sick with the healthy, and, not unfrequently, the living with the dead. Several instances having occurred of a lifeless corpse being dragged for miles chained to a wretched comrade, who could obtain no relief from the merciless conductor until they arrived at the nightly halting-place, when the chain was unlocked and the body removed for sepulture, a favour not always granted. In some instances the corpse was thrown out to the prowling hyenas and jackals.

From the memoranda I made on conversing with the gentlemen from Mangulore, I find two different accounts of the fate of General Mathews, and the officers above the rank of lieutenant, so treacherously surrounded at Bednore: that the field-officers, captains, and commissaries of the army were all put to death, there remained no doubt. The manner in which the tyrant's orders were executed is not so clearly ascertained. By some it was asserted that General Mathews, another field-officer, and Mr. Charles Stewart, the head commissary, and formerly a resident at Onore, were summoned to Tippoo's durbar, and received with respectful politeness, which he well knew how to assume. After being seated on the carpet they were each presented with a cup of poisoned coffee; it was offered first to the general, as of the highest rank:

guessing its cruel purport, he hesitated to take it. Mr. Stewart, better acquainted with the sultaun's character, advised him to acquiesce, otherwise insult would be added to cruelty, and taking the cup intended for himself, drank it off, and was in a few minutes either carried out in the struggles of death, or expired at the tyrant's feet. His example was then followed by his fellows in misfortune, which speedily terminated their misery!

There seems some improbability in this story; not that any deed of death was too cruel for Tippoo's character, but I believe it is not very common for the sentence to be executed in the presence of an oriental sovereign. That such instances have occurred, the Persian annals, and those of the house of Timur, sufficiently testify; and Tippoo's favourite mechanical tiger affords great reason to suppose he would have enjoyed the direful spectacle. Nothing more strongly marks his savage propensity than this toy; for it was no more. Although the registers of cruelty, exceeding even Tippoo's refinement, furnish instances of death by similar mechanism, where the devoted wretch met his fate in the embrace of a lovely female; where the automaton, smiling at his terror, plunged a dagger in his heart. The plaything of the Mysore tyrant, equally evincing his diabolical disposition, had at least a more innocent tendency. The mechanical tiger was found in a room of the sultaun's palace at Seringapatam, appropriated for the reception of musical instruments, and hence called the ragmehal. It was sent among the presents to his Britannic Majesty, and thus described:

"This piece of mechanism represents a royal tiger in the act of devouring a *prostrate European*. There are some barrels, in imitation of an organ, within the body of the tiger, and a row of keys of natural notes. The sounds produced by the organ are intended to resemble the cries of a person in distress, intermixed with the roar of a tiger. The machinery is so contrived, that while the organ is playing, the hand of the European is often lifted up, to express his helpless and deplorable condition. The whole of this design was executed by order of Tippoo Sultaun, who frequently amused himself with a sight of this emblematical triumph of the *Khoodadaud* (or God-given) sircar over the English."

A human being, who could pass his hours of relaxation and amusement in this savage manner, may be easily supposed to have enjoyed the death of an European who unhappily fell into his power, whether effected by poison, sword, or bow-string. Tacitus, desirous to paint Domitian's cruelty in the blackest colours, thus contrasts his character with another imperial monster: "Nero had the grace to turn away his eyes from the horrors of his reign; he commanded deeds of cruelty, but never was a spectator of the scene. Under Domitian, it was our wretched lot to behold the tyrant, and to be seen by him, while he kept a register of our sighs and groans. With that fiery visage, of a dye so red, that the blush of guilt could never colour his cheek, he marked the pale languid countenance of the unhappy victims, who shuddered at his frown."

How far Tippoo imitated Domitian's refinements in cruelty, I cannot determine. I received my account of the poisoned coffee in the durbar from a gentleman who had just arrived from Mangulore. He also communicated an additional instance of the tyrant's rigid and cruel discipline during the siege of that fortress. The sultaun, on being informed that the killedar who commanded it when taken by the English, had since treated them with kindness, determined to sacrifice him: for which purpose, ordering his regular troops from the trenches, and assembling them with the rest of his army, on a hill within view of the Mangulore ramparts, he rode before the lines, surrounded by his guard of silver lances, and all the state insignia. A gallows having been previously erected, the order of death was issued, and the killedar conducted to the spot. While standing under the gibbet with a halter round his neck, Mahomed Ally, an officer of high rank, and a great favourite of the late nabob, Hyder Ally, came forward, and in the most earnest manner supplicated for a pardon, which being indignantly refused, Mahomed Ally ordered his brigade to follow him in an imprudent attempt to prevent the execution. They were soon overpowered, and a dreadful example immediately followed, in the presence of the two generals. The officers and colour-bearers were blown from the guns; the noses and ears of the sepoys were cut off; and Mahomed Ally, after beholding the execution of his friend, was ordered into confinement, and cut off on the road by a private order from the sultaun. Thus perished two of the best and bravest officers in his service. Their only crime consisted in having shewed too much humanity to the English during the siege of Mangulore; who, from the ramparts, were witnesses of this melancholy spectacle.

The other account of the fate of the British officers captured at Bednore, was, that all above the rank of lieutenant were put to death; by what means was not particularly stated, excepting in the case of General Mathews, who being closely confined, and suspecting he was to be taken off by poison, refused for many days to taste the food prepared by his keeper, being kept alive by the compassion of a servant, who shared his small allowance with the general. This was connived at by the officer placed over him, until he was himself threatened with death if his prisoner any longer survived. This being communicated to the general, he ate the poisoned food, which in a few hours terminated his sufferings. The other officers belonging to the Bombay establishment were supposed to have shared the fate of their commander about the same time. A few subalterns, in hopes of better treatment, passed themselves off for officers of higher rank, from a mistaken idea of deference to situation among the Asiatics: this deception cost them their lives, as they would otherwise have been sent with the subaltern officers to their respective settlements at the conclusion of the peace.

In comparing the characters of Hyder Ally and Tippoo Sultaun, the former has greatly the advantage, especially considering his neglected education. Tippoo, born a prince, was educated as heir to a throne, which the Mysore usurper vainly imagined was fixed on a solid foundation; a musnud surrounded by tributary kings and conquered provinces, constantly accumulating. Like other short-sighted mortals, he little imagined the commencement and termination of his dynasty would be comprized within half a century. Sic transit gloria mundi!—For the despotic sovereignty of this empire, Tippoo was trained by his ambitious father. Hyder could neither read nor write; not that he was of that low origin frequently mentioned: on the contrary, his ancestor first brought into notice, went to India from Arabia, about the middle of the seventeenth century; some fix the period A. D. 1660, when he was appointed mullah, or priest, at the musjeed of Viziapore. Hyder must have been born about the year 1718, as it is said in the manuscript found at Nellore, that his father Futty Naik, who commanded a considerable body of horse and foot in the service of Abdul Russul Khan, nabob of Sirpy, fell in battle in 1728, when Hyder, Futty Naik's youngest son, was ten years of age. An elder brother and an uncle of Hyder having engaged themselves in the service of the rajah of Mysore, Hyder accompanied them in all their military operations; thus engaging, from a child, in active scenes, his education was neglected; and, whether from thoughtlessness on one side, or idleness on the other, Hyder Naik, as he was then called, was not taught either to read or write, nor did he afterwards ever acquire any literary knowledge.

When thirty years of age, Hyder, as a soldier of fortune, at the head of fifty matchlock peons, and five horses, offered his services to Nunderauz, commander in chief and duan to the rajah of Mysore: here properly commenced his military career. In less than three years he increased his troops to one hundred horse, and five hundred sepoys, whom he armed with European firelocks, and attached two field-pieces to his own little corps.

Another account, taken like the above, chiefly from Mahomedan historians, says, that in the year of the Hejira 1140, A. D. 1727, Futty Naik, the father of Hyder Ally, with a corps of a thousand men, entered into the service of the rajah of Seringapatam; or more properly Srirungaputton, so called from the temple of Sriunga, dedicated to the beautiful Hindoo deity Sri, the goddess of fecundity, similar to the Ceres of Greece. This city was then the capital of a powerful kingdom, governed by a Hindoo rajah; who, on the death of Futty Naik, gave his son Hyder the command of his own corps; where under the patronage of Munderauz he made a rapid progress in the path of ambition and glory. It is not my intention to follow him in this career: " *exaltation,*" say the oriental historians, " was inscribed on his forehead." By a chain of good fortune, assisted by singular talents, he at length filled the situations of his friend and patron Nunderauz, as duan (or vizier), and commander in chief of the army. Not content with those high dignities, he aspired to the throne, usurped the sovereignty, and imprisoned the rajah and his family in a hill-fort called Mudgery, situated on a strong rock, sixteen coss from Bangalore: this was in the year 1762. From that period he took the title of nawaub, or nabob, Hyder Ally Khan Bahauder; and pursuing his conquests in many of the surrounding countries, he added Bednore and its valuable territory, the Soondah country near Goa, and other considerable districts to the Mysore empire.

Establishing himself at Seringapatam, Hyder made that city the metropolis of his dominions; he enlarged and strengthened the fortifications, erected a new palace and other public buildings, and increased its population by every means in his power; still keeping up the garrisons at Bednore, Bangalore, and the different strong-holds in his extensive empire. Mangulore was his principal sea-port; Onore and some smaller towns near it hardly meriting that appellation; although Onore, especially as connected with Mirzee and Barcelore, has been always a place of considerable trade. This caused Tippoo's indignation at the English taking and defending Mangulore and Onore so bravely against his army, and counteracting his wily manœuvres. Hyder had always a great predilection for Mangulore: here he built all his large ships, with timber brought down from the Ghaut forests in the rainy season, by means of two rivers, which uniting near Mangulore, flow into the salt lake generally called Mangulore river. This settlement would be of much greater value were it not for the accumulation of sand during the south-east monsoon, forming a bar which renders the passage dangerous. Among other valuable articles of commerce, a great quantity of rice is annually exported from Mangulore.

Mangulore was the great deposit for marine stores of every description for the use of the sultaun's navy; Seringapatam contained the grand military arsenal, where they cast cannon, and fabricated all kinds of arms, in the oriental and European fashion. Most of the cannon cast during the reign of Tippoo, were ornamented with the representation of a tiger devouring an European; emblematical of his tyrannical and revengeful disposition. It is remarked by an intelligent writer, that "Tippoo's thoughts were constantly bent on war and military preparations; he having been frequently heard to say, that in this world he would rather live two days like a tiger, than two hundred years like a sheep. He adopted as the emblem of his state, and as a species of armorial bearing, the figure of the royal tiger, whose head and stripes constituted the chief ornaments of his throne, and of almost every article which belonged to him. This throne was of considerable beauty and magnificence. The support was a wooden tiger as large as life, covered with gold, in the attitude of standing. His head and fore legs appeared in front and under the throne, which was placed across his back. It was composed of an octagonal frame, eight feet by five, surrounded by a low railing, on which were ten small tiger heads made of gold, beautifully inlaid with precious stones: The ascent to the throne was by small silver steps on each side. From the centre of the back part, opposite the large tiger's head, arose a gilded iron pillar, seven feet high, surmounted by a canopy, superbly decorated with a fringe of pearls. The whole was made of wood, covered with a thin sheet of the purest gold, richly illuminated with tiger stripes and Arabic verses. The *huma* was placed on the top of the canopy, and fluttered over the sultaun's head. This bird, the most beautiful and magnificent ornament of the throne, was sent by the Marquis Wellesley to the Court of Directors. It was about the size and shape of a small pigeon, and intended to represent the fabulous bird of antiquity, well known to all Persian scholars; a bird peculiar to the east, supposed to fly constantly in the air, and never to touch the ground. It is looked upon as a bird of happy omen, and that every head it overshades will in time wear a crown. The tail of the huma on Tippoo's throne, and its wings, were in the attitude of fluttering. It was formed of gold, entirely covered with diamonds, rubies, and emeralds."

" Tippoo Sultaun seems to have adopted Ally as the guardian genius, or tutelary saint, of his dominions; as the peculiar object of his veneration, and as an example to imitate. His selection of the tiger as an emblem, appears to have been intended in honour of Ally; for the natives of Hindostan make no distinction between a lion and a tiger. Hyder, which also signifies a lion, but interpreted by the natives of Hindostan, tiger, is another title of Ally; it was likewise the name of Tippoo Sultaun's father. The name of Hyder, thus distinguished by the triple circumstance of its being the title of Ally, the name of Tippoo Sultaun's assumed emblem, and the name of his father, the founder of his dominion, was introduced by him on every occasion; and either the word at length, or its initial letter, was stamped upon every article belonging to him."

I have read many letters from Hyder and Tippoo on various subjects, and on a former occasion introduced one from Hyder to Colonel Wood, strongly characteristic of his determined and war-like disposition. I have also given an extract of a bigotted epistle from his son, very much in the same spirit with a prayer prefixed to a foolish superstitious dream, thus entered in his diary: "On the seventh day of the month Jaufre, of the year Shaudaub 1217 from the birth of Mahomed, (answering to August 1790) when encamped at Sulaumabad, before the attack upon the in-trenchments of Ram Nayer, and after evening prayers, I made invocation to the Deity, in these terms: 'Oh God! the damned infidels of the hills forbid fasting and prayer, as practised by the Mussulmans; convert them at once to the faith, so that the religion of thy prophet may acquire strength.' In the course of the night, and towards the morning, I had a dream," &c.—This dream is not worth relating, nor shall I give a translation of the cruel mandates sent to the commanders of his forts respecting the English prisoners in the year 1783, particularly one (as I was credibly informed) ordering Captain Mathews and Lieutenant Wheldon to be turned out in a forest, and hunted to death by dogs, trained for such a purpose. These epistles are too sanguinary for insertion: they are equally cruel, but less energetic and concise than many similar compositions; especially that from the caliph Haroun-al-Rashid, to Nicephorus, emperor of Constantinople, which Gibbon styles of such tremendous brevity.

"In the name of the most merciful God! Haroun-al-Rashid, commander of the faithful, to Nicephorus the Roman dog:

"I have read thy letter, O thou son of an unbelieving mother. Thou shalt not hear, thou shalt behold my reply."

A reply, which was indeed written in characters of blood and fire, on the plains of Phrygia!—Similar was the language of Hyder to his enemies; equally laconic and sanguinary his epistles to the government of Madras; followed up by his conquering cavalry, carrying death and destruction to the very gates of Fort St. George!

I will dwell no longer on these melancholy scenes.—Sir James Sibbald, who resided eleven years in Hyder's dominions, and was for some time in a public character at his durbar in Seringapatam, as well as in habits of intimacy with Tippoo Sultaun, during the life of his father, has often entertained me with a description of the splendid pageantry and ostentatious ceremonies in the newly established durbar, where he carried his authority with a high hand; sometimes profuse in his entertainments and princely in his presents, at others equally mean and sordid. These Mahomedan sovereigns seemed anxious to revive the magnificence of former times, in the palace at Seringapatam; but they had neither taste, judgment, nor wealth, to follow the example of the Mogul and Patan courts in India, still less to vie with the splendor of the Abassides, or the Moorish sovereigns in Europe, the former of whom they seemed desirous to imitate; especially Tippoo, who wished to add the character of sanctity to his other princely virtues. Rising at break of day, he always employed his first hour in reading the Koran; how far its religion and morality influenced his life, is evident from these unconnected memoirs. He then gave audience to the civil and military officers who had particular business to transact; and before breakfast visited the jamdar khana, or treasury, containing his jewels, gold and silver ornaments and utensils, curious arms, and new mechanical inventions, on which he lavished large sums; but his museums and collections are said more to have resembled the heterogeneous mixtures of Asuph-ul-Dowlah, at Lucknow, than the valuable deposits of the Mogul emperors in their days of splendour.—After breakfast, arrayed in rich apparel, he gave public audience, and sometimes administered justice, reviewed the troops, hunted with the cheta, or superintended the arsenals; these and similar pursuits generally employed the succeeding hours in his capital. In camp, or severe marches, no soldier in his army could bear more fatigue: war was his delight, and every thing tending to it engaged his first consideration.

Among the chief curiosities in his treasury and wardrobe, were the arms and war-dresses; some of the latter formed complete suits of armour, in chain-work, and other heavy encumbrances for man and horse, of more shew than use. Among the articles of a war-dress sent to the Duke of York was one of the sultaun's turbans, (perhaps more of a helmet) which had been dipped in the sacred fountain of Zum-Zum at Mecca, and on that account was supposed to be invulnerable: this was called a *tuburrook*, or holy gift. Altogether the jewels, treasure, and valuables, which the eastern sovereigns have laid up in store, from the days of Solomon to Tippoo Sultaun, fell very short of general expectation at the capture of Seringapatam. Indeed all Indian wealth and magnificence, since Nadir Shah's plunder of Delhi, even the brilliant huma, pearly canopy, and varied gems of the tiger throne, dwindle into comparative insignificance, when mentioned with the splendid luxury of the Arabian caliphs. The name of Haroun-al-Rashid is familiar to every reader of the Arabian Nights' Entertainments; nor are the descriptions of his palace, gardens, and pavilions, altogether fictitious. The successes of the Arabian prophet soon laid aside the patriarchal simplicity which distinguished his character. Every authentic history of Mahomed confirms the remark of Gibbon, " that his good sense despised the pomp of royalty; *the man styled the apostle of God* submitted to the menial offices of the family; he kindled the fire, swept the floor, milked the ewes, and mended with his own hands his shoes and his woollen garment. Disdaining the penance and merit of a hermit, he observed, without effort or vanity, the abstemious diet of an Arab and a soldier. On solemn occasions he feasted his companions with rustic and hospitable plenty, but in his domestic life, many weeks would elapse without a fire being kindled on the hearth of the prophet. The interdiction of wine was confirmed by his example; his hunger was appeased with a sparing allowance of barley-bread; he delighted in the taste of milk and honey; but his ordinary food consisted of dates and water. Perfumes and women were the two sensual enjoyments in which he chose to indulge, and his religion did not forbid; affirming that the fervor of his devotion was increased by these pleasures."

In little more than a century after the death of Mahomed, the

Abassides then established at Bagdad, forgetting the origin and example of their prophet, and disdaining his abstinence and frugality, began to emulate the splendour of other oriental monarchs. The character of Hyder Ally and Tippoo Sultaun are, in many respects, not unlike those of Mahomed and his early successors; especially in their zeal for converts and rage for conquest. Ambition and extent of empire were the ruling passions of Hyder; to these his son was desirous of annexing the titles of apostle, priest, and prophet. He gloried in being himself a religious author, and certainly possessed a library superior to that of any modern prince in Hindostan. He was at the same time vain, ostentatious, and deficient in the noble qualities of a sovereign; his own capricious cruelties, and those sanctioned by his authority, have been mentioned. He affected a splendid pageantry, and marshalled his choicest troops before his durbar on the introduction of a new ambassador at the Mahomedan festivals, and other public occasions; but all his ostentatious parade was trifling, compared with the wealth and splendor of the caliphs of Bagdad, or the Moorish kings in Spain, of which Abulfeda has given two remarkable instances: one of them peculiarly applicable to Tippoo Sultaun. The first exhibits the entrance of a Greek ambassador at the court of Moctader, on the decline of the Arabian caliphs. The latter presents a short, but striking, trait in the character of Abdalrahman, one of the great Moorish kings in Spain; who constructed the city, palace, and gardens of Zehra, near Cordova.

Abulfeda, as quoted by Gibbon, relates that when the Greek ambassador repaired to the palace of Moctader, "the caliph's whole army, both horse and foot, was under arms, which together made a body of one hundred and sixty thousand men. His state officers, the favourite slaves, stood near him in splendid apparel, their belts glittering with gold and gems. Near them were seven thousand eunuchs; four thousand of them white, the remainder black. The porters or doorkeepers were in number seven hundred. Barges and boats, with the most superb decorations, were seen swimming upon the Tigris. Nor was the palace itself less splendid, in which were hung up thirty thousand pieces of tapestry; twelve thousand five hundred of which were of silk embroidered with gold. The carpets on the floor were twenty-two thousand. A hundred lions were brought out, with a keeper to each lion. Among the other spectacles of rare and stupendous luxury, was a tree of gold and silver, spreading into eighteen large branches; on which, and on the lesser boughs, sat a variety of birds, made of the same precious metals, as well as the leaves of the tree: while the machinery affected spontaneous motions, the several birds warbled their natural harmony. Through this scene of magnificence the Greek ambassador was led by the vizier to the foot of the caliph's throne."

The reflection, if not the magnificence of Abdalrahman, is interesting; and each of these anecdotes not only merit their place in the Decline and Fall of the Roman Empire, but illustrate oriental manners and customs at the present day.—" Abdalrahman's buildings at Zehra were sustained or adorned by twelve hundred columns of Spanish and African, of Greek and Italian marble. The hall of audience was incrusted with gold and pearls, and a great bason in the centre was surrounded with the curious and costly figures of birds and quadrupeds. In a lofty pavilion in the gardens, one of those basons and fountains, so delightful in a sultry climate, was replenished, not with water, but with the purest quicksilver. The seraglio of Abdalrahma, his wives, concubines, and black eunuchs, amounted to six thousand three hundred persons; and he was attended to the field by a guard of twelve thousand horse, whose belts and scimetars were studded with gold." We may profit by the experience of this monarch; for after his decease this authentic memorial was found in his closet: "I have now reigned above fifty years in victory or peace, beloved by my subjects, dreaded by my enemies, and respected by my allies. Riches and honours, power and pleasure, have waited on my call, nor does any earthly blessing appear to have been wanting to my felicity. In this situation I have diligently numbered the days of pure and genuine happiness which have fallen to my lot: they amount to FOURTEEN! O man, place not thy confidence in this present world!"

This reflection of Abdalrahman corresponds with the pathetic exclamation of VANITY from another voluptuous sovereign, renowned above all oriental princes for wisdom, wealth, and magnificence. The short dynasty of Hyder, the annihilation of the Mogul empire, the prostrate thrones, and tottering crowns of so many European monarchs, all within the short space of twenty years, wonderfully evince the fallacy of mundane speculations, and confirm the sublime line of the poet:

"He builds too low, who builds beneath the skies!"

It is but justice to the celebrated historian to add his remark on Abdalrahman's memorial, that "the confession of the Arabian monarch, the complaints of Solomon, and the happy *ten* days of the emperor Seghed, will be triumphantly quoted by the detractors of human life. Their expectations are commonly immoderate, their estimates are seldom impartial. "If I may speak of myself, (the only person of whom I may speak with certainty) my happy hours," says Gibbon, "have far exceeded, and far exceed, the scanty numbers of the caliph of Spain; and I shall not scruple to add, that many of them are due to the pleasing labour of composing the History of the Decline and Fall of the Roman Empire."—With honest pleasure, as with equal truth, I may make the same assertion respecting the many delightful days I have spent in compiling these memoirs, and delineating their illustrations.

It is not probable that the Mysore sovereigns, who gave rise to these reflections, enjoyed many happy hours, in the true sense of the expression. The splendors of royalty, especially in Asia, dazzle the eye of the spectator; he beholds the purple and fine linen, the brilliant tiara, stately palace, and obsequious nobles. His imagination carries him to the interior apartments, where beauty, wealth, and pleasure, obey the imperial nod. But did he at the same time oppose the fear, distrust, and jealousy of despotism, he would exclaim with our immortal bard:

"Unweary lies the head with such a crown!
O polish'd perturbation! golden care!
That keeps the ports of slumber open wide
To many a watchful night!
—What stronger breast-plate than a heart untainted?
Thrice is he arm'd that hath his quarrel just;
And he but naked, though lock'd up in steel,
Whose conscience with injustice is corrupted."

The truth of Shakespeare's observation is abundantly confirmed by Dr. Buchanan's picture of the inner apartments of Tippoo's palace: "From the principal front of the sultaun's palace at Seringapatam, which served as a revenue office, and as a place from whence he occasionally shewed himself to the populace, the chief entry into the private square was through a strong narrow passage, wherein were chained four tigers; which, although somewhat tame, would, in case of any disturbance, become unruly. Within these was the hall in which Tippoo wrote, and into which very few persons were ever admitted. Immediately behind this was the bedchamber which communicated with the hall by a door and two windows, and was shut up on every other side. This door was strongly secured on the inside, and a close iron grating defended the windows. The sultaun, lest any person should fire upon him while in bed, slept in a hammock, which was suspended from the roof by chains, in such a situation as to be invisible through the windows. In the hammock were found a sword and a pair of pistols.

That this suspicion and anxious dread pervades the whole despotic system, from the imperial musmud to the durbar of every inferior oppressor, is evident from the general construction of the great houses in Hindostan, which are full of dark passages, close narrow stairs, and short turnings, from whence the dagger of the assassin may best execute the meditated blow. Too true, I fear, is the melancholy picture of Sir William Jones in most parts of the world, but in Asiatic regions it applies with tenfold force—it formed part of a letter to Lord Teignmouth, written from Bengal in 1793.

"Of European politics I think as little as possible; not because they do not interest my heart, but because they give me too much pain. I have goodwill towards men, and wish peace on earth; but I see chiefly under the sun, the two classes of men whom Solomon describes, the *oppressor* and the *oppressed.* I have no fear in England of open despotism, nor of anarchy."

This distrust and suspicion in some measure accounts for the custom in India, especially among the Mahomedans, that in default of children, and sometimes where there are lineal descendants, the master of a family adopts a slave, frequently a *Haffshee*, Abyssinian, of the darkest hue, for his heir: he educates him agreeably to his wishes, and marries him to one of his daughters. As the reward of superior merit, or to suit the caprice of an arbitrary despot, this honour is also conferred on a slave recently purchased, or already grown up in the family; and to him he bequeaths his wealth, in preference to his nephews, or any collateral branches. This is a custom of great antiquity in the east, and prevalent among the most refined and civilized nations. In the earliest period of the patriarchal history, we find Abraham complaining for want of children, and declaring that either Eliezer of Damascus, or probably one born from him in his house, was his heir; to the exclusion of Lot, his favourite nephew, (for whom he had just fought with the king of Elam and his confederates) and all the other collateral branches of his family.

The arrival of our ill-fated countrymen from Mangulore, during our stay at Tellicherry, replete with anecdotes of Tippoo's cruelty, and the distresses they had sustained in that fortress, aggravated by what they heard of the dreadful sufferings of the officers and privates marched through the Mysore dominions, so engrossed conversation, that little attention could be given to any other subject. The failure of British policy and intrepidity in the late unfortunate expedition to Bednore, and the loss of the flower of the Bombay army, were universally deplored. This, added to the sacrifice of all our northern possessions, to obtain an ignominious peace with the Mahrattas, threw a gloom over the oriental hemisphere on our departure from India. Important and advantageous have been the succeeding events in that quarter of the globe, where those fatal catastrophes are now so happily reversed. Tippoo destroyed, Mysore restored to the descendant of its ancient rajahs, many of the Guzerat purgunnas once more in possession of the Company, and British protection extended over the greater part of the rich and populous regions of India, in a retrospective view leave the mind absorbed in wonder, looking forward in incalculable conjecture.

I never visited Tellicherry without a sigh to the memory of an amiable female, with whom in my juvenile years I had the happiness of being intimately acquainted. At a season when youth, beauty, innocence, decked her virgin form with superior charms, and attracted universal love, a sable cloud, commencing its portentous aspect at this settlement, obscured her brighter prospects; and after a scene of accumulated sorrow, led her an early victim to the grave, which to her was indeed a haven of repose; an asylum where " the wicked cease from troubling, and the weary are at rest." The mournful history of the lovely Maria would call forth the sympathetic tear from every heart of sensibility. It is suppressed from delicacy to the survivors; for the same reason the following lines are veiled in ambiguity; they were suggested by reading some stanzas in *La Pitié*, by De Lille, one of the most beautiful poems in the French language. C'est la Pitié elle-meme! The tale of woe to which they allude has frequently employed my pen in the tropical shades of Malayala, (or Malabar) and the romantic scenery of her native Salopia.

LINES ON MARIA.

Ah hapless maid! sweet nymph of Salop's vale!
Whoe'er has heard, and not deplor'd thy tale?
Alas! while Hymen nuptial garlands wove,
To crown the blushes of thy virgin love,
As some gay flower that decks the verdant mead,
Relentless Death mow'd down thy blooming head!

Yet not like vulgar nymphs shall die thy name,
Unwept by Pity, undeplor'd by Fame:
No—let these lines, embalm'd, thy virtues keep,
That pensive Memory still may wake to weep.
How small the tribute!—On some future day
May sculptur'd marble mourn upon thy clay!
The votive urn thy pious friends shall rear,
And souls congenial hallow with a tear,
In Albion's isle shall deck the solemn grove,
Bedew'd by Sympathy, enwreath'd by Love!

And oft as o'er Malaya's wilds I stray,
Or through her cassia groves explore my way,
Whether the bulbul's notes salute my ear,
Or noisy baya's pensile nests appear,
Whether Alhinna scents the passing gale
Or softer zephyrs Mogree's sweets exhale,

Still shall Maria's sainted form be nigh,
And dove-ey'd Pity heave her tender sigh!

O! if there be some valley deep retir'd,
Some sacred spot by Innocence desir'd,
Untrod by Envy, Jealousy, and Strife,
Unknown, unruffled by the storms of life,
There, let us celebrate, from tumult free,
A fête as pure and innocent as thee!
Thence let us banish all the empty shew,
Unfeeling pomp and ornament of woe.
There blooming maids with wreaths of cypress crown'd,
Shall oft assemble on the hallow'd ground,
When summer suns unfold the buds of spring,
And scattering roses o'er thy urn shall sing.

"Hail, nymph belov'd!" shall chant the virgin choir,
"Hail! of our sex, the honour, grace, desire!"

"Time, which destroys, renews fair Nature's face,
Repaints each hue, retouches every grace,
Recalls the zephyr, renovates the bower,
Again resuscitates the faded flower,
Ne'er shall record upon the sculptor'd shrine
More soft and lovely traits than once were thine!

"Hope of thy parents! glory of thy age,
What anguish could thy angel look assuage!
Bright as the morning star in beauty drest,
Thy charms attracted every feeling breast!
In thy warm heart those soft sensations stole,
Which, unperceiv'd, too oft enthral the soul;
Honour and love, another's fame to save,
Led thee, a victim, to th' untimely grave!

"Adieu, sweet nymph, adieu! may thy blest shade
Sometimes revisit this sequester'd glade!

For thee shall Philomel each note prolong,
And choose her sweetest, most entrancing song;
Zephyr shall follow through the silent dell,
And Echo call thee from her rocky cell.

"Adieu! when garlands crown returning spring,
We will return, and vernal offerings bring:
Accept, to sooth thee in Elysian bowers,
Our hymns, our tears, our sorrows, and our flowers!"

Chara Maria, vale!

The General Elliot was to receive her final dispatches for Europe from the governor and council at Bombay, by a cutter to be sent after us to Tellicherry. This vessel arrived on the 17th of February, with the packets for the court of directors, and orders for our immediate departure to St. Helena and Europe, without touching at the Cape of Good Hope. By this opportunity I received a letter from the government secretary at Bombay, enclosing a copy of a paragraph from the governor and council's address to the court of directors, dated the 10th of February 1784, per ship General Elliot, which closed my public career in the company's service. Self-respect and a laudable pride of character, induce me to insert in these memoirs the most pleasing recompence I could have received for having zealously devoted to them the best years of my life, and suffering much from the enervating influence of the climate.

"In the month of December last Mr. James Forbes, senior merchant on this establishment, addressed us a letter, requesting permission to proceed to England for the benefit of his health, and enclosing a certificate from the late surgeon of the Baroche factory, pointing out the same as necessary for the re-establishment of a relaxed constitution, occasioned by frequent attacks of bilious fevers. In November 1775, Mr. Forbes had occasion to solicit our permission to proceed by the Betsey snow to the Cape of Good Hope, and from thence to England, for the same complaint; we have therefore complied with Mr. Forbes's request to take his passage in the General Elliot; and as he has on all occasions afforded us much satisfaction, and proved himself a diligent and faithful servant to his employers, we beg leave strongly to recommend that he be permitted to return to India without prejudice to his rank in the service, whenever his health may permit of his soliciting you for that purpose.

" Attested to be a true copy,

James Hatley, Secretary."

Our cargo being entirely completed, and the packets from the chief and council of Tellicherry closed, they finally dispatched the Governor Elliot on the 18th of February. We sailed the next morning for Chetwa, a Dutch settlement on the Malabar coast, a little to the southward of Calicut, and fifteen leagues north of Cochin. There we filled up our water casks, received a large supply of poultry and fresh provisions, previously provided, and parted from a valuable friend, who had thus far accompanied his wife and children, on their way to England. He returned to Bombay with two other gentlemen, who then left us, in a vessel detained for the purpose.

We neither landed at Chetwa nor Calicut; the latter was in

the possession of Tippoo Sultaun, and the English factory withdrawn. The external appearance of Calicut remained much the same as when formerly described. The Dutch, Portugueze, and Danish flags waved over their respective factories, while the Mahomedan colours usurped the place of the zamorine's standard, in this once celebrated emporium, which was completely conquered by the sultaun of Mysore, now become one of the first potentates in India; while the zamorine of Calicut, so great and powerful a sovereign when De Gama arrived here, was annihilated—or, like the queens of Allinga, and other Malabar princes, enjoyed only the name and shadow of royalty. The zamorines, or kings of Calicut, according to the Nellore manuscript, were ascertained to have maintained twelve hundred brahmins in their household; and until they had been first served with victuals, the zamorine never tasted any himself. It was an etiquette, also, that he never spoke to, nor suffered a Mahomedan to come into his presence. Hyder Ally, after taking Calicut, sent a complimentary message, and desired to see the zamorine, but was refused: he, however, admitted Hyder's head brahmin to speak to him, and carry his answer back to his master, then waiting at some distance from them. After this interview, Hyder, instead of sending rice sufficient for the daily food of twelve hundred brahmins, ordered only enough for five hundred; this they dispensed with. The second day he diminished the allowance to a sufficiency for three hundred; and on the third they received only enough for one hundred. All further supplies were afterwards refused; nor did the conqueror take any notice of the zamorine's complaints and applications. The unfortunate prince, after fasting three days, and finding all remonstrances vain, set fire to his palace, and was burned, with some of his women, and three brahmins, the rest having left him on this sad reverse of fortune.

On the zamorine's death, Hyder Ally garrisoned Calicut with two thousand foot and five hundred horse, and marched with the remainder of his army to Coimbatore, forty coss on his route to his own country. About two months after the nabob's departure, the late zamorine's brother appeared before Calicut with twenty thousand men, and having got possession of it, he put every man of Hyder's army to death, except about three hundred, who fled to a temple for safety. As soon as this news reached Hyder, he detached Assut Khan, with five thousand foot and one thousand horse, to retake Calicut; who, after two engagements, forced the Hindoos to abandon the country, and kept the town for Hyder. Within three months they returned with greater force, retook the place, cut off Assut Khan's head, and killed a number of his people. This was after my visit to Calicut in 1772, and previous to the year 1776; but I cannot ascertain the exact date. Before the expiration of many months, Hyder Ally himself marched for Calicut with two thousand horse and six thousand foot; but when he had proceeded two days towards it, he gave the command of that force to Sevajee Row, a Mahratta general in his service. The zamorine's brother again tried his fortune in the field, and was again defeated. He then left the country, the inhabitants of Calicut evacuated the place, and Sevajee immediately took possession.

These extraordinary events having taken place since my former voyage on the Malabar coast, and description of this celebrated emporium, I thought a brief recital would be interesting. They may be said to complete its oriental history; for Calicut, with all the extensive districts included under the appellation of the Malabar province, are now subject either to the power or influence of the East India Company, under whose settled government and mild administration, the natives must be happy. Nor can I quit this interesting spot without contrasting the cruel behaviour of Hyder Ally, in withholding food from a conquered sovereign, the last of a noble Hindoo dynasty, who had never offended him, with the generous conduct of the British government to the descendants of the Mysore usurper, who are allowed every thing becoming their royal descent, except the liberty of treading in the bloody footsteps of their ancestors, and fomenting wars and rebellions in their native country.

The particular assignments to the family and descendants of the late Tippoo Sultaun, and the sums appropriated to the zenana, the legitimate and illegitimate children, and dependants of every description on the Mahomedan sovereigns of Mysore, have been so fully detailed in recent publications as to render it unnecessary to insert them in this place. They are liberal and benevolent, becoming the conquerors of a despot with whom they were compelled to engage for the preservation of their own existence in India, and the restorers of the ancient line of Hindoo rajahs, from whom the sovereignty of Mysore had been usurped by the unjust ambition and cruel policy of Tippoo's father.

Taking advantage of the land-breeze, we sailed from Chetwa for Europe, soon after midnight on the 22d of February, and at sun-rise the next morning I beheld, for the last time, the coast of India, exactly eighteen years from my first arrival at Bombay, where I landed on the 23d of February 1766. This diversified and interesting period of life I recollect with heartfelt delight; nor did I take a final view of the cloud-capt mountains of Malabar without strong sensations. Nineteen passengers had embarked from England on the same ship with myself, full of youthful ardour, and eager to obtain their respective situations in the civil, military, and marine departments of the company's service. I never read Camoen's Lusiad without a peculiar interest in that pathetic description of the Lusitanian youth embarking with De Gama in his first voyage to India. It is a scene truly pathetic; from which I long ago connected a few detached lines, and fashioned them to the modern departure of an Indiaman full of passengers, for those distant shores; with youthful hearts and warm imaginations impatient to encounter their future trials and enter the path of glory.

Urg'd by ambition, or allur'd by fame,
To gain a fortune, or to raise a name,
Through Albion's youth the kindling ardours roll,
And glory dawns o'er each aspiring soul:
All eager to perform their destin'd race,
Oceans immense and foreign shores to trace;
Where spicy gales from sunny mountains blow,
And forest trees with splendid foliage glow;
Gay wreaths of flowers, of fruitage, and of boughs,
Unknown in Europe, crown their lofty brows:
Where various monsters of the wild are seen,
And birds of plumage azure, scarlet, green:
High sounds the voice of India's pearly shore,
Golconda's gems, and Delhi's countless store:
For these through realms remote they seek to roam,
For these they leave the dear delights of home.

Safe through the deep, where every yawning wave
Still to the sailor's eye displays his grave;
Through howling tempests, and through gulfs untried,
O mighty God! be thou their watchful guide!

Of the nineteen youths with whom I thus commenced my juvenile career, seventeen died in India many years before my departure; one only besides myself then survived; with him I formed an early friendship, which continued without interruption to his death, for he also has since fallen a sacrifice to the climate, and I have been for nearly ten years the only survivor! Many in this country who have participated in the generous, hospitable, and social virtues of the late Daniel Seton of Surat, will unite in this little eulogy to his memory, and lament that he was not permitted to return home, and enjoy the delights of domestic happiness with his amiable family, who left him some years before, to acquire, under the eye of maternal affection, those accomplishments which cannot be attained in India. This separation of families is a great alloy to a residence in that distant country, where parents are obliged to part with these sweet pledges of connubial love; or a fond mother is compelled, as it were, to divide herself in the performance of her tenderest duties.

I greatly admire a passage in Pliny's letters on the subject of human mortality. The sentiments of that amiable and virtuous heathen are as exalted and noble as can be conceived in a mind unassisted by divine revelation. Happily a Christian's view of immortality is of a more sublime and durable nature, extending beyond the bounds of time to a scene of endless duration.

" Within what narrow limits are the lives of so great a multitude confined! To me therefore, the royal tears shed upon a reflection of this kind, seem not only pardonable, but worthy of praise; for they say, that Xerxes, upon a review of his immense army, wept to consider, that of such a number of men, in a very little time, not one would be living. But this ought to incite us to employ our time, fleeting and transitory as it is, if not in great actions, yet certainly in study: and as it may not be permitted us to live long, let us leave something behind to shew that we have lived. Noble is the contention, when friends, by mutual exhortations, spirit up each other to the love of immortality!"

On this melancholy occasion I cannot withhold a most pathetic observation, still more distressing, mentioned by Captain Williamson, on the mortality of Europeans in India, which I would rather give in his words than my own, after what I have said respecting the state of British society and manners in that part of the world, on different occasions, in these memoirs. I have no doubt of the truth of this quotation, but I have reason to hope the portrait no longer exists to such an extent; on the contrary, the manners and customs at Bengal are much improved.

"I cannot give a better idea of the state of society in Bengal upwards of twenty years ago, than by observing, that I was one of a party, not exceeding sixteen in number, who met to dine with a friend in the south barracks of Berhampore, in 1796; when, happening to meet with some friends we had not seen since occupying the same quarters in 1782, we casually mentioned our old comrades at the same place; but were generally found to wind up our retrospective details, with "Ah poor fellow, but he's dead!" The frequent repetition of the apostrophe induced two of us to take pen and paper; when, one reckoning up those among our lost friends who had occupied the north, and the other recording the obituary of the South Rangers, we found that in the space of little more than twenty years, we had lost one hundred and sixty-three in one list, and one hundred and fifty-seven in the other! It is worthy of remark, that our record was confined to such officers and staff, as had occupied the cantonments during three years only; and that more than three hundred officers had never been quartered at any one time at the station! What adds to the wonder of such an occurrence is, that for the greater part of the time very little change took place; the same corps being fixed for several years!—With the exception of a few prudent men, whose moderation rendered them contemptible in the opinion of the major part of us, who were greatly attached not only to sport, but to every species of debauchery, I believe few quitted Berhampore in those days untainted by disease, or without some serious injury to their constitutions. Happily an entire reform has long since taken place throughout India."

The exception to the prudent and moderate men abovementioned, is in my opinion entitled to more emphatic consideration than is there allowed to it. In the following observation I do not intend the smallest reflection, in contrasting the conduct of the company's servants, civil and military, during my residence in India. In each of those establishments were many noble characters, eminently virtuous and praiseworthy in all respects. I therefore only wish to point out the principal cause, which in my opinion produced so material a difference in the character and career of the youth sent to India: this was the employment of time, especially in a morning. The writers at the period of my arrival at Bombay, and during the whole time of my officiating in that capacity, were fully engaged from nine o'clock to twelve, when they retired from their respective offices to dinner, which was then at one o'clock in every class of English society. At two the writers returned to their employment until five; when, after a dish of tea, a social walk on a fine sandy beach, open to the salubrious western breeze, gave us a keener appetite for supper than our scanty pittance of thirty rupees per month could furnish. Such was our constant practice six days in the week. The cadets, on the contrary, who were then soon promoted, and whether stationed at the presidency or the subordinate settlements, perhaps mounted guard once or twice a week, and did no other duty, had abundance of leisure time. On those idle days, the morning was generally occupied in calling upon each other at their different quarters, and at each visit taking a draught of punch, or arrack and water; which, however cool and pleasant at the moment, was succeeded by the most deleterious effects; indeed from its fatal consequences it might be called a slow poison; and from this cause alone, it may be confidently asserted, that a number proportionate to the Berhampore estimate, were annually committed to an untimely grave.

There were many amiable exceptions of youth in the military department, who devoted their morning hours to professional studies, music, drawing, literary improvement, and other rational pursuits, who became eminent in their profession, and are now enjoying the fruits of their wise conduct, independent and happy in their native country. I do not mean to infer that physical causes have no effect upon the European constitution in India; I know from long experience they are often very powerful; and it must be admitted, that, notwithstanding the utmost care and circumspection, they frequently produce a gradual and melancholy effect, especially on delicate females, who uniformly lead a life of temperance, tranquillity, and virtue. But in that class of Asiatic society which I allude to, I am persuaded that moral evil produces far more fatal consequences than any physical cause whatsoever.

I can illustrate my position by two anecdotes, trifling perhaps in themselves, but not totally irrelevant to the purpose. The introduction of such circumstances sometimes throws more light upon a subject than learned and laborious discussion.

I was one day in company at Bombay, with twelve other gentlemen, in the civil service, most of them considerably under thirty years of age, when the conversation turning upon the mortality of Europeans in India, one of the company made use of the old remark, that there was something ominous in the number thirteen at a convivial meeting, and that certainly one of us would die before the anniversary of that day in the following year; the probability of which was certainly much in his favour in a climate deemed so inimical to European constitutions. I was, at the moment, cutting open the leaves of a book with an ivory paper-cutter; and merely to keep in mind the predicted death of one of the company within twelve months from the assertion, I wrote down on the ivory the name of each individual comprised in the fatal number: this was in the year 1770. The ensuing year passed over without the completion of the prophesy; not one of the company died. In 1780, ten years after I made my nomenclature, the whole thirteen were in perfect health. The party consisted of the secretary, deputy secretary, and eleven assistants in their office, writers in the Company's service; several of them are now filling useful and honourable situations in the three different divisions of the United Kingdom, wherein they were born.

This fact evinces the advantages of moderation, employment, and diligence. The following, which is introduced purposely to show the effects of the contrary system, can give no offence; because the thoughtless youth has long since been numbered with the dead. And should the gentleman who wrote it from Tellicherry to his friend at Bombay in the year 1772, and has since appeared both as a senator and an author, peruse these memoirs, he will possibly recollect that he sent this humorous description of a morning visit on the island of Durmapatam, in a letter containing something of much greater importance, which was the cause of its being preserved.

Tellicherry, 14*th January*, 1772.

"On sunday last after dinner I accompanied some of our friends belonging to this settlement on a visit to the island of Durmapatam. There was nothing interesting in the excursion, either as to the appearance or natives of the country; but it was impossible to help being diverted with the singularity of an European to whom I was introduced. I must however premise that our mirth was mingled with pity at this degradation of human nature. The person I allude to was no other than lieutenant B—, who is stationed in the fort at Durmapatam. He received us with great cordiality, and entreated us all, five in number, to be seated in a bungalow, where there were only two broken chairs. This compliment therefore we could not accept of: he then ordered five sneakers of a mixture which he denominated punch, but which had a nearer resemblance to a mess composed of sugar, dirt, and water. He informed us that he liked his situation prodigiously. I observed to him that it was lonely, and that he must sometimes wish for company. "Oh sir!" he replied "all that is nothing; I have one of the finest prospects in India; and plenty of alligators to shoot at in the river; and as for company, by Jupiter, I prefer a little black Tivettee-girl to all the company in the world." We congratulated him on his prospect, his game, and his company; and returned to Tellicherry under a deluge of blessings and good wishes for my happiness in Europe. We sail with the land wind to night, and in three days expect to take our final departure from Cochin."

I conclude this subject with a copy of verses, written by a young lady of great sensibility, on reading the preceding pages in manuscript; especially that passage which mentions my being the only survivor of nineteen passengers who embarked with me on our juvenile career to India.

LINES WRITTEN MAY 19, 1812.

Oh! never can the scenes of other days
Which fancy oft in vivid light arrays,
Arise like visions of the midnight hour,
And pass unheeded, and unfelt their power.

Resistless they awaken pensive thought,
And are with long-forgotten pleasures fraught:
In lonely musing then the heart is blest,
And faded joys in brilliant hues are drest.

Again the blossoms of the Spring appear,
Though age, like winter, has despoil'd the year:
Again the sunny haunts of youth we roam,
Though ling'ring near the grave, our final home:
Again with fervent joy our bosoms glow,
Or throb with hope, or pine in cheerless woe·
Again Ambition's glorious prospects dawn,
And we exult in life's propitious morn;
Retrace the paths of danger and of fame,
Enkindling emulation's dying flame;
Or pausing oft, amid his bright career,
We find remember'd grief still claims a tear.
Perhaps o'er Love's sepultur'd joys we mourn,
Or from our heart some cherish'd bliss is torn;
Perhaps some friend, who shar'd our early toils,
And blended counsel with benignant smiles,
Whose dear regard and ardent love of truth,
Directed and sustained our erring youth,
Has left us long for his eternal rest
No more reposing on our aching breast.

Oh! relative beloved! thou wilt not deem
These, wayward follies, and an idle dream.
Oft through the twilight paths of other days
Thy memory wanders, and thy fancy strays;
E en there thou lov'st to pause, and linger last,
And fondly think o'er joys and sorrows past.
What mingled forms, what varied scenes appear,
To greet remembrance, and to claim a tear!
An ocean's vast expanse, and foreign shores,
Again thy retrospective glance explores;

Gives back the precious hopes that blossom'd there,
And more than bless'd a stripling's fervent prayer;
Gives back the solemn groves and fav'rite flowers,
The brahmins' lonely walks, and sacred bowers;
Gives back the FRIEND, who shar'd each lov'd retreat,
And render'd every passing moment sweet;
And Oh! restores the agony of soul
(His pleading voice can never more control)
When he in manhood's noble vigour died,
And thou bereav'd in solemn anguish sigh'd:
But yet he lives within thy "heart of hearts,"
And consolation's heavenly balm imparts;
Sustains the hallow'd hope within thy breast,
That thou shalt share his beatific rest.
Remember'd blessings 'mid this gather'd gloom,
A renovated lustre now assume.
Preserv'd from perils, and from conflicts past,
Protected wheresoe'er thy lot was cast,
And to thy country and its joys restored,
To live belov'd, and ah! to die deplor'd!
When all thy dear associates are no more,
Who left their kindred and their native shore
With expectation ardent as thine own,
Nor thought to leave thee in thy path alone.

Illumin'd thus by Memory's brightest rays,
Thou meet'st the faded flowers of other days,
And, looking upward to their azure skies,
Adores the SOURCE from whence these blessings rise! MARIANNE.

These affectionate lines, sent to me as the sheets were going to press, have indeed awakened the feelings they express, in my bosom—they have done more, they have induced me, even in this late stage of the work, to make a further selection, from an arrangement made near thirty years ago, on my voyage to England in the General Elliot; when I destroyed every letter and paper, which seemed no longer of importance, and preserved a few tokens of friendship and affection, from a correspondence of near twenty years, passed in the country I was then leaving, at the most interesting and delightful season of life. The originals were deposited with my descriptive letters and drawings; and formed, in my estimation, the choicest part of the collection. They were afterwards rejected from the papers intended for publication, from an idea of their being generally of a private nature, and in some respects irrelevant to the principal purport of the publication. But on further consideration, after receiving the preceding lines, I resolved to make a still more limited selection from the manuscripts then preserved. It is now indeed confined to a very small number of letters which passed during the lapse of a few months, between the sacrifice of Baroche and the northern purgunnas, and our final departure from Tellicherry to Europe. In these memoirs, which are intended as a medium between the dignity of history, and the hasty language of epistolary correspondence, this little selection may not be altogether without interest, especially to those readers who have resided in India. The letters display an unpremeditated and desultory portrait of the Anglo-Indian character, and exhibit a warmth of heart and liberality of sentiment, perhaps not inferior to late publications of the correspondence of celebrated individuals of both sexes in France and England. I formerly inserted a few letters from my Asiatic friends; these, except in one instance, are from my English associates during the short period abovementioned.

EXTRACT FROM A LETTER DATED MARCH 1783.

"Alas! my Friend, to what a scene of misfortune are we reduced! I have received some very confidential letters from Bombay; where the particulars of the treaty lately concluded between the English and the Mahrattas had arrived, from Mr. David Anderson, ambassador from the Bengal government to Mhadajee Sindia, through whose mediation it was effected. There seem to have been two separate treaties; one between the East India Company and the Poonah durbar, the other between the Company and Mhadajee Sindia only. The former is by no means so favourable as that concluded by colonel Upton in 1776; because Jamboseer and every other cession and conquest from the Mahrattas and Guicawars, since the commencement of the Mahratta war, are to be relinquished, except Salsette, Caranjah, and the smaller isles in Bombay harbour. All our possessions in the Concan are vanished; no territory remains to Surat; nor is the promised country of three lacs any louger to be expected. These sacrifices might have been anticipated, but to gratify Mhadajee Sindia for procuring this peace, the governor general and council have been pleased to grant him, by a separate treaty, the city and purgunna of Baroche, a pretty douceur of near one hundred thousand pounds per annum.

"Most heartily do I execrate this inglorious convention; for nothing surely could be more unjust than thus sacrificing the Bombay presidency to the interests of the other two. But our part, my friend, is submission; and I feel the effects of the treaty far more for the general loss and disgrace to the service, and the interest of those individuals so essentially hurt, than anything that respects myself, except the dishonourable mode of quitting a station which I have held for seven years. I greatly suspect no provision whatever is made for our private property, except the usual one of liberty to remove or dispose of it: a cruel case indeed; but should a resident be left for mercantile affairs, it may be somewhat softened. Could I confer this magic power on you, we might soon people Malabar hill with the late happy inhabitants of your sweet village near Baroche; but alas! my friend, these must be left behind us!

I am now enabled to send you a translation, by a native linguist, of the inglorious treaty, executed at Tellowgaum, in 1779; which is not only the foundation of all our present misfortunes, especially in the loss of Baroche, but will probably, at some future period, be considered a curiosity; as such you may wish to preserve it in your valuable collection.

Articles of agreement between Mhadarow Narrain Pundit Purdhun, Peshwa of the Mahrattas, on the one part; and the English Company on the other part.

"That in the time of the late Mhadarow matters went on peaceably; since which the English obtained possession of several places belonging to the Sircar; such as Salsette, Ouran, (or Caranja), Jamboseer, the mahauls and purgunnas of Baroche, belonging to the sircar and the Guicawar. The English aided Ragobah, and war having commenced, Colonel Upton came from Calcutta, with full power, and made an agreement; according to which matters were to go on between the Company and Sircar; but which was not adhered to by the English; they having aided Ragobah, and making preparations for the war, mounted the Ghauts, invaded the districts of the Sircar, and began hostilities; on which the Sircar also prepared for war. That in the district of Worgaum near Tellowgaum, Messrs. Carnac and Egerton of the Select Committee at Bombay, being fully empowered, did depute Messrs. Farmer and Holmes; that the old friendship between the English and Sircar being interrupted, Colonel Upton made an agreement, but according to which matters did not proceed; and therefore that treaty was annihilated. So that on the same footing as the English and the Sircar were in the time of Mhadarow, they are henceforth to remain, and the cause of Ragobah to be given up; nor any aid to be afforded to the enemies of the Sircar.

"The islands and places abovementioned are to be given up; and to go on and remain as in Mhadarow's time; and it is stipulated that in the above case good faith is to be observed on the part of the Sircar. That Ragobah by his own free consent committed himself with all his effects to Tookajee Holcar and Mhadajee Sindia. That the English army at Worgaum shall be permitted to proceed with all its effects to Bombay; and as security for it on the part of the Sircar, two persons shall proceed, belonging to each of the abovementioned Sirdars, to conduct the army to Bombay; for which purpose troops shall be sent or not with the army, as the army please; and that the army shall not molest any one on the road.

"That the Anterwad and Bundywad provinces and their Sirdars being ever under the Sircar, no damage must be done to them. The English army from Calcutta having passed the Nerbudda, and now at Hussingabad, must not be permitted to proceed further, but must be sent back to Calcutta, no one being molested by them on the road.

"The above was framed by the mediation of Tookajee Holcar and Mhadajee Sindia; and according to this matters must in future go on without failure; to which they pledge the English faith to observe, and it is stipulated the Sircar must also observe it, and that no aid or protection shall be afforded to the French.

Signed in the English camp, by

JOHN CARNAC,
CHARLES EGERTON.

Signed in the Mahratta camp, by

THOMAS HOLMES,
W. G. FARMER."

Dated at Worgaum near Tellowgaom, 27th Jilkyjee, or 13th January 1779.

Separate Agreement of John Carnac and Charles Egerton, the English Committee from Bombay, with Mhadajee Sindia.

"After falling out with the Sircar of Mhadarow Narrain, Pundit Purdun, we with an English army from Bombay came upon the Ghauts, and encamped at Tellowgaum; on which you ordered a fighting, and we, both parties, did fight; in which we were defeated, returned back, and encamped at Worgaum with Dada-Saheb (Ragobah); from whence we could not in safety retreat to Bombay with our army and stores. Considering all this, we sent Messrs. Farmer and Holmes to you, desiring you would come and get the Sircars and our treaty settled as before, and conduct us and the English army to Bombay. You came between us, and got the Sircar's and English treaty settled, and you promised to conduct us and the army to Bombay, without molestation from any one. You made our escape entirely. All this we took into our consideration, and were very glad. You are a principal officer with the Sircar, and a well-wisher to the English government, which has induced us to keep a friendship with you; this came into our mind, and we were satisfied that you made us free from the Sircar, and every body's molestation, and got this treaty settled, as beforementioned, without any molestation from the Sircar; therefore we thought we should serve you; and for this reason we have of our own free will and accord, agreed under the king and the company's seal, to deliver up to you the fort of Baroche, with its purgunna and government, in the same manner as the Mogul did hold it; which fort is now in the English possession, and which we have given to you. We further agree that we will, on our arrival at Bombay, obtain the governor's dustuck (or order) under the king's seal, to the killidar of Baroche, to deliver the fort and country to you, in the manner the Mogul did hold it; under oath, no dispute shall arise in this; we promise solemnly; and we have left Mr. W. G. Farmer and Mr. Charles Stewart with you, as hostages for the performance of this agreement. We will let no dispute arise; this we agree to in writing.

(Signed) JOHN CARNAC,
CHARLES EGERTON."

*Dated at Worgaum near Tellowgaum, 27th Jilkyjee,
13th January,* 1779.

From Dhuboy, 8th April, 1783.

From Damoder Madonjee, Purvoe and Linguist, to James Forbes, Esq.

"I HAVE received your favour of yesterday, my honoured master, and I shall observe the contents therein mentioned. All the people in Dhuboy are extremely sorry to hear such news, that the Mahratta government are going to have this place again. All the poor subjects both in the town and in the purgunnas were happy under the English Company and your government; but now they are all sorry, and hope God will not make this news true. This year especially, from master's kindness in settling light the jumma-bundy, when God had not given the latter rain, and the batty and some other grain all come spoiled, the subjects will remember your goodness and pray for you for ever, because master considered the poor, and made the subjects happy until the next season. And now such news as shall take this happiness from us, makes us all too much sorry; but it is what God pleases; what the subjects say I have only to acquaint you, Sir.

"We still hope God Almighty will make this news become false, the same as when such report was in Guzerat last year. Then all the subjects will again be happy; otherwise very sorry, but it depends upon God. The news in Dhuboy is, that the Bengal gentlemen are doing this bad business; therefore only acquaint you, Sir. I told Mogut Ram and the other dessoys and jamadars what you mentioned about the peace with the Mahrattas; they also, and all the brahmins and Mahomedans, who sit on the carpet of justice, hope God Almighty will make this news false, and that the purgunnas will remain as they are. Such news the jamadars hope to hear; and then, the moment they find it true that the English government shall remain as it is, they will divide sugar and sweetmeats among all the people in the cutcheree; then every body will speak sweet words. They have also promised to make ceremonies in the pagodas, and give charity to the brahmins: they say they have all been happy under you for more than three years, and make their abaddee this season also. Therefore with all they say I only acquaint you, Sir, &c."

From J. Forbes, at Dhuboy, 23*d April*, 1783.

"No more, my dear friend, shall I address you from Dhuboy; this is probably the last day of my government, as I am in hourly expectation of a Mahratta despot, with his greedy train, to take possession of this city, and all the adjoining districts; all eager to tax and oppress a quiet set of people, whom it has been my study to render happy. How melancholy an appearance does every thing now wear, from that which delighted you four months ago, when we enjoyed our party with the chief, through these pergunnas. The higher orders of people in the city have actually laid aside their long robes, and put on more humble apparel. The banians in general have shut up their shops in the bazar, and many of them are gone off. The rest of the inhabitants await their doom in mournful silence, or melancholy converse without the Gate of Diamonds; where you and myself have so often witnessed their happiness. Yet even this is trifling, compared with the sacrifice of Baroche to Mhadajee Sindia; it never did belong to the Mahrattas; and as the inglorious treaty of Worgaum never took place, the cession of Baroche was disgraceful to the Company, prejudicial to Bombay, and a cruel stroke on the individuals stationed at that pleasant and advantageous settlement. It was a situation which we looked upon as permanent as the presidency of Bombay itself; and I must say, our acutest feelings are excited at the idea of leaving all those who have sought the English protection, and emigrated from other countries to purchase lands, build houses, and establish new manufactures, under the flag of Baroche; there to enjoy the lenity of our laws, and a security of property unknown under other governments; these, as well as our numerous dependants and domestics, who cannot accompany us to Bombay, must be left to the mercy of an arbitrary rapacious Mahratta chieftain.

"My feelings, I freely confess, are far more for others than myself. I have almost attained the fruition of my wishes, and should not have remained more than another year in India. Dalton and my sister will now accompany me home, as they have no further prospects of advantage in this part of the globe. I have been fortunate to recover every rupee due to the Company from the revenues of my districts, and shall not leave a single concern unsettled at Dhuboy: it will be far otherwise at Baroche; where we have houses, landed property, and many outstanding concerns not provided for in the late treaty. I have written you these particulars, in which I know you will take a great interest, because my letter cannot reach you before your arrival at Canton: whither you intended sailing soon after your return to Bombay from Guzerat; and where I hope you will in a few years finish your fortune."

To J. Forbes, from the Commanding officer at Dhuboy, dated 28th April 1783.

" I do indeed rejoice, and that most sincerely, my dear Sir, at your wonderful escape from the Gracias, and safe arrival among your anxious friends at Baroche: but when you wrote to me you knew not half the extent of the robbery and murders among your people, by those cruel banditti: ere this you must have heard the melancholy particulars, which I will not recapitulate. Nothing but the lucky circumstance of your setting out from hence so many hours earlier than usual prevented your falling into the hands of those merciless wretches. They were afraid, as I am informed, of being too early at the rendezvous, lest you should get intelligence of it, and disappoint them; but they reached the destined spot very soon after you left it. The whole tribe of Gracias in this part of Guzerat are concerned in this horrid plot; Mandwa, Vazeria, Veloria, Rampoor, Meah, and many others. They have ever since posted a couple of horsemen in all the villages round Dhuboy, to give them the earliest intelligence of our motions.

" Yesterday we had a flying report that in consequence of the Mahrattas having captured one of the Company's vessels with several king's officers on board, there would be a renewal of the war, and consequently no cession of these purgunnas. This being rather confirmed by your last letter, I immediately communicated the news to the principal inhabitants, who solicited me to fire a salute on the occasion, that the happy intelligence might be communicated far and near: this, however, I declined, fearful of its ultimate consequence to the petitioners, should the report prove to be unfounded, and a Mahratta chief still succeed you. I thought the grateful venerable Ardeseer, tandar of Zinore, would have died with joy when he heard the news; and your purvoe damoder put on the first smile visible on his long face since your departure. He much regrets having dismantled your apartments in the durbar; and in consequence of the favourable report, I am replacing the copper bolts and bars which I had taken from the powder magazine, being determined not to leave them for the Mahrattas. I am most truly concerned to hear of the shocking conspiracy and mutiny at Baroche; but I do not so much wonder at it, when I consider the hatred of the Mahomedans to a Mahratta government, although so timely discovered; it is a peremptory duty to make a severe example of the ringleaders both among the conspirators and sepoy mutineers."

From Baroche, 2d July 1783.

"We detained your halcarra, my dear Sir, to inform you of the transactions in council yesterday, as you could not leave your residency to be present. It was our last meeting; and our final resolutions respecting this ill-fated settlement, closed the consultation. This morning we are to assemble at a full Court of Adawlet, and after settling the causes, dissolve the court; all prisoners confined for just debts are to be delivered over to the new government. The chief is to do as he thinks right with the natives committed by him as a magistrate. About twenty pieces of ordnance one hundred barrels of powder, and shot in proportion, are to be lent to Bascar Row for Mhadajee Sindia, with which he seems much pleased.

"Bascar Row, the provisional governor appointed by Mhadajee Sindia to take charge of this valuable cession, arived at Baroche on Saturday evening, visited the chief on Monday, and will, I imagine, take possession of the fortress on Friday next, if the weather will permit of our journey to Surat; but at present the rains fall so heavy as to render our departure doubtful.

"Corkran and myself paid Bascar Row a long visit; he seems a shrewd sensible man; his observations were generally just, and he shewed great penetration in many instances. For a Mahratta he is polite and agreeable; his conversation affable, and sometimes jocose. Lullabhy hardly ever leaves the new pundit, and seemed particularly inclined to be present at our interview; an honour which we dispensed with, and during his absence Corkran gave Bascar Row many traits of his character; a confidence he was well pleased with, and requested another conference. With this our friend is equally delighted; because he will remain here as English resident, and hoist the British colours on the factory house when they are struck on the fort, to give place to the Mahratta flag.

"Bascar Row has already noticed his intentional proceedings on taking charge of the settlement. After paying his devotions at the pagoda, the following edicts are to be immediately issued from the durbar.

"First, that no cow, bullock, or calf, shall evermore be killed in Baroche, on pain of death; nor beef to be eaten by any person whatever.

" Secondly, That no Hollocore, Derah, or Chandala caste, shall upon any consideration come out of their houses after nine o'clock in the morning, lest they should taint the air, or touch the superior Hindoos in the streets.

" Thirdly, To encourage sobriety, no person whatever is to distil or sell mowah arrack, or other spirits, to any person whatever.

" Fourthly, No prostitutes or disorderly women of that description shall reside within the walls of Baroche.

" These appear to be a very extraordinary set of edicts from an oriental governor, and are not likely to conciliate the Mahomedan and Parsee subjects to their new administration. The former have been accustomed to eat beef from the first conquest of the Moguls, and the latter to drink mowah arrack; from which, in moderation, they are not prohibited by any religious tenets. As to the poor chandalas and Frass caste, the order seems cruel in the extreme; but the last respecting the cyprian corps has caused the most astonishment among all classes of society, being perfectly novel in the system of Asiatic jurisdiction. In consequence of the late conspiracy, mutiny, and confusion, which reigns throughout the city on this cruel change, except in council, I have been generally silent. It would be needless to interfere with measures which we can neither prevent nor redress; and as to the new edicts, I think them totally inconsistent with my ideas of Mahratta policy, rapacity, and morality: nor have I a doubt that money well applied at Bascar Row's durbar, will cause a repeal of the whole; even that relating to the inexpiable sin of eating beef.

From L. C. Esq. Resident at Baroche, dated 16*th July* 1783.

"I CANNOT tell you, my dear friend, what I suffered after seeing you all cross the Nerbudda, and finding the settlement forsaken by that social circle which so lately enlivened it. Your letter gave me some pleasure in finding the weather favourable, and the roads tolerable, considering the late heavy rains. Your hospitable reception at Surat I had no doubt of; it is the characteristic of India, and your host is particularly renowned for that virtue. I have written fully to Dalton of Bascar Row's infamous conduct in reversing several late decrees by the English judges in the Court of Adawlet at Baroche, justly awarded during their government.

"That insidious and complicated oppressor Lullabhy, whose power was so humanely curtailed under the English administration, has entirely ingratiated himself with Bascar Row, and is hourly pointing out to his ready ear some new victim of oppression. Lullabhy has completely besieged him; every man in the durbar is his creature, and Bascar Row the instrument of his tyranny. This ungrateful banian, so patronized by many of our late Board, is now constantly hinting that the English acted with too much lenity in favour of several individuals; at the same time urging him to overset the decrees, or at least to pretend to do so, that money may flow into the coffers of himself and Bascar Row.

"A few days ago a Pinjaree, named Rhaman, formerly an inhabitant of Baroche, but who on account of some dispute with Lullabhy left the place of his nativity, and lived at Duan, was sent for by Bascar Row, and at the instigation of Lullabhy, met with an extraordinary reception. Rhaman, a bold enterprizing fellow, during the time of the late nabob of Baroche was famous for jaunsaw, and other noble feats in the purgunnas. Rhaman thinking himself ill used by Lullabhy, and not obtaining satisfaction, in the reign of Gulam Shah, came from Duan, in the spirit of revenge, to dispatch that of the sanctified banian, into the body of a cow; but being betrayed by one of his comrades, Lullabhy complained to the English chief, who confined him in the chowkey, and put him in irons, which he contrived to get off, and with them knocking down the European centinel taken by surprise, made his escape. After this transaction, Lullabhy was with great reason suspicious of Rhaman, until a reconciliation took place between them about three years ago upon the death of the Ahmood rajah. On this occasion the treacherous banian presented the open-hearted Rhaman with a considerable sum of money, in token of his entire reconciliation. On Bascar Row's late appointment to Baroche, Lullabhy sent an express to Rhaman at Duan, inviting him to Baroche, and promising to procure him a good appointment under the new pundit. In consequence of this friendly summons the unsuspecting Rhaman came hither a few days ago, was immediately made a jemadar, and honoured with the command of fifty men. Short indeed was his enjoyment of this situation. Lullabhy had now accomplished his infamous purpose; and poor Rhaman, without the shadow of a crime either against Bascar Row or the Mahratta government, was, upon the secret instigation of Lullabhy, condemned to death in this despotic durbar, and ordered to be blown from the mouth of a cannon, which sentence was executed two days ago without the east gate of the city. This brave fellow in his way to execution, exultingly and loudly exclaimed, that he had friends who would revenge his death on the treacherous banian. You and I are pretty well acquainted with Lullabhy's character, though I believe I know the most of his villainy. I have lately been reading Fielding's Life of Jonathan Wild the Great; the more I see and reflect upon the character of Lullabhy, the more I think him entitled to the glorious epithet of the *Great Man.* The proclamation, issued under his auspices by Bascar Row, is likely to be altogether as permanent as the general moral system of Lullabhy. Notwithstanding its recent and solemn promulgation, the privilege of distilling and vending arrack for one year, was farmed three days ago for seven thousand rupees to the sircar, and one thousand *soocry,* (a douceur) to Bascar Row. Yesterday the annual customs collected at the Baroche phoorza, were farmed to a banian from Malwa, for ninety-one thousand rupees, and five thousand soocry. It is plain the man came from a far country; for should the trade continue as flourishing as under our government, of which there is no prospect, the farmer must lose from twenty to thirty thousand rupees; of this you, who was so many years phoorza-master at Baroche, must know the truth.

"You may guess my situation among this rapacious and oppressive people; hourly hearing of grievances I cannot redress, and cruelties I cannot mitigate. I particularly lament the fate of the worthy Afsaram, and many other of our native friends, who, at the vile instigation of Lullabhy, are now under the displeasure of the new pundit for their grateful attachment to us. They are almost forbidden to visit me, especially poor Afsaram, who feels it much. In short, no government can be more tyrannical. Fines are inflicted on the most frivolous pretences, to gratify the malice of Lullabhy, and enrich the coffers of Bascar Row, who it is said is only a temporary governor, until a favourite of Sindia comes from Oojeen; consequently he cares not by what means his fortune is made. The wretched inhabitants deplore the blessings of the British government, as much as I do the loss of that society you still enjoy with our former delightful associates; especially our four charming English ladies, who will enliven Surat, and the Bengal cantonments during the monsoon.

"At all events, my worthy friend, continue your correspondence, and let me know what is going on in the world; place yourself in my solitary situation, and I well know how it will operate in my behalf. As soon as you had all crossed the river, the Mahratta troops marched into the garrison, and on hoisting Sindia's flag on the flag-staff tower, saluted it with one gun; on which I immediately hoisted the British colours on the house formerly the Dutch factory, now appropriated to the English resident.— Conceive my feelings!"

Extract from the Answer, dated Surat, the 19th of July, 1783.

"YOUR letter, my worthy friend, reached me yesterday evening. I am sorry the halcarrah lost mine to you of the 11th, not that it was of any further consequence than to convey our united tribute of friendship and affection on our departure from Baroche. At a season when my mind was most open to tender impressions, I could not help inditing the effusions of a heart warmly interested in your welfare and happiness. I well knew how you would feel our separation. Those who remain on the spot alway suffer more than those who take their departure; whose attention is more or less engaged with a variety of new objects, as was our case in the journey to Surat. I therefore feel much for you, placed among such detestable characters, and compelled to witness distresses you cannot relieve; but the downy wings, and (allow me to say) the balmy comforts of religion, united to the active duties of a commercial career, to commence with the opening of the fair season, will I trust alleviate the miseries which now surround you. You must, my friend, look at the magnifying end of the telescope, the brilliant medium of the glass called Claud Lorraine: behold the pleasing scenes that await you a few years hence in England. Call in the pleasures of imagination; remove the veil which obscures the bright prospect and enviable pleasures we have so lately talked of enjoying together in our native isle; which ere long will I hope be realized. The lovely rose is often encompassed by thorns; and seldom does the cup of humanity contain an unmingled potion. You must therefore consider your situation for two or three years to come, as a road, which, although a little rough and dreary, will ultimately lead you to all that is most desirable in this sublunary vale.

"An elegant sufficiency, content,
Retirement, rural quiet, friendship, books,
Ease and alternate labour, useful life,
Progressive virtue, and approving Heaven."

Now, my friend, let me not preach in vain; knowing you sometimes dwell too long on the sombre scene, and indulge a little too much of what is emphatically styled the English malady (happily not very common in this country), it is the duty of friendship to brighten the prospect; and I have no doubt when things are properly represented to Mhadajee Sindia, you will find your situation more pleasant and advantageous.

"I not only feel for you, but most sincerely do I pity the worthy Afsaram, Dowlat Roy Dessoy, and our former native friends; indeed the whole city and purgunna of Baroche claim our compassion; because when malice and rapacity, uncontrolled, unite hand in hand, as they do with your two *great men*, dreadful must be the consequences. At the same time that I lament the fall of Baroche, I cannot but exquisitely feel for my friends at Dhuboy now suffering under similar calamity. Should Assaram or the Dessoy be allowed to visit you, remember us to them in the kindest manner; not so to their oppressor, who I have no doubt will soon fall, and that too from a lofty pinnacle, to make his overthrow the more conspicuous. Such a fate to Lullabhy would not only correspond with the general system of Asiatic policy, but is frequently permitted by Providence for the punishment of the culprit, and an example to others. His cruelty to the unfortunate Rhaman indelibly marks his character. Nor can all his ostentatious charities, glittering pagodas, and magnificent wells, wipe off the stain of murder, cruelty, and oppression. The tears of the widows and orphans whom he has reduced to that calamity, mingling with the blood of Rhaman, form a different stream, and exhibit a sad contrast to the Persian inscription over his beautiful well, without the Jerasseer gate of Baroche, the very spot selected for poor Rhaman's catastrophe!"

Bengal Cantonments, near Surat, 21*st August,* 1783.

"MANY thanks, my dear Sir, for your favour of the 10th, and kind congratulations on my convalescence. Thank God, I am now nearly recovered from the severest fever I ever had in my life, in which I was for many days in great danger; and my trembling hand will still convince you of my weak state. I came about a week ago, by the physician's advice, for change of air to the Bengal camp, and have since been gradually gaining appetite and strength. Our four Baroche ladies, with their husbands, are also staying with their friends in camp; those from Surat are frequent visitors; and the only two Bengal ladies belonging to that establishment do every thing in their power to render it agreeable.

"I know not the full meaning of the word *cantonment*, and a camp this singular place cannot well be termed; it more resembles a large town, being many miles in circumference. The officers' bungalos on the banks of the Tappee are large and convenient, generally consisting of three rooms and verandas; some of more: all built in wooden frames, filled up with bamboos or neat straw work, lined with coloured chintz or white calico, and the floors covered with cotton carpets. Each bungalo has its own garden, poultry-yard, stables, and out-houses. The soldiers' quarters and every part of the cantonment are equally neat and regular; without seeing it I should have formed a very imperfect idea of the comfort and luxury of a Bengal encampment. For, although I cannot much enter into it, I assure you here is a constant succession of amusements for morning, noon, and all night long. The former is occupied in hunting, shooting, cock-fighting, and dog-fighting. Feasting at dinner from one till three o'clock, when horse-races commence, quite in the English style, on a very good course. Between the heats, fighting-rams, dancing-bears, ladies running races on elephants, and more varieties than I can tell you of, fill up the intervals. When the horse-race finishes, the company leave the stage, to drink tea in an adjoining tent, from whence they retire to their respective bungalos, to dress for the ball; which is given every evening by subscription from the principal officers in the commandant's bungalo; a large mansion, excellently suited to the purpose. A concert sometimes precedes the dance before supper, an entertainment equally elegant and abundant. After which dancing, singing, music, and masques continue until four in the morning. These festivals have already lasted four days, they are to terminate to-morrow; a fortunate circumstance for the principal actors, who I should imagine would not hold out much longer. We purpose returning to Surat in a few days, and sailing from thence for Bombay about the beginning of September."

Extracts on leaving Bombay.

"The enclosed, my dear Forbes, is the promised letter to my best friend, to whom you want no introduction. Take yours in your hand, and tell mine he is as worthy a man as ever left India; a character congenial to his own: that I sincerely wish

Dalton and your sister all health and happiness, is most true; no wish rises nearer my heart than that for the welfare of you all. Keep me in remembrance as one who has a just sense of your worth and virtues, and who will esteem it as one of the first pleasures England can hereafter afford—the renewal of our intimacy in that happy isle, without the idea of another separation

"But when my destiny will lead me thither I dare not venture to pronounce; I hope however within four or five years. This side of India has now very few profitable situations in the company's service; and by the loss of Baroche, and all our valuable possessions, the prospect is altogether gloomy. We are weighed down by an enormous debt, unnecessary expenses, and a great scarcity of cash. No payments to any civil department of the service; the military swallow up our whole resources. Transfer is now at thirty-three per centum, with a prospect of being worse as soon as the army accounts are liquidated."

"Accept my sincere thanks for your beautiful painting of flowers, which I shall preserve until we have again the pleasure of meeting in England—yet I am almost sorry you are going to that happy country where we all so much wish to be; but that proceeds from too selfish a principle to be cherished: for believe me, my dear friend, there are not two persons in the world in whose success I more rejoice than yours and Dalton's. I am well assured neither of you will forget me, but on the contrary I shall frequently receive letters from you both. I have hinted to my sister that you have many volumes of drawings and descriptions of every part of India in which you have been, which would be very entertaining to her, and give them all a better idea of India than any thing I know besides.

"I THINK it very probable you may meet our friend C— at Tellicherry or Cochin, in one of the Portugueze ships from Macao, which generally arrive about this time. You have heard of his late misfortunes, but it is possible you may not know by what means his affairs are likely to be retrieved; and therefore with exquisite delight I relate an anecdote which does honour to human nature. The story is true, and in my opinion equals any thing of the kind upon record. You, who were formerly so well acquainted with this worthy man in India, know that he afterwards resided many years highly respected at Canton and Macao; where a sudden reverse of fortune lately reduced him from a state of affluence to the greatest necessity. A Chinese merchant, to whom he had formerly rendered service, gratefully offered him an immediate loan of ten thousand dollars, which the gentleman accepted, and gave his bond for the amount; this the Chinese immediately threw into the fire, saying, "When you, my friend, first came to China, I was a poor man; you took me by the hand, and assisting my honest endeavours, made me rich. Our destiny is now reversed: I see you poor, while I am blessed with affluence." —The by-standers had snatched the bond from the flames; the gentleman, sensibly affected by such generosity, pressed his Chinese friend to take the security, which he did, and then effectually destroyed it. The disciple of Confucius, beholding the renewed distress it occasioned, said he would accept of his watch, or any little valuable as a memorial of their friendship. The gentleman immediately presented his watch; and the Chinese, in return, gave him an old iron seal, saying, "Take this seal; it is one I have long used, and possesses no intrinsic value: but as you are going to India to look after your outstanding concerns, should Fortune further persecute you, draw upon me for any sum of money you may stand in need of, seal it with this signet, sign it with your own hand, and I will pay the money."

The Macao ships did not arrive during our stay at Tellicherry, consequently we had not the pleasure of meeting Mr. C—, whose commercial concerns turning out advantageously, he returned to Europe with an independent fortune. On inquiring the name of the generous Chinese, I was informed it was *Chinqwa*. It is a name which deserves to be recorded on a rock of adamant, and an action which will ennoble him for ever.

With this triumph of virtue, before I close this little selection from an oriental correspondence, it may be equally proper to mention the downfal of prosperous vice. Lullabhy, the opulent banian of Baroche, so often mentioned in these memoirs, and lately introduced as an oppressive zemindar, and the murderer of the unfortunate Rhaman, when he had nearly reached the pinnacle of his ambition and accumulated wealth, sufficient even to gratify a rapacious Mahratta chief, was seized on one of those ready pretences in an oriental durbar, his immense property was confiscated, and himself banished to a distant fortress, not celebrated for the goodness of its water. There, either by the change of beverage, or some speedier method, he fell a sacrifice to his crimes.

"I now return all the books you lent me, together with your drawings and manuscripts, as I fear the hour approaches when you will pack them up for Europe. The latter are not only beautiful, but extremely interesting; your descriptions are pleasing, your observations just, and the whole collection does great credit to your taste and judgment. Without partiality or flattery to my friend, I think myself rather competent to decide on this point after upwards of thirty years residence in this country. You ought, in justice both to yourself and friends, to devote more of your leisure hours to the Muses, who seem so well inclined to be propitious to your invocation. Allow me to request a copy of the poetical epistle from Dhuboy to your amiable sister at Baroche; it is truly pathetic and descriptive.

"And now, my friend, I have a further favour to ask of you. I well remember the assortment of seeds you procured a few years ago for Dr. Fothergill from the Baroche gardens, and all the neighbouring districts. I do not think of a collection to such an extent, in your present unsettled situation, but Sir Joseph Banks is so zealous for the improvement of botanical knowledge, that I think it meritorious to contribute to the utmost in my power to forward his endeavours; and you cannot more singularly oblige me than by exerting your ingenuity to enable me to comply with a request in his last letter; in which he says, the jac I sent him by Major Wood was the first which had been imported into England, at which the king expressed a more particular satisfaction than usual on such occasions; and Sir Joseph further desires me to send him seeds of the common fruits, flowers, and drugs of India, of which there are yet but few in the English conservatories. In this you must assist me, and if I can succeed in a similar request to another friend, I shall trouble you with the packet to the worthy baronet."

"Accept, my dear friend, of the enclosed, as the truest mark of a confirmed esteem; and believe me when I tell you I think I pay my own heart one of the highest compliments when I say it is filled with the warmest sentiments towards you; and that they will continue during our separation. Take with you my warmest wishes for the perfect restoration of your health, and happy meeting with all those you respect and love in our native country.

"I trust, my worthy friend, it will not be long before I follow your example. Your sentiments have always coincided with my own as to the proper period of leaving India. Long have I firmly fixed that period in my own mind; and now, as the time approaches, did I not carry my intentions into execution, I should degrade myself in my own opinion, for want of that firmness and resolution, which I think not to possess is a disgrace to the human character. Was my fortune collected and advantageously remitted to England, I should now have fully sufficient for a man of my disposition, who courts the shade of retirement, and has no taste for fashionable dissipation, or ostentatious vanity. I should be able to gratify every wish of my heart; and wealth, accumulated for any other purpose than the promotion of happiness, I hold in sovereign contempt. I am most sincerely concerned when I see some of my very particular friends, at the expense of their constitutions, heaping up riches, far beyond what their own occasions can ever require. This disposition I cannot but regard as a bias that will ultimately destroy their happiness, because they cannot find that consolation in futurity, and those anticipated enjoyments, for which, by an unnecessary self-denial, they now sacrifice so many real and present comforts. You, my dear friend, are not one of those, and most heartily do I congratulate you that you are not."

"I CANNOT, my excellent friend, allow you to leave India without a few lines, especially as I do not think you received a letter which I lately wrote on the subject of your health. I was truly concerned to find you had been so dangerously ill at Surat, and not entirely free from a relapse of fever at Bombay. You certainly never have enjoyed perfect health in this climate, and now that you are leaving it, I would advise you not to sit too much at the desk, and to use more exercise. Wherever your lot may be cast, let me entreat of you to walk out early in a pure air, on a dry soil; gentle riding on horseback will also be extremely beneficial to you. Be careful in your diet, and do not lead so sedentary a life as you have been accustomed to from the heat of the climate in India; your writing and drawing, however fascinating, must not engage so much of your time; by inactivity the fibres are relaxed and debilitated, the humours of the body more viscid and abundant, and consequently when attacked by a disorder it will be the more severe. The habit being weakened, and the humours accumulated, nature, even with the assistance of art, finds it more difficult to throw off the morbid load.

"On your arrival in England let me recommend you to drink the Cheltenham waters; they are extremely efficacious in bilious complaints. The water at Dazagon is not exactly of the same tendency, but you must remember the great benefit you derived there some years ago. I wish you could have found time to try the baths at Vazarabhy, as well as to have drank the waters before leaving Bombay, as you had no advantage of that kind in Guzerat. You would have had time after your return from Salsette, and they would have strengthened you for the passage to Europe. I have great pleasure in complying with your wishes, by enclosing an account of the hot wells at Vazarabhy, drawn up some time ago by our friend B——, as you wished it for your collection. I have not altered a word from the original paper in my possession.

An Account of the Hot Wells at Vazarabhy.

About twenty-five miles north of Beunda, a town at the head of Tannah river, formerly considerable for its trade, in a pleasant extensive valley, surrounded by mountains, stand the pagodas of *Ramexauar* and *Bhemexauar*, famous for their natural hot springs; which are preserved in baths elegantly made of hewn stone. The face of the country, in the month of November, was rural and wild, and the soil fertile to the last degree. But delightfully pleasant as the weather was, and agreeable our situation, we soon found by experience that the month of November was a very improper season for this excursion: a kind of epidemical fever pervaded every village near us, and soon seized our servants to such a degree, that before we had passed three weeks in our tents we were left almost destitute of their assistance; and had not a more disagreeable event (the dangerous state of health of one of our party) happened, to cause our sudden departure, we must shortly have been under the necessity of decamping on that account alone. The natives informed us that these fevers visit them annually, after the rains cease, and continue until the warm weather sets in.

The productions of the country are rice, gram, and a small dark grain used by the poor Columbees for food; they also plant a little tobacco, and a sort of bean something like the caravance. They have a few lime-trees, mangos, plantains, and guavas; the mango abounds in the country, the other fruit-trees are only planted round the pagodas. It is entirely owing to the lazy disposition of the natives, who live barely from hand to mouth, that the earth is not as famous for most oriental productions as it is for the surprizing springs with which Providence has so kindly and profusely furnished it. Something indeed may be said for the present confused state of the country, and the unhappy constitution of the government, which does not permit them to make a proper use of the riches nature has lavished on them; but industry was never the character of a Mahratta. The grass grows to a surprizing height, and the earth every where abounds with flowers and fragrant herbs of various sorts. The branches of the lime-trees about the pagoda Ramexauar, we found bowed to the ground with their golden produce, and every thing seemed to flourish in the highest perfection. We pitched our tents under the friendly shade of a noble banian tree, which overshadowed a space of an hundred and thirty paces in circumference, and completely sheltered us from the heat of the sun.

Within a few yards of the pagodas runs a small river, remarkable for the sweetness of its water. To the brink of this river a number of tigers, hyenas, wild hogs, deer, and other creatures, flock in the night from the neighbouring mountains to drink; and although the tigers frequent it every night, as we constantly observed by their fresh tracks, the country people regard them with no other fear than lest they should destroy their cattle; instances of which are even rare in this lovely valley. Pigeons and doves abound here, also partridges and snipes; but the high grass prevented our success with the latter; the banian-trees are enlivened by green-pigeons, squirrels, and monkeys. Reptiles of various descriptions are found in abundance; the most remarkable is a very beautiful snake, which lies among the branches of the burr-tree, where a monstrous species of spider spreads a strong and extensive web from bough to bough, and fiercely attacks every thing that touches it.

The natives rear large herds of cattle, which they drive into their houses every evening, and men, women, children, cows, and buffaloes all sleep together. In our journey from the wells we put up in a Mahratta village; and rather than expose ourselves to the dew when we could get under cover, accepted an offer from the patell of his house to sleep in; and a most uncomfortable night we had. No sooner was the lamp out, after the whole village had satisfied their curiosity in seeing us eat our supper, than we were beset by a numerous army of hungry Bandicoote rats, almost as large as sucking pigs, which kept a continual squeaking and fighting the whole night, running over us with the greatest familiarity.

These we should have despised, had not the lowing of a great buffalo calf, close at our feet, kept us from dropping asleep. We thought the night tedious, and about two o'clock determined to rise and decamp; for this purpose, while searching about to open the door, and awake the palanquin bearers, I found myself furiously attacked by the head of a cow, which obliged me to make a precipitate retreat, and remain quiet until the lord of the castle awoke and procured a light, which we found it very difficult to persuade him to.

In our journey from Beunda, we passed several of these wretched villages of Columbees (people who till the ground). Those near the hot wells are Ankalulee, half a mile to the south-west; Chambalee, a few paces beyond it; Kellang, to the westward; Gerad, to the north-west; and Vazarabhy at the distance of two miles to the south-west. The last village is the most considerable, and there resides Vittelpunt, the subahdar. He is at present superintending the building of a magnificent pagoda, designed also as a fortress in that part of the country. The pagoda, which is nearly finished, is elegantly designed and highly executed: but the engineers are very inferior to the civil architects, and in their choice of this ground have proved themselves so. For although they have, at a great expense, fortified one hill with a strong square stone wall, forty-three feet high, with a parapet and embrasures (in the midst of which stands the pagoda) they have entirely disregarded two more which hang directly over it, and absolutely command every inch of ground they have fortified; nay, so great is their error in this respect, that a stone rolled from the top of the nearest hill, must fall directly into the fort; for the side of this hill, cut down and cased with stone, forms the fourth side of it.

About three miles from Vazarabhy, in a low swampy valley, stands the pagoda Bhemexauar, very neatly designed, with two handsome baths before it. These baths are little frequented, on account of their bad situation; but the waters appear to be of the same nature and virtue with those of Ramexauar. Within a mile of this pagoda, in the midst of the river, or rather in the bed of it, (for except in the rainy season it does not deserve the name of a river) are two of the hottest springs that perhaps were ever known. They are preserved in two hollow cavities, formed by nature in the rock, and are equal in heat to the source of the emperor's bath at Achen, raising the thermometer to one hundred and thirty-six degrees of heat, which are sixteen degrees higher than the kings bath at Bath, in Somersetshire; and the same number of degrees higher than the hottest well at Ramexauar. We could scarcely bear to dip our hands in; and actually took out a snake from one of them whose flesh was turned white, as if it had been boiled, and fell to pieces as soon as touched with a stick; how long it had been boiling we could not tell.

The birds in the woods which surround this pagoda, deserve to be particularly mentioned for their harmonious notes, approaching something to a regular tune. It is true their notes are few, and have little variety, but their manner of mocking each other with those few, has a pleasing and singular effect.

The last and most frequented pagoda is called Ramexauar.

Within three hundred yards of this structure, at the bottom of a flight of steps leading to the river, lies a small cistern, equal in heat to the king's bath at Bath, which raises the thermometer to one hundred and twenty degrees; and, according to several experiments and observations made on the spot by two medical gentlemen, they evidently proved that these waters are of the same composition, nature, and quality with the Bath waters, in every respect except one: these have no impregnation of iron, and those at Bath a very small one; but so very small, that according to Dr. Lucas's account, it is not of the least importance in respect to their virtue. The waters of the last described cistern we used for drinking, being by much the clearest and best. Two yards from this we found another cistern, choked up with mud, and disregarded on that account. We cleared it out of curiosity, but made no use of the water. There are three other wells in the midst of the river, which are entirely overflowed in the rains. Besides these there are many small springs in the river itself, which warmed the water near them very perceptibly.

The country people destroy the efficacy of these waters on themselves by constantly bathing in them. The brahmins, banians, women and children, resident in the neighbouring villages, resort to them morning and evening; they are crowded from all parts on festival days, and the brahmins who live at the pagodas are alternately bathing in them all day long.

On a comparison between the experiment made by Dr. Lucas with the Bath waters, and those made with the hot spring at Ramexauar, the latter is found to contain sixteen grains of solid contents; about six of which are earth, and ten salt: these are united in a fluid, heated about twenty degrees above the blood of man in an ordinary healthy state; and with respect to the heat, the earth, and the salt, are exactly the contents of the Bath waters.

"I HAD the pleasure of receiving your last letter from Goa, and embrace the only opportunity that will now occur, of writing a few lines before you finally leave India, by the vessel which conveys the General Elliot's dispatches. Most sensibly, my valuable friend, do I feel the truth of all you said in your affectionate sheet. Absence and death alone reveal to us those feelings which only transiently affect us when present with the object of our esteem or love. I now find that a long intimacy and strict acquaintance with the virtues and qualities of any person, leaves a very sensible and lasting impression on the mind. We are formed (at least the valuable part of mankind) for the enjoyment of friendship and mutual benevolence; nor are there any sentiments more truly noble, generous, and elevating, than these. Human nature, unfortunately, admits not, or very rarely, of too close a connection. The seeds of petulance, pride, folly, and caprice, are sown even in the most liberal and exalted breasts, with a lavish hand; and we are too apt, when continually together, to find some occasions of vexation and disgust; but in absence it is just the reverse: we view our friend at a distance with other eyes; his faults are no more remembered, while we amplify or enlarge his amiable and elegant qualifications. We eagerly seize the only medium of communication which now remains, and think we never can sufficiently express in letters the warm affection which actuates our hearts. As this is a faithful picture of my feelings, so I will flatter myself that it is not a very erroneous one of yours. I know of no person in India, to whom I have been so long and uniformly attached; and I shall hope ever, though we should meet no more, to retain a warm place in your remembrance. You will ever live in mine!"

These unpremeditated effusions, at the period of separation between persons long united in the bonds of friendship and affection, will not I trust be deemed irrelevant to their present situation. Were they introduced only to gratify my own feelings, they would need an apology; but they are inserted from a nobler motive. They evince, in a variety of individual characters, a mind superior to the fascinations of ambition, wealth, and luxury, in a part of the globe where these passions are supposed to be amply gratified; and by many incompetent judges in England are presumed to engross almost the whole pursuits of their countrymen in India. From an intimate correspondence of nearly twenty years I might have adduced many other proofs of sound judgment, extensive knowledge, and liberal sentiment, which do honour to our national character, but I have limited myself to our correspondence during the last months of my residence in India, in which, although I may have gratified private feeling, I have also given undeniable proofs of the noblest virtues being deeply rooted, and residing, in the hearts of Britons settled in the oriental regions.

After leaving the Malabar coast we had a continuance of fair winds and pleasant weather, until we passed the line; where, instead of the calms so often experienced, a strong western gale carried us across the equator, on the third of March, with a hundred and ten miles on the board. These are delightful circumstances in a monotonous India voyage, both to sailors and passengers, but afford no topic for the descriptive pen.

> " La mer n'est plus qu'un cercle aux yeux des matelots,
> " Ou le ciel form un dôme appuyé sur les flots."

From this period light winds and calms prevailed alternately for near a fortnight; until, in the latitude of 13° south, we met the south-east trade wind, which wafted us on our course at the rate of seven miles an hour; so that we had generally from a hundred and sixty to a hundred miles in our day's reckoning. This, in the twenty-eighth degree of southern latitude, increased to a severe gale, which blew with unremitting fury four days; then gradually subsiding, it left us with fair winds and fine weather. These favourable gales continued until the 12th of April, when they entirely forsook us, and instead of the easterly winds common at that season, we encountered strong wintry blasts from the north-west, which drove us to the latitude of 38 degrees south; where during eight days we experienced three dreadful storms. One of them was a scene of horror and very great danger.

These hurricanes were succeeded by a faint lull, a short deceitful change, which carried us into soundings on the great southern bank of Africa; but the captain having positive orders not to stop at the Cape, we began to anticipate the more circumscribed pleasures at St. Helena, after our late anxiety; when, for twenty-six days together, the dead-lights were shut in, and very often no victuals could be dressed. The situation of the ladies and children was then truly lamentable, and the whole scene distressing.

We now thought our trials over, but a storm more tremendous than any I had ever witnessed, suddenly broke upon us from the north-west, and continued with unabated fury for several days. In former voyages I had never beheld any thing so dreadful: the raging billows seemed more like moving mountains of a black metallic substance, than an undulating fluid; while the sky, hard, dark, and dismal, was without a cloud. Language is too faint to describe this awful scene on the grandest theatre of nature. Camoens' Lusiad, in Mickle's translation, was my frequent companion on the voyage, especially during the tempests raging round this Cape of Storms. The sublime description of the Lusitanian bard was then completely realized, and I inserted the following lines in my journal, as presenting a faithful picture of the tremendous scenery.

"To tell the terrors of the deep untried,
What toils we suffer'd, and what storms defied;
What rattling deluges the black clouds pour'd,
What dreary weeks of solid darkness lour'd;
What mountain surges mountain surges lash'd,
What sudden hurricanes the canvas dash'd;
What bursting lightnings with incessant flare,
Kindled in one wide flame the burning air;
What roaring thunders bellow'd o'er our head,
And seem'd to shake the reeling ocean's bed;
To tell each horror on the deep reveal'd,
Would ask an iron throat with tenfold vigour steel'd:
These dreadful wonders of the deep I saw,
Which fill the sailor's breast with sacred awe;
And which the sages, of their learning vain,
Esteem the phantoms of the dreamful brain."

After experiencing for several weeks the reality of this sublime poesy, in doubling the southern promontory, we at length enjoyed a favourable gale; which settling in the regular south-east trade wind soon wafted us to St. Helena, where we passed near three weeks in all the pleasure and variety which this small but cheerful island amply affords. Having fully described it in a former voyage, I have now little to add: eight years had elapsed since my first visit, during which the cultivation of the island was considerably improved, especially in the growth of potatoes. This valuable root now supersedes the yam in the estimation of the islanders, and the numerous vessels that stop there for provisions. Many farmers raise two crops a year, from four to five hundred bushels each; the medium price was now six shillings per bushel. The surface of the island contains about thirty thousand acres; six thousand were then said to be under cultivation. When Lord Valentia visited it twenty years afterwards, the cultivation was increased to between seven and eight thousand acres.

Exclusive of the tutelary saint from whence St. Helena derives its name, the two Grecian goddesses of Crete and Delos unequally divide their sway over the inhabitants of this Atlantic isle, and one of them exerts no small influence over its visitors. The goddess of Chastity, whose votaries in a voluptuous climate are probably not very numerous, gives her name to the loftiest mountain in this romantic region, Diana's Peak being near three thousand feet above the picturesque valley which contains the little metropolis, where the queen of Love and her mischievous boy exert their sway, and wound the hearts of their itinerant votaries, who forgetting the transient nature of their abode in this Circean retreat, in the course of a few days frequently commence and conclude a union, which is to last for life. To those who have been long accustomed to the antelope eyes, jetty locks, and brunette complexions of Asiatic damsels, the fair and sprightly nymphs of St. Helena appear in twofold charms.

During our short stay at St. Helena, three of these entanglements took place. One triumphantly carried off his bride from her native rocks, to the fashionable circles in England. Another I believe succeeded in the same manner. The third concerned one of my most particular friends returning from another part of the East in the prime of life, and possessed of a noble fortune. Captivated by one of these blooming beauties, an offer of marriage was proposed and accepted: one of the little quarrels not uncommon between lovers, occasioned a procrastination, and the affair not being accommodated so soon as wished for by one of the parties, the vessel weighed anchor, and the gentleman was reluctantly carried on board by his exulting friends, who did not approve of the attachment. I well knew his feelings on this occasion, and sincerely pitied him. Absence, a sea voyage, and an English beauty, in time reconciled him to a life, which, on taking a last view of the retreating mountains of St. Helena, he thought would be insupportable.

> The slave that quits his native land,
> And bids for aye adieu,
> Oft turns to view the barren strand,
> And oft his sighs renew.

Though keen the pangs that rend his heart,
His pangs are nought to mine,
Doom'd by hard fate from thee to part,
And every joy resign!

To persons not under the immediate influence of the Cyprian deities, and no otherwise connected with the natives of St. Helena than by an interchange of friendly offices, and the usual weekly account, this island would be a very monotonous residence for any length of time. But during the period of an Indiaman's detention, its novelty and rural scenery amuse the passengers; and the supply of fresh meat, fruit and vegetables, which are sent off every morning to the vessels, refresh the sailors. More cattle and poultry might certainly be reared, and more fruits and vegetables produced, by attention and encouragement; the great increase of ships resorting to this small spot has enhanced the price of every thing, and the scarcity is sensibly felt by vessels that have not previously touched at the Cape. The latter once more belongs to the English, and long may it continue in their possession, because in every point of view its political and commercial advantages are of the greatest importance. The value of St. Helena to the East India Company, especially during a war with Holland, was inestimable; yet it is maintained at a moderate expense, the annual charge of the civil and military establishments and contingencies never exceeding forty thousand pounds.

Properly to estimate the importance of St. Helena, it must be considered as rising in the midst of the ocean, far from all other shores, in the immediate track of the homeward-bound Indiamen. A fair wind for those ships blows constantly throughout the year;

a winged harbinger, called the St. Helena pigeon, announces the mariner's approach long before it is discovered by the telescope. The bay near the town affords safe anchorage, and receives a fine stream of fresh water, with conveniences to fill the empty casks of the vessels. The interior prospects are truly romantic, and want only richer woods and more copious streams, to rival the sublime and beautiful landscape of Switzerland. Bleak and rocky mountains form a stupendous frame to verdant uplands, dotted with neat farms, groves and gardens; intersected by pastoral vallies, animated with flocks and herds; while through some majestic opening appears the azure main, to finish the interesting view.

A fellow-passenger, with whom I had been intimate many years in India, being then an invalid and unable to bear the busy scenes in St. James's Valley, retired as soon as possible to one of those charming solitudes; from whence he wrote me a pressing invitation, with an attractive description of his retirement in Swan's Valley.

"I WISH very much to see you here, if you could spare me two or three days, before we return on board the General Elliot; an event which I confess I do not anticipate with pleasure; though I never can forget the friendly attentions you have shewn me ever since we embarked. Never have I recovered the effect of those dreadful storms we encountered in doubling the Cape, when for so many weeks confined to my cabin. On arriving here yesterday I found my feelings more resemble those of health than any I have been blessed with during the voyage. My lot, even to myself, does not yet appear to be absolutely decided; I may do well; I may see my country, my friends, and beloved relations; but, although I own it to be with great concern, yet without horror or anxiety, I believe the chances at least three to two against me, for I know too much of the human frame, and the disorders it is afflicted with, to be materially deceived. My spirits are yet good, and I have no great bodily pain, though a constant heavy one in my right side, and parts adjacent. I continue at times to have a slow dispiriting fever, and violent headach: my appetite is gone, my sleep indifferent, and not refreshing. I will do every thing in my power to combat my disorder; but if the Sovereign Disposer of all has determined that mine shall be a sickness unto death, his will be done!

" My reason for wishing to see you in Swan's Valley, is not wholly from selfish motives. To a mind, like yours, fond of rural amusements, and sublime and tranquil scenery, these hills and vallies would afford real delight. It is true the country boasts neither of rich woods, nor meandering streams; but the inequality of the landscape, dressed in a smiling garb of vivifying green, would please you much; while the elastic freshness of the air would produce a sensible effect on your constitution. I must say we have had very English (which is the most descriptive term I can use) and to a valetudinarian, rough weather; but I found it somewhat congenial to my mental feelings, and was pleased to have my mind invited to solemn musings; which the prospect of an immense ocean, and these vast hills when clothed in storms, naturally inspire. I regret I did not bring Ossian on shore with me; I should here have perused it with double pleasure."

In justice to the salubrity of St. Helena, I must remark, that my valetudinary friend, during a fortnight's residence in Swan's Valley, greatly recovered his health, which still improved on the voyage to England, where he lived some years after our arrival.

I spent several days in different parts of the interior scenery, and sometimes found a little cascade, which formed a purling rivulet beneath the romantic cliffs, sufficient for a cold bath; one of the greatest luxuries we could experience after a fatiguing voyage. The heat in the middle hours of the day was rather unpleasant, but the cool serenity of the evening constantly produced those solemn musings my invalid shipmate alludes to in his letter. I found a spot particularly favourable to mental contemplation, anticipating the delights of love and friendship, in a reunion with those from whom we had been so long separated. When all the plantation slaves had retired to rest, and a sweet tranquillity reigned throughout the romantic scenery, when

> The glowing orb beneath the western main,
> Descending, calls to rest the weary swain:
> Mild Cynthia rising from Endymion's arms,
> With azure mantle veils her blushing charms;
> Come, Contemplation, on thy pensive wing,
> And with thee dreams of love, of rapture bring;
> Bid sacred Friendship close the smiling train,
> While Truth respondent swells the melting strain:
> So shall my soul from every passion free,
> Save Love and Friendship, fondly turn to thee:
> With thee retrace each happy scene long flown,
> And chide the hours that part me from my own!

We left St. Helena without regret, and sailed for England on the 23d of May. When I last embarked for India, and had formed some judgment of my future prospects in that part of the world, I promised my parents, that should it please the Almighty to bless me with a moderate competency, no flattering situation of wealth or power should induce me to remain there after I had attained my thirty fifth year: as a sound constitution, an independent fortune, and the happiness of their society, were to me of far greater value than all the wealth of India, united to the consequences of a longer residence in the torrid zone. I kept my promise, and spent that anniversary of my birth in the wilds of St. Helena.

A fair wind wafted us in seven days from St. Helena to Ascension, another island, which like it has been produced by volcanic fire. Ascension is about half the size of St. Helena; entirely uninhabited, except by sea-fowl and turtle.

> "No human footstep marks the trackless sand."

Diospedea, procellaria equinoctialis, and various birds of the ocean, build in the volcanic cliffs of Ascension; while what epicures deem the best kind of turtle nightly frequent the beach, and afford the ships that touch there a large supply of this nutritious food; but the Company's orders being positive against such an indulgence, to prevent a contraband trade between their homeward-bound shipping and the Americans, we were reluctantly obliged to leave this delicacy to vessels not under such a restriction.

The trade-wind continued until we crossed the equinoctial line on the third of June, which we lost shortly afterwards in the latitude of 5° north, when for a few days light airs and calms retarded our progress until we met the north-east trade; which blew fresh through the tropic of Cancer, to the 28th degrees of north latitude and 43d of west longitude, when it finally left us, in what is called the *Sargasso*, or Grass-sea; so named from the prodigious number of fuci and other marine plants which almost cover the ocean, from the 18th or 20th degree of north latitude, to 30 and 32, and extend for fifteen degrees of west longitude from 25 to 40°. It is generally supposed these marine plants are carried by the winds and currents from the Gulf of Mexico. This is disputed by philosophers; and in one of Barrow's voyages he rationally observes, that the plant has neither roots nor fibrils of any kind to indicate that it ever was attached to rocks or shores; but its central stem, buried in the midst of its leafy branches, makes it sufficiently evident that it vegetates while floating on the surface of the fathomless deep; some of these plants are many feet in diameter, others only a few inches; all appear in a growing state, covered with fish, worms, insects, and testaceous animals of various descriptions.

A track so much frequented affords very little for a modern voyager to describe. Dolphins, albacores, and bonettas, the coryphæna or dorado, scomber thynnus, and scomber pelamis, are now as well known as the icthyology of Europe. We had one opportunity of seeing an amazing sword-fish, (xiphias gladius) which often does dreadful damage to the hull of a ship, by darting in the sword or horn, from whence it derives its name; this being frequently broken off, and torn from the head by the violence of the shock, the sea becomes stained with blood, without any apparent cause; until when docked, at the conclusion of the voyage, several instances have occurred of the weapon being found transfixed through the strongest planks of oak, which had the enraged animal been able to withdraw, the ship must inevitably have foundered; such may possibly have been the fate of the Aurora frigate, and other vessels, whose loss has never been ascertained. The saw-fish, (squalus pristis) is more common, but we met with none very large, though sometimes I believe it equals the sword-fish in size; and they are not unfrequently from fifteen to twenty feet long.

The most interesting scene of animated nature on the ocean, is the shoals of flying-fish (exocoetus evolans) abounding in particular latitudes, and flying in every direction to escape from a watery foe, become an easy prey to an aerial enemy. In the Hindoo metempsychosis, where the bodies of the dove, the bee, the ant, and other favourite animals, are assigned as the temporary abode of tender, affectionate, and tranquil spirits, and lions, tigers, and hyenas for those of a ferocious disposition, the body of the flying-fish would be a fit receptacle for those malicious envious souls, who, like the arch-fiend they imitate, are continually going about seeking whom they may devour. The flying-fish are very beautiful, in form and colour not unlike the grey mullet, (mugil cephalus) but of a silvery hue, and more brilliant colours, varying from grey to blue and purple. They are sometimes from twelve to eighteen inches long, and even larger; but generally eight or nine. In some the long pectoral fins are beautifully spotted; by means of these wings, occasionally dipped in the sea, they continue their flight, mostly in a horizontal direction, a few yards above the surface, for a considerable distance; but cannot fly more than a hundred yards at a time without wetting their fins. I have sometimes seen them fall upon the deck, and dressed for table; but as there was seldom more than one at a time, and that divided among many claimants for a taste, it is difficult to define its excellence in that respect: it seemed more delicate in flavour than the other ocean fish. In Dr. Shaw's Systematic Natural History, one of the most scientific and entertaining zoological works in Europe, he quotes an observation by captain Tobin, respecting the habits of the exocoetus evolans, which appears very curious. "The lower half of the tail in the flying-fish, is full twice the length of the upper; the use of it has always appeared evident to me. I have by the hour watched the dolphins and bonettas in pursuit of them; when, without wholly immersing themselves, which would have proved fatal to them, they have disposed in their progressive motion the lower part of the tail in such a manner as to supply their wings with moisture, so as to support them above the surface. I never saw one exceed the distance of one hundred yards in its flight, without being obliged to dip for a fresh supply."

I should have had no other occurrence to mention in this voyage, had it not been for a dreadful storm, which came upon us after losing the north-east trade wind: it was not of long continuance, but dreadfully terrific, and we had every reason to suppose the ship must inevitably perish. The prognostics were singular, and the alarming aspect gave some little time for preparation, which was not the case on a similar occasion mentioned in a former voyage to England, near the Azores. Such scenes are extremely difficult to describe; nor should any effort of my pen or pencil have attempted it from my own journal; but there is an exact counterpart of it by Mr. Clarke, in a note to his beautiful edition of Falconer's Shipwreck, a work in which the noble spirit of poetry, the uncommon naval erudition, the subject itself untrod, and intractable as it should seem to numbers, the tender sympathy of wounded friendship and separated love, all conspire to rank the author high in the list of fame, and to draw the tear of sensibility from the compassionate reader. Much as the poem itself deserves encomium, the language of his commentator must be allowed to possess all the warmth and energy of orientalism in the description of the storm to which I allude.

"We were cruizing off *Ushant*, in the *Impetueux*, during an evening at the close of October, and the dreary coast so continually present to our view, created a painful uniformity, which could only be relieved by observing the variations of the expanse that was before us. The sun had just given its parting rays, and the last shades of day lingered on the distant waves, when a sky most sublime and threatening, attracted all our attention, and was immediately provided against by the vigilant officers of the watch. To the verge of the horizon, except where the sun had left some portion of its departing rays, a hard, lowering, blue firmament presented itself; on this floated light yellow clouds, tinged with various hues of crimson, the never-failing harbingers of a gale. A strong vivid tint was reflected from them on the sails and rigging of the ship, which rendered the scene more dreadful. The very calm that prevailed was portentous—the sea-bird shrieked as it passed! As the tempest gradually approached, and the winds issued from the treasuries of God, the thick darkness of an autumnal night closed the whole in horrid uncertainty."

> "It was a dismal and a fearful night;
> And on my soul hung the dull weight
> Of some intolerable fate!" COWLEY.

This concluded our adventures on the voyage from India to Europe; for after encountering the last storm, and getting clear of the Sargasso, we were favoured by strong westerly gales, which conveyed us seven or eight miles an hour without intermission, until the 13th of July; when perceiving the water to be discoloured, we sounded, and had ground at eighty fathoms. On the 15th we saw the verdant hills on the coast of Devonshire, and I once more experienced those emotions of pain and pleasure which sicken the heart: they are only to be felt on such occasions, nor can language describe them. When I considered the age of my venerable parents, the uncertainty of their being yet alive, and the variety of circumstances which awaited me at this important era, I found every nerve of sensibility awakened. On landing at Portsmouth, on the 17th, I met a friend, who informed me that all our friends were well, and with fond impatience expecting their long absent children. We were soon restored to their embraces; and at their respective rural residences enjoyed the most ineffable sensations of love and friendship in the bosom of tranquillity, in the sweetest season of the year; with nothing to diminish the joy of returning to our native country but a regret for the absence of those friends whom we had left behind us in the torrid zone.

> "O quid solutis est beatius curis!
> Quum mens onus reponit, ac peregrino
> Labore fessi, venimus larem ad nostrum
> Desideratoque, acquiescimus lecto. CATULLUS.

"Ah what so happy as a mind at rest,
When cares no more lie heavy on the breast;
When, tir'd of foreign travel, we return
To our own country, and at length discern
The place which first we knew, which most we love,
And in the bed which nurs'd us sleep!"—

"OMNIA DEO!"

CHAPTER XLII.

IMPORTANT SUBJECT OF THIS CONCLUSION; RETROSPECTION OF THE ENGLISH EAST INDIA COMPANY'S FIRST SETTLEMENTS IN HINDOSTAN; THEIR PROGRESSIVE IMPROVEMENT, AND FLOURISHING STATE OF THE BRITISH EMPIRE IN INDIA, IN 1812.

REFLECTIONS ON THE CHARACTER OF THE HINDOOS, AND THE IMPORTANCE OF CONVERTING THEM TO CHRISTIANITY.

"From ills, that painted, harrow up the breast,
(What agonies, if real, must they give!)
Preserve thy votaries; be their labours blest!
Oh! bid the patient Hindoo rise and live.
His erring mind, that wizard lore beguiles,
Clouded by priestly wiles,
To senseless nature bows, for nature's God.
Now, stretch'd o'er oceans vast, from happier isles,
He sees the wand of empire, not the rod:
Ah! may those beams that Western skies illume,
Disperse th' unholy gloom!
Meanwhile, may laws by myriads long rever'd,
Their strife appease, their gentler claims decide;
So shall their victors, mild with virtuous pride,
To many a cherish'd grateful race endear'd,
With temper'd love be fear'd;
Though mists profane obscure their narrow ken,
They err, yet feel, though pagans, they are men."

SIR WILLIAM JONES.

CONTENTS.

castes, corroborated by other writers—opinion of Sir William Jones, Lord Teignmouth, Holwell and others—charge of Sir John Mackintosh at Bombay—paramahansa, a caste who eat human flesh—parricide and infanticide—blessings of Christianity, in time and eternity—illustrated by many eminent characters—its benevolence contrasted with the cruel policy of the Hindoo religion in various instances—Om, or Aum—druidical mysteries—ignorance of the lower castes of Hindoos—interesting anecdotes, prayers, and religious opinions of Sir William Jones and Lord Teignmouth—Lord Valentia's sentiments on Hindoo conversion, and the example of Europeans in British India—difficulty of converting the higher castes—great power of the brahmins—necessary moderation in all attempts to proselyte—many brahmins have embraced christianity—its progress in India—its sublimity and consolation—wretched state of the Chandalas—the Hindoos compared with the Greeks and Romans when Christianity was preached among them—Cornelius—Paul's sermon at Athens state of fallen man—modern philosophy—religious sentiments of Socrates, Plato, Seneca, and other eminent heathens—appeal for Hindoo conversion from various motives—happiness of Christians compared with unbelievers—state of the world at its promulgation—examples of the effects of true religion, in life and death, in time and eternity! Conclusion.

CONCLUSION.

" Sweet is the harp of prophecy; too sweet,
Not to be wrong'd by a mere mortal touch:
Nor can the wonders it records be sung
To meaner music, and not suffer loss.

" O! scenes surpassing fable, and yet true,
Scenes of accomplish'd bliss! which who can see,
Though but in distant prospect, and not feel
His soul refresh'd with foretaste of the joy?
Rivers of gladness water all the earth,
And clothe all climes with beauty. No foe to man
Lurks in the serpent now ———
All creatures worship man; and all mankind
One Lord, one Father! Error has no place:
One song employs all nations; and all cry,
" Worthy the Lamb! for he was slain for us!"

" Behold the measure of the promise fill'd;
See Salem built, the labour of a God!
Bright as the sun the sacred city shines;
All kingdoms, and all princes of the earth
Flock to that light. Thy rams are there,
Nebaioth; and the flocks of Kedar there:
The looms of Ormus, and the mines of Ind,
And Saba's spicy groves pay tribute there.

"Praise is in all her gates: upon her walls,
And in her streets, and in her spacious courts,
Is heard SALVATION!" COWPER.

HAVING, by the Divine blessing, been favoured with health and leisure to pursue my allotted task, and finish the selection from the manuscripts and drawings mentioned in the preface, I now take leave of my readers, in a concluding chapter; which I hope will not be deemed obtrusive, or irrelevant to the general tenor of these volumes.

At this eventful period, every reflecting mind must be convinced, whether in a political or religious point of view, that something extraordinary is carrying on in the counsels of that Omnipotent Being, "whose way is in the sea, and his paths in the great waters, and whose footsteps are not known." I have neither talents nor inclination to venture on such an interesting topic: in the awful events now taking place, some prophecies are doubtless fulfilling, from which time will withdraw the veil. Many attempts have been made to develope those ancient predictions; not always satisfactorily; and the mind is still left in uncertainty and conjecture. In this state of precocity I should deem it presumptuous to enter the field; but there is a subject connected with this important epocha, in which I am warmly interested, and my mind is so deeply impressed with the necessity of avowing my sentiments, (feeble as may be my endeavours) that I cannot remain in a state of neutrality. It has been pronounced by the highest authority, "He that is not with me, is against me! whosoever shall be ashamed of me, and of my words, in this adulterous and sinful generation, of him also shall the SON OF MAN be ashamed, when he shall come in his own glory, and in his Father's, and with the holy angels."

In discussing the important subject contained in this chapter, I shall avail myself of every assistance from the various sources of information which have been lately opened, and now flow in copious streams through this highly favoured island: which seems to be selected by Infinite Wisdom and Goodness for the preservation of liberty in Europe, and the diffusion of truth and knowledge throughout the dark regions of the earth.

It is now one of those predicted periods when there should be wars and rumours of wars, when nation should rise up against nation, and kingdom against kingdom; and there should be famine, and pestilence, and earthquakes, in divers places. In the arcana of Infinite Goodness and Infinite Power, much good may be ordained to spring up from the unparalleled events and calamities now overwhelming the continent of Europe, which are felt in a greater or less degree throughout the British empire. "Dulce mihi nomen pacis!" May the blessings of peace, of an honourable and lasting peace, be restored! May my native country be providentially the means of restoring that choicest good to exhausted Europe! May England rise in triumph, to promote the glory of God, and the happiness of man; to dispel the mists of ignorance, superstition, and idolatry, and diffuse the light of Revelation to the remotest corners of the earth. If I may be deemed the humblest instrument in promoting this great design, by any thing which may be offered in the ensuing pages, it will afford me a heartfelt satisfaction, which language could ill express.

My mind is solemnly impressed with the importance of the object, my heart, I trust, "is inditing of a good matter," and I hope to be excused for bringing in so many auxiliaries.

I have often been struck with the simple language, good sense, and piety, in a dedication to Sir Francis Walsingham, secretary to queen Elizabeth, by Richard Hakluyt, the celebrated author of the early voyages and discoveries of the English nation, imprinted in the year 1599. It appears to be in some degree so connected with the general purport of these volumes, and particularly with the contents of this concluding chapter, that I shall transcribe a part of that excellent letter, because I trust I have been actuated by the same spirit; and shall be truly happy if I may, in one instance especially, contribute in the smallest degree to the fulfilment of his pious and almost prophetical wishes for the accomplishment of an event which he so ardently desired to behold in the reign of his peerless mistress. Although not permitted to take place at that memorable period, it is, I trust, reserved for the liberal and enlightened epoch of the nineteenth century.

"Right honourable, I do remember that being a youth, and one of her majesty's scholars at Westminster, that fruitful nursery, it was my hap to visit the chamber of Mr. Richard Hakluyt, my counsin; a gentleman of the Middle Temple, well known unto you, at a time when I found lying upon his board certain books of cosmography, with an universal map. He seeing me somewhat curious in the view thereof, began to instruct my ignorance, by shewing me the division of the earth into three parts, after the old account, and then, according to the latter, and better distribution, into more. He pointed with his wand to all the known seas, gulfs, bays, straits, capes, rivers, empires, kingdoms, dukedoms, and territories of each part; with declaration also of their special commodities, and particular wants, which by the benefit of traffic, and intercourse of merchants, are plentifully supplied. From the map he brought me to the Bible, and turning to the hundred and seventh psalm, directed me to the twenty-third and twenty-fourth verses, where I read, "that they which go down to the sea in ships, and occupy by the great waters, they see the works of the Lord, and his wonders in the deep." Which words of the prophet, together with my cousin's discourse, containing things of high and rare delight to my young nature, took in me so deep an impression, that I constantly resolved, if ever I were preferred to the University, where better time and more convenient place might be ministered for these studies, I would, by God's assistance, prosecute that knowledge and kind of literature, the doors whereof (after a sort) were so happily opened before me.

"It cannot be denied, but, as in all former ages, there have been men in our nation full of activity, stirrers abroad, and searchers of the remote parts of the world; so in this most famous and peerless government of her most excellent majesty queen Elizabeth, her subjects, through the special assistance and blessing of God, in searching the most opposite corners and quarters of the world, and to speak plainly, in compassing the vast globe of the earth more than once, have excelled all the nations and people of the earth.

"Lucius Florus, in the very end of his history, "De gestis Romanorum," recordeth as a wonderful miracle, that the Seres, which I take to be the people of Cathay, or China, sent ambassadors to

Rome, to intreat friendship, as moved with the fame of the majesty of the Roman empire. And have not we as good cause to admire, that the kings of the Molucca, and Java major, have desired the favour of her majesty, and the commerce and traffic of her people? Is it not as strange that the born naturals of Japan, and the Phillipines, are here to be seen, agreeing with our climate, speaking our language, and informing us of the state of their eastern habitations? For mine own part, I take it as a pledge of God's further favour both unto us and them: to them especially, unto whose doors I doubt not in time shall be by us carried the incomparable treasure of the truth of Christianity, and of the Gospel, while we use and exercise common trade with their merchants. I must confess to have read in the excellent history entitled, Origines de Joannes Goropius, a testimony of king Henry the Eighth, a prince of noble memory, whose intention was once, if death had not prevented him, to have done some singular thing in this case; whose words, speaking of his dealing to that end with himself, he being a stranger, and his history rare, I thought good, in this place, verbatim to record. "Ante viginti et plus eo annos ab Henrico Kneutto Equite Anglo nomine Regis Henrici arram accepi, qua convenerat, Regio sumptu me totam Asiam, quoad Turcorum et Persarum Regum commendationes, et legationes admitterentur, peragraturum. Ab his enim duobus Asiæ principibus facile se impetraturum sperabat, ut non solum tuto mihi per ipsorum fines liceret ire, sed ut commendatione etiam ipsorum ad confinia quoque daretur penetrare. Sumptus quidem non exiguus erat futurus, sed tanta erat principi cognoscendi aviditas, ut nullis pecuniis ad hoc iter necessariis se diceret parsurum.

O Dignum Regia Majestate animum, O me felicem, si Deus non ante et Kneuettum et Regem abstulisset, quam reversus ab hoc peregrinatione fuissem, &c."

"But as the purpose of David the king to build a house and temple to God was accepted, although Solomon performed it; so I make no question, but that the zeal in this matter, of the aforesaid most renowned prince, may seem no less worthy (in his kind) of acceptation, although reserved for the person of our Solomon, her gracious majesty; whom I fear not to pronounce to have received the same heroical spirit, and most honourable disposition, as an inheritance from her famous father.

"Whereas in the course of this history, often mention is made of many beasts, birds, fishes, serpents, plants, fruits, herbs, roots, apparel, armour, boats, and such other rare and strange curiosities, which wise men take great pleasure to read of, but much more contentment to see; herein I myself to my singular delight have been as it were ravished in beholding all the premises gathered together with no small cost, and preserved with no little diligence, in the excellent cabinets of my very worshipful and learned friends Master Richard Garthe, one of the clerks of the petty-bags; and Master William Cope, gentleman-usher to the right honourable and most prudent councellor (the Seneca of our Common-wealth) the Lord Burleigh, High Treasurer of England.

"This being the sum of those things which I thought good to admonish thee of, good reader, it remaineth that thou take the profit and pleasure of the work; which I wish to be as great to thee, as my pains and labour have been, in bringing these rare fruits unto their ripeness; and in reducing these loose papers into this order."

Such were the pious and liberal sentiments of Hackluyt, on the publication of his work upwards of two hundred years ago. Mine is now brought to a conclusion; after a period of forty-seven years, since my first juvenile attempts in the descriptive letters and drawings, which constitute the foundation of these memoirs. During that time the most extraordinary events have occurred in India; many of which are alluded to in the preceding pages.

It has not been my object, neither have I talents to discuss the political, commercial, and military systems in British India; the aggrandisement of that part of the empire has of late years been rapid and wonderful. Reverting to the middle of the seventeenth century, we find the English possessions in India consisted of two factories, situated on the banks of the Hughly river; with an ensign's guard of thirty men, stationed there for the protection of property; they were limited to this number by the jealous policy of the emperor Aurungzebe and his predecessors, who would not allow the factors to build even the slightest garden wall, from a fear of its being converted into a fortification. Such was the commencement of the British establishment in Bengal.

In the year 1638, Mr. Langhorne, agent for the English East India Company, purchased the village of Madras-patana, with a small district on the sea-coast of Coromandel, from the Hindoo rajah, for the East India Company. This village was soon after surrounded by a wall, and a castle called Fort St. George was erected there in 1640. This being a purchase, no objection was made to the circumvallation. And from this small beginning arose the extensive dominions now belonging to the East India Company, under the Presidency of Madras, or Fort St. George.

In less than thirty years after these petty establishments in Bengal and Coromandel, the island of Bombay was ceded to the English, on the marriage of Charles the Second with the princess Catherine of Portugal: this was the foundation of the Bombay government, and all its subsequent appendages on the western side of the Indian peninsula. The whole of these settlements, and every other British factory in India (including those retained in the eastern islands after the cruel massacre of the Company's servants at Amboyna, by the Dutch) were subordinate to the Governor and Council at Surat; established there, with a supreme authority, by the East India Company in England.

It would be foreign to these memoirs to enter on a detail of the history of the English East India Company, or the aggrandisement of the British nation, in the remote regions of Hindostan. This history became generally interesting about the middle of the eighteenth century, in consequence of the unparalleled cruelty of the nabob of Bengal, and the sufferings of the English in the *Black Hole* at Calcutta, an event which was soon followed by the memorable battle of Plassey, and other gallant exploits in Bengal, by Robert, Lord Clive, the first of that title; which not only amply revenged the perfidious cruelty of the Mahomedan despot, but gave the Company power, wealth, and territory, in the finest provinces of India, where from a set of licensed foreign merchants they became sovereigns of the country.

The wars which subsisted at that period between the native princes of India, on the coast of Coromandel, aided by English and French troops, opposed to each other as auxiliaries, under experienced commanders of both nations, and the consequences of such interference to the British nation, are admirably related by Orme, justly styled "the elegant historian of India." The subsequent conquests by other generals, and the more recent victories in which the name of WELLESLEY is so conspicuous, have added an immense domain to the British empire. These invaluable territories, acquired by British valour, are maintained by sound policy, moderation and justice; the extent of our territorial power and influence excites the wonder of Asia; and the effects are sensibly felt by all the maritime nations of Europe, whose consequence in India declined as the British empire triumphed, until, at this extraordinary period, not a single possession remains to any potentate of Europe, except Goa and some insignificant seaports belong to the Portugueze, and the Spanish settlement at Manilla.

The transactions in India since the termination of Orme's memoirs, open an ample, diversified, and interesting field, for the pen of the historian. That is a subject on which I have not presumed to enter, nor am I competent to discuss the luminous and extensive scale of policy, commerce, literature, and science, which dignified the administration of WARREN HASTINGS, the first governor-general of India, who was appointed to that high situation in 1774; it is a theme frequently adverted to with great delight in these volumes; and whatever opinion may be entertained of this great man in England, so long as the name of Britain exists in

India, so long will that of HASTINGS be remembered with admiration, gratitude, and love!

My pen can add no lustre to the exalted character of Marquis Cornwallis; the necessary wars in which he engaged, and the vigorous and comprehensive system which he pursued, brought new acquisitions of wealth and power to his native country. His mild and equitable government was peculiarly adapted to gain the confidence and friendship of the Indian sovereigns; his amiable manners conciliated the respect and affection of the Company's servants in every department; and his benevolent heart dispensed general happiness among all classes of natives in those remote regions.

The high sense entertained of Marquis Wellesley's administration in India, is best expressed in the energetic language of those who so well know how to appreciate his merits; it forms part of the address signed by upwards of six hundred European inhabitants of Calcutta, on the governor-general's departure for England in August 1805.

"The events of the last seven years have marked the period of your Lordship's government as the most important epoch in the history of European power in India. Your discernment in seeing the exigencies of the country, and of the times in which you were called to act, the promptitude and determination with which you have seized on the opportunities of acting, your just conception and masterly use of our intrinsic strength, have eminently contributed, in conjunction with the zeal, the discipline, and the courage of our armies, to decide upon these great events, and to establish, from one extremity of this empire to the other, the ascendancy of the British name and dominion.

"We are impressed with a firm persuasion, that you have governed with a direct view to the glory of your country, and to the prosperity of its possessions; and with no other personal feeling than the honourable ambition of obtaining its applause as your reward. To the community at large, no doubt, it belongs to fill up the measure of that reward; but it is a duty incumbent upon those among whom you have lived and acted; whose personal concern, in the course of your government, has enabled them to appreciate its character, to declare before the nation their sense of your public services.

"It is under the impression of this duty that we address you, and with the desire to mark, in the most authentic manner, that you carry with you to our common country the respect, the regard, and the confidence of your fellow-subjects; a confidence which is undiminished at the last hour of your administration; a respect and a regard which are founded on our long experience of your ability, of your unsullied integrity, of your impartial and honourable use of power, and of your high and liberal spirit in the conduct of public affairs."

In addition to this unequivocal testimony of the Marquis Wellesley's excellent administration in India, I must not pass over his institution, and paternal care, of the college at Fort William: which, however it may have been condemned by the Court of Directors, or by individuals, for its magnitude and expense, must be allowed to be one of the wisest, and ultimately, perhaps, one of the most philanthropic establishments ever adopted, for promulgating knowledge, literature, and science, throughout an extensive empire, especially in promoting a jurisprudence founded on the principles of the Mahomedan and Hindoo codes, improved by the spirit of those laws which form the glorious constitution of Great Britain. Without adulation to any living character, as without invidious reflection on the memory of men long since called to their final audit by an unerring Judge, who thought so very differently of one of these distinguished benefactors, I cannot suppress my own estimation of such inestimable advantages to the British empire in India, nor withhold the conclusion of Marquis Wellesley's address to the students of the college at Fort William in 1805, wherein the noble visitor asserts, that "the due administration of just laws within these flourishing and populous provinces, is not only the foundation of the happiness of millions of people, but the main pillar of the vast fabric of the British empire in Asia; the main-spring of our empire is situated here; and it is supplied and guarded by the laws and regulations of this government. From the prosperity of these provinces are derived all the sources of our revenue and commerce and public credit; and the origin and stability of that prosperity are to be found in the code of laws which you are now directed to study, and hereafter destined to administer, to expound, and to amend.

"Subject to the common imperfection of every human institution, this system of laws is approved by practical experience, (the surest test of human legislation) and contains an active principle of continued revision, which affords the best security for progressive amendment. It is not the effusion of vain theory, issuing from speculative principles, and directed to visionary objects of impracticable perfection; but the solid work of plain, deliberate, practicable benevolence; the legitimate offspring of genuine wisdom and pure virtue. The excellence of the genuine spirit of these laws is attested by the noblest proof of a just, wise, and honest government; by the restoration of happiness, tranquillity, and security, to an oppressed, and suffering people, and by the revival of agriculture, commerce, manufacture, and general opulence, in a declining and impoverished country.

"Contemplating these benevolent views, and animated by the prospect of the great and exalted duty to which you are called, I trust that you will derive from this institution the most effectual means of preserving and securing to the inhabitants of these prosperous regions, that primary object of all good government, the greatest blessing attainable by any people, an impartial administration of just laws."

Thus the luminous administration of a Hastings; the wise and virtuous governments of a Teignmouth and Cornwallis; the extensive policy, promptitude, and decision of a Wellesley, united with the military talent and enterprise of a Wellington, have placed those distinguished characters on a glorious eminence. How highly exalted do they appear when opposed to D'Acughna and the unworthy successors of Gama and Albuquerque, the Portuguese conquerors of India! Those monsters of iniquity, by their rapacity, oppression, and cruelty, brought disgrace and ruin on that once celebrated nation; the patriotic and benevolent virtues of the delegated administrators of British sovereignty, will endear their names to the latest posterity!

To the preceding characters, I must, in the same spirit of truth and candour, add the eminent names of Lord Pigot, Lord Macartney, the second Lord Clive, Lord William Bentinck, and their successors in the respective governments of India; who will be recorded in history as bright examples of British virtue, cooperating with the supreme administration in conducting the Asiatic empire; which, commencing with a few Banians and factors in a mercantile warehouse, now extends over an immense territory, (exclusive of our latest oriental conquests) inhabited by upwards of sixty millions of people!

Under the general name of Hindostan, throughout these volumes, I have included the whole peninsula of India, agreeably to the geographical boundaries in the Ayeen Akbery. Several modern writers comprise it within a smaller compass, including only the provinces north of the Deccan, extending to the frontier mountains. As I did not thus understand it during my residence in India, I have not since adopted it. The best standard for this subject, seems to be the country thus distinguished by Abul Fazeel. "Hindostan is washed by the ocean on the east, the west, and the south; to the eastward lies Malacca, together with Sumatra, the Moluccas, and many other islands. On the north are high mountains, part of which forms the boundary of Hindostan, on that quarter; the rest belong to Turan and Iran. Beyond these mountains, as far as Chinese-Tartary, are several fertile territories; particularly Cachemeer, the two Thibets, and Kushtwar. The north side of Hindostan is plentifully supplied with rivers; so that it may be said to have water on all quarters.

"The whole extent of this vast empire is unequalled for the

excellency of its waters, salubrity of air, mildness of climate, and temperate constitutions of the natives. Every part is cultivated, and full of inhabitants, so that you cannot travel the distance of a coss (or two miles) without seeing towns and villages, and meeting with good water. Even in the depth of winter, the earth and trees are covered with verdure: and in the rainy season, which in many parts of Hindostan commences in June, and continues till September, the air is so delightfully pleasant, that it gives youthful vigour to old age."

In another part of the Ayeen Akbery we find that the imperial dominions, in the fortieth year of Akber's reign, consisted of one hundred and five Sircars, or provinces; subdivided into two thousand seven hundred and thirty-seven kusbahs, or townships. The grand Soobah divisions and subordinate purgunnas of the empire have been already mentioned. The revenue of the whole was then settled for ten years, at the annual rent of three aribs, sixty-two crore, ninety-seven lacks, fifty-five thousand, two hundred and forty-six dams, or sicca rupees 9,0743881, upwards of eleven millions, three hundred thousand pounds sterling. At the death of Aurungzebe, in 1707, from major Rennel's accurate memoir, "the Mogul empire comprehended a tract of country, extending from the tenth to the thirty-fifth degree of north latitude, and produced a revenue of thirty-two millions sterling; which, in a country where the products of the earth are about four times as cheap as in England, is an enormous annual amount."

What infinite advantage, what incalculable benefits, must accrue from a wise and liberal administration over those extensive realms which now form a part of the British empire, is not for me to discuss. What immense good was done by the wise policy of the Bombay government alone, during a late famine, we learn from the address of Sir James Mackintosh to the Grand Jury of that island, in 1804; no other language than his own can be adopted on this interesting subject; it indirectly points out the object I have often mentioned; the amelioration of the natives of India by the introduction of religion, laws, art, science, and civilization, in their best and most comprehensive sense.

This upright and able magistrate, after descanting upon famine in general, enters into the particulars of that in the Concan, occasioned by a partial failure of the periodical rains in 1802, and from a more complete failure in 1803, from whence, he says, "a famine has arisen in the adjoining provinces of India, especially in the Mahratta territories, which I shall not attempt to describe; and which, I believe, no man can truly represent to the European public without the hazard of being charged with extravagant and incredible fiction. Some of you have seen its ravages; all of you have heard accounts of them from accurate observers. I have only seen the fugitives who have fled before it, and have found an asylum in this island. But even I have seen enough to be convinced that it is difficult to overcharge a picture of Indian desolation.

"I shall now state, from authentic documents, what has been done to save these territories from the miserable condition of the neighbouring country. From the 1st of September 1803, to the present time, there have been imported, or purchased by government, four hundred and fourteen thousand bags of rice; and there remain one hundred and eighty thousand bags contracted for which are yet to arrive; forming an aggregate of nearly six hundred thousand bags, and amounting to the value of fifty lacs of rupees, or six hundred thousand pounds sterling. During the same time there have been imported by private merchants four hundred and eighty thousand bags of rice; making in all an importation of a million of bags, and amounting in value to one million pounds sterling.

"The effects of this importation on the population of our own territories, it is not very difficult to estimate. The population of Bombay, Salsette, and Caranja, and of the city of Surat, I designedly under-estimate at four hundred thousand. I am entitled to presume, that if they had continued subject to native governments, they would have shared the fate of the neighbouring provinces, which still are so subject. I shall not be suspected of any tendency towards exaggeration, by any man who is acquainted with the state of the opposite continent, when I say, that in such a case an eighth of that population must have perished. Fifty thousand human beings have, therefore, been saved from death in its most miserable form, by the existence of a British government in this island. I conceive myself entitled to take credit for the whole benefits of the importation; for that which was imported by private merchants, as well as for that which was directly imported by the government; because, without the protection and security enjoyed under a British government, that commercial capital and credit would not have existed by which the private importation was effected.

" The next particular which I have to state, relates to those unhappy refugees who have found their way into our territory. From the month of March to the present month of October, such of them as could labour have been employed in useful public works, and have been fed by government. The monthly average of these persons, since March, is 9125 in Bombay, 3162 in Salsette, and in Surat a considerable number; though from that city I have seen no exact returns.

" But many of these miserable beings are on their arrival here, wholly unable to earn their subsistence by any, even the most moderate, labour. They expire on the road before they can be discovered by the agents of our charity: they expire in the very act of being carried to the place where they are to receive relief. To obviate, or at least to mitigate, these dreadful evils, a *Humane Hospital* was established by government, for the relief of those emigrants who were unable to labour. The monthly average of those who have been received since March into this hospital, is 1030 in Bombay, about 100 at Salsette, and probably 300 at Surat.

" I myself visited this hospital in company with my excellent friend Dr. Scott; and I witnessed a scene, of which the impression will never be effaced from my mind. The average monthly mortality of the establishment is dreadful; it amounts to four hundred and eighty. At first sight this would seem to argue some monstrous defects in the plan or management of the institution; and if there were great defects in so new an establishment, hastily provided against so unexampled an evil, those who are accustomed to make due allowance for human frailty, would find more to lament than to blame, in such defects. But when it is considered that almost all these deaths occur in the first four or five days after admission, and that scarcely any disease has been observed among the patients but the direct effects of famine, we shall probably view the mortality as a proof of the deplorable state of the patients, rather than of any defects in the hospital; and instead of making the hospital answerable for the deaths, we shall deem it entitled to credit for the life of every single survivor.

"Those who know me, will need no assurances that I have not made these observations from a motive so unworthy of my station and my character, as that of paying court to any government. I am actuated by far other motives. I believe that knowledge on subjects so important cannot be too widely promulgated. I believe, if every government on earth were bound to give an annual account, before an audience whom they respected, and who knew the facts, of what they had done during the year for improving the condition of their subjects, that this single and apparently slight circumstance would better the situation of all mankind; and I am desirous, if any British government in India, should ever, in similar calamitous circumstances, forget its most important and sacred duties, that this example should be recorded for their reproach and disgrace.

"Upon the whole, I am sure that I considerably understate the fact in saying, that the British government in this island has saved the lives of ONE HUNDRED THOUSAND persons; and, what is more important, that it has prevented the greater part of the misery through which they must have passed before they found refuge in death; besides the misery of all those who loved them, or who depended upon their care.

"The existence, therefore, of a British government in Bombay, in 1804, has been a blessing to its subjects. Would to God, that every government of the world could with truth make a similar declaration!

"Many of you have been, and many will be, intrusted with authority over multitudes of your fellow-creatures. Your means of doing good will not indeed be so great as those of which I have now described to you the employment and the effect. But they will be considerable. Let me hope that every one of you will be ambitious to be able to say to your own conscience, I have done something to better the condition of the people intrusted to my care. I take the liberty to assure you, that *you will not find such reflections among the least agreeable or valuable part of that store which you lay up for your declining years.*"

It is impossible to read this statement without admiring the feelings of the heart which dictated it. The last paragraph ought to make a strong impression upon every man who has acted a part on the public theatre of India: to him the concluding words must be peculiarly affecting. Under this idea, I am more emboldened to add the following observations which deeply engaged my attention on terminating these memoirs.

On my first arrival in India, struck with the novelty and apparent simplicity of the Hindoo character, I faithfully pourtrayed it to the best of my knowledge. I particularly admired the retired life, and applauded virtues of the religious brahmins, at their sacred groves and temples; and was delighted with the patriarchal manners of the natives, at a distance from European settlements, and Mahomedan oppressors.

In those days we had no Asiatic Researches; made few inquiries into the antiquities of India; and knew but little of the mythology and literature of the brahmins. The Institutes of Menu, the Geeta, and Heetopades, the depositaries of their ethics and morality, were not translated. The Sastras and Vedas, the most sacred brahminical volumes, mysteriously concealed from even the lower classes of Hindoos, were veiled still closer from Europeans; the language in which they were written was confined to the priesthood, and strangers seldom interfered with their religious or moral institutions. At the period of my arrival in 1766, the pursuits of the English in India were chiefly confined to commerce, or defensive war: the hostilities in Bengal and the Carnatic had only been lately settled, and the Company's territory and influence were comparatively small.

After the appointment of Mr. Hastings to the supreme government of India, in 1774, a new scene opened to the intellectual view; his enlightened mind, corresponding with his exalted station and powerful influence, exerted every means for the acquisition of knowledge, not only in the dominions immediately under his jurisdiction, but in foreign countries; his researches in remote, and hitherto unexplored regions, were rewarded by a rich increase from their treasures of literature, art, and science. In these pursuits the governor-general was assisted by many eminent characters; above all, by that bright oriental luminary, Sir William Jones, whose name alone it is sufficient to mention, and whose loss is irretrievable.

From that memorable epoch in Anglo-Asiatic history, new sources of oriental knowledge flowed to Europe; the stores of brahminical learning were no longer concealed; their sacred books, for ages veiled in impenetrable secrecy, were brought to light; their poetry, drama, history, astronomy, art and science, have been translated by able hands into our own language; and the English are now, perhaps, better acquainted with the ancient and modern history of Hindostan, than with that of many contiguous nations in Europe.

A variety of opinions prevails, both in Europe and Asia, respecting the introduction of Christianity into India: it is a subject which has been frequently alluded to in these volumes; some able writers maintain there is no necessity for extending its influence to those remote regions: one asserts, that "*on the broad basis of its own merits, the Hindoo system little needs the meliorating hand of Christian dispensations, to render its votaries a sufficiently correct and moral people, for all the purposes of civil society.*" After extolling the religion and morality of the Hindoos, he adds, "*whenever the Christian religion does as much for the lower orders of society in Europe, as that of Brahma appears to have done for the Hindoos, he shall cheerfully vote for its establishment in Hindostan.*"

This may certainly be the opinion of a few individuals; but it never can be considered as the prevailing sentiment of the British nation. One of its brightest intellectual luminaries, emphatically styled the Colossus of literature, thought very differently; and I trust his powerful language conveys the decided opinion of thousands, and tens of thousands, who truly estimate the value of Christianity.

"I did not expect to hear that it could be a question amongst Christians, whether any nation, uninstructed in religion, should receive instruction; or whether that instruction should be imparted to them by a translation of the holy books into their own language. If obedience to the will of God be necessary to happiness, and knowledge of his will be necessary to obedience, I know not how he that withholds this knowledge or delays it, can be said to love his neighbour as himself. He that voluntarily continues ignorant, is guilty of all the crimes which ignorance produces; as to him that should extinguish the tapers of a light-house, might justly be imputed the calamities of shipwreck. Christianity is the highest perfection of humanity; and as no man is good but as he wishes the good of others, no man can be good in the highest degree, who wishes not to others the largest measure of the greatest good. To omit for a year, or for a day, the most efficacious method of advancing Christianity, in compliance with any purposes that terminate on this side of the grave, is a crime of which I know not that the world has yet had an example."*

In minutely describing the tenets and influence of the Hindoo religion, in a chapter mostly written at Chandode in the brahminical solitudes on the banks of the Nerbudda, I alluded to a question which has been often asked me by wise and good men both in Europe and Asia. "What benefit will the Hindoos derive from being converted to Christianity? Why should we not leave them

* Dr. Johnson.

as we found them?" A question of a similar tendency was last year addressed to a member of the Society for promoting Christianity among the Jews, by Manasseh, a learned, and respectable character under the Mosaical dispensation. "What advantages, relative to their present and future happiness, will the Jews derive from their conversion to Christianity?" I avail myself of the answer to this interesting question, to strengthen what is said throughout this chapter on the conversion of the Hindoos.

"Previous to any remark on the subjects alluded to in your letter, I must, for myself and those with whom I am connected, sincerely and affectionately declare, that in whatsoever point of view our endeavour may appear to yourself, or others of your brethren, we are solely actuated by the pure motive of regard and tender anxiety for what we believe to be the true interest and happiness of all those who have not embraced Christianity. That very religion, by which we ourselves hope to be saved, enjoins it as a fundamental duty on Christians, to endeavour, by every lawful and charitable method, to bring all men to the knowledge of the gospel of Jesus Christ. We certainly do aim at your conversion from an undue and misplaced reliance on mere forms and ceremonies, to that salvation through the Messiah, whom the prophet Isaiah describes as "a man of sorrows, and acquainted with grief; who was stricken, smitten of God, and afflicted; wounded for our transgressions, and bruised for our iniquities."

"In answer to the advantages that will be derived from this conversion, allow me, with the greatest solemnity, and sincerity of heart, to reply, 'much every way.' We believe, that by your conversion to Christianity, you would be freed from the slavery of a mass of superstitious traditions, by which you are at present held in the greatest intellectual bondage: that you would be restored to the enjoyment of those privileges in the favour and communion of God, which you have so long utterly lost. That you would be, in the hands of the Lord Jehovah, the happy instruments of bringing multitudes of the unbelieving Gentiles to the standard of the Messiah, Jesus Christ: and above all, that you would, by a cordial, (for I never mean a merely nominal) reception of the truths of Christianity, have a certainty of that eternal salvation which we are taught to expect *only* through the name, merits, and sufferings of Jesus Christ.

"We view the present situation of your people, when spiritually considered, as peculiarly awful and dangerous; whilst we also believe, that by a real conversion to Christianity, you would be delivered therefrom, and brought into one which comprehends the highest and happiest privileges; both as it concerns your well-being and well-doing in this world; and your everlasting blessedness in that which is to come.

"Those who so anxiously labour and pray for your conversion to Christianity, are united and constituted on the broad and liberal basis of the *Church Universal:* they carry their ideas and designs far beyond that of proselyting to any particular sect or denomination of Christians. Many classes of Christians, differing indeed in a few matters avowedly of lesser importance, but all agreed in owning and worshipping Jesus Christ as the true Messiah, are united in endeavouring to accomplish the great end of bringing the Jews, by argument and persuasion, to do the same; looking to God alone to bless their aim and design.

"These Christians are all agreed in viewing those points of worship, or opinion, wherein they differ, as being of infinitely less importance than the grand tenet in which they all unite, viz. that Jesus Christ is the Messiah, and that faith in him is essential to salvation. They are all agreed in their present cordial endeavour to bring the Jews to their acknowledgement of this same truth, as the foundation of their union with the Christian church; leaving it to the subsequent determination of the converts, into what particular community of professing Christians they may, after mature reflection, feel it their duty to enter.

"We are looking forward to that period, of which the prophets have spoken, when "the earth shall be full of the knowledge of the Lord, as the waters cover the sea. And in that day there shall be a root of Jesse, which shall stand for an ensign of the people; to it shall the *Gentiles* seek, and his rest shall be glorious. And it shall come to pass in that day, that the Lord shall set his hand again the second time, to recover the remnant of his people, which shall be left from Assyria, and from Egypt, and from Pathros, and from Cush, and from Elam, and from Shinar, and from Hamath, and from the islands of the sea. And he shall set up an ensign for the nations, and shall assemble the outcasts of Israel, and gather together the dispersed of Judah from the four corners of the earth. The envy also of Ephraim shall depart, and the adversaries of Judah shall be cut off; Ephraim shall not envy Judah, and Judah shall not vex Ephraim." ISAIAH.

"At that period, which may God hasten! all lesser distinctions shall vanish in one true knowledge and love of God the Father, and Jesus Christ whom he hath sent. We hope that the very subject of the conversion of the Jews is proving, and will prove a bond of union, whose influence will be peculiarly happy in strengthening the universal cause, and promoting the firm establishment of one united body of Jews and Gentiles in true church fellowship. You will judge for yourselves about things of lesser importance hereafter: in the mean time hearken to him, who declares, "I, even I, am the Lord; and beside me there is no Saviour; come worship in his holy temple!"

"Thus we Christians invite you to the examination and reception of the truths of the gospel, regardless of our own inferior points of difference, and anxious on every principle of duty to God, and love to man, to manifest our perfect union, in wishing you to enjoy the blessing of that faith in Jesus Christ, concerning which we have but one and the same common feeling amongst us all. We all worship God in the same spiritual temple; and we, likewise, with one heart and voice, say to you, come and worship with us in that holy temple!"

This excellent reply to Manasseh seems to comprise all that is essentially necessary to the subject of conversion in general: surely those who object to that of the Hindoos in particular cannot have considered it in this light.

"Redemption! 'Twas Creation more sublime!
Creation's great superior, Man! is thine:
Thine is Redemption!
And is there, who the blessed Cross wipes off
Like a foul blot, from his rebellious brow?
If angels tremble, 'tis at such a sight!" Young.

The unprejudiced mind will allow that a real Christian has, at least, as much charity and liberality of sentiment, as the deist or unitarian: he embraces all mankind as his brethren, and strives to render them as happy as himself, but he certainly views the most important of all concerns very differently from a modern philosopher. His mind having, by divine grace, been prepared for the awful truths of Christianity, he is assured, that without this knowledge, all other acquisitions are comparatively of trifling importance. *"If," as a modern divine well observes, "our taste were the most correct, our learning the most profound, our information the most enlarged, and our fame the most illustrious that the world ever saw; if we could understand all the curiosities of science, and all the treasures of literature were poured at our feet; if we could embrace all that the restless mind ever conceived, so that nothing remained for the imagination to invent, or the desires to pursue;—still, what is all this, if we are ignorant of ourselves, and of Christ and holiness? "What shall a man be profited, if he gain the whole world, and lose his own soul? or, What shall a man give in exchange for his soul?" What indeed are all the fading scenes of this momentary world? The time is at hand, when the heavens shall pass away with a great noise, and the elements shall melt with fervent heat. The period is hastening apace, which will for ever put an end to this world and all its concerns; which, like a flood, will sweep away its pain and its pleasure, its applause and its frown, its learning and its ignorance, its distinctions and its disgrace, its good and its evil. The awful glories of the last judg-

* Wilson.

ment will ere long be here; when the humble and penitent inquirer, who has endeavoured to do the will of God, and by faith to receive that stupendous grace which the doctrine of Christ reveals, shall be eternally saved; while the merely speculative student, whose secret love of sin, and wilful neglect of God, have led to his disobedience to the gospel, shall, notwithstanding his barren notions and schemes, his abortive designs of amendment, and his presumption of final impunity, be for ever undone. In a word, the hour will soon arrive, when every veil will be torn aside; and they that have done good, shall arise to the resurrection of life, and they that have done evil to the resurrection of condemnation!"

I now come to the principal point intended in this conclusion; and with a desire to obviate any objection which may arise from a seeming alteration of my opinion of the Hindoo character, from that given in the former part of these memoirs, it may be necessary to remark, that my sentiments changed progressively, as I became more acquainted with the higher castes of Hindoos. There was a time when I loved and venerated the character of a brahmin, leading a tranquil, innocent, and studious life, under the sacred groves which surrounded his temple. Few readers, perhaps, have been more delighted than myself with Sir William Jones's little "unvarnished tale" of Rhadacaunt, a pundit in Calcutta, who refused to accept the office of pundit to the Supreme Court of Justice, when offered by Mr. Hastings, even if the salary were doubled.

"My father (said the worthy pundit) died at the age of a hundred years; and my mother, who was eighty years old, became a *Sati*, and burned herself to expiate sins. They left me little besides good principles. Mr. Hastings purchased for me a piece of land, which at first yielded twelve hundred rupees a year; but lately, either through my inattention or through accident, it has produced only one thousand. This would be sufficient for me and my family; but the duty of brahmins is not only to teach the youths of their sect, but to relieve those who are poor. I made many presents to poor scholars, and others in distress; and for this purpose I anticipated my income. I was then obliged to borrow for my family expenses, and I now owe about three thousand rupees. This debt is my only cause of uneasiness in this world. I would have mentioned it to Mr. Shore, but I was ashamed."

The introduction of this little anecdote is a proof of that kindness and sensibility which Sir William Jones ever felt for distressed merit. It is superfluous to add, what the reader will have anticipated, that the disposition to relieve his wants was not suffered to evaporate in mere profession.

When I visited the Hindoo villages in the Concan, and enjoyed the pleasant interview with Ragojee Angria and Govindsett, mentioned on my journey through that district, I was charmed with the simple manners of the brahmins, the liberal sentiments of the prince and his philanthropic vizier, the venerable Mahomedan at Ram-Rajah, and many other amiable characters, replete with novelty and interest. I wrote from first impressions, in the same manner as I afterwards pourtrayed the natives of Malabar, and the inhabitants of Surat and the northern cities, where I occasionally resided; especially while sojourning in the Mahratta camp, and travelling to Ahmedabad, through the delightful province of

Guzerat. In my letters on those occasions, I related events as they occurred, without much reflection, or comparison with other countries. Every incident had the charm of novelty; and, like some other travellers, I might have viewed passing events superficially, and formed hasty conclusions.

In subsequent situations, particularly when collector of Dhuboy, and acting as judge in that district, I had much greater opportunities of scrutinizing the Hindoo character. In this investigation my opinion materially changed, and a further intercourse with the religious brahmins at Dhuboy and Chandode, did not raise them in my estimation. Nor did the moral conduct of the Yogees, Senassees, and other devotees frequenting the jattaras of the Nerbudda, prejudice me in their favour. But when I developed the character of the secular brahmins and Hindoos of various description, employed in the revenue department, from the consequential zemindar to the village patell, how was I astonished! Their cruelty, avarice, craftiness, and duplicity, occasioned a thousand grievances, which I could neither counteract nor redress; and displayed such shocking traits, rooted and strengthened by religious opinions, prejudice of caste, and habits of oppression, as baffled all my endeavours to relieve the poor ryots, suffering under their tyranny. I mentioned these things as they occurred; they were written at the moment, and are so fully confirmed by enlightened French and English travellers, during the two last centuries; by recent documents of the Reverend Dr. Claudius Buchanan, and observations of the discriminating Dr. Francis Buchanan, that I hazard nothing in differing from the representation of other writers, who, I doubt not, from the best motives, have written so very favourably of the Hindoos.

To avoid prolixity, I shall only make a few short extracts from the most respectable writers on the Hindoo character. Such assistance is necessary, when philosophers and sceptics are endeavouring to undermine Christianity, and exalt paganism. It then behoves every person who has acquired a knowledge of those pagans, and been happily taught the truths of Christianity, to support religion, purity, and virtue, against priestcraft, superstition, and error. To those advocates for Hinduism, I must, in the first instance, oppose the high authority of Sir William Jones, whose judgment and impartiality are universally acknowledged. In the preface to his Institutes of Menu, this learned orientalist allows that code to possess "a spirit of sublime devotion, benevolence, and tenderness to all sentient creatures; that the sentiments of independence to all beings but God are truly noble; and prove that the author adored, not the material sun, nor any symbolical representation of the Deity, but that divine light, which illumines all, and delights all; from which all proceed, and to which all must return." This beautiful and rational thesis cannot fail to delight every pious mind, but candour renders it necessary to transcribe another passage on the same subject, from the same authority. "This code is also a system of despotism and priestcraft, both indeed limited by law, but artfully conspiring to give mutual support, though with mutual checks. It is filled with strange conceits in metaphysics and natural philosophy; and with a scheme of theology most obscurely figurative, and consequently liable to dangerous misconceptions."

Such is the decision of Sir William Jones, one of the most amiable benevolent men that ever existed; partial to oriental manners, literature, and poetry, from early youth; and formed, in all respects, for those researches which were his grand pursuit in India. Lord Teignmouth, a character most truly amiable and respectable, from a personal knowledge of the Hindoos, says, "Individuals in India are often irritated by petty provocations, to the commission of acts which no provocation can justify; the result of vindictive pride, and ungoverned violence of temper." On a former occasion I mentioned Governor Holwell's decided opinion that "the Gentoos are as degenerate, crafty, superstitious, litigious, and wretched a people as any in the known world; and especially in the common run of brahmins."

A more accurate observer, or a more upright judge than Sir James Mackintosh has, perhaps, never appeared in any country. Part of his charge to the grand jury of Bombay has been introduced; the following observation must not be omitted: "The accomplished and justly celebrated Sir William Jones, who carried with him to India a prejudice in favour of the natives, which he naturally imbibed in the course of his studies, and which in him, though not perfectly rational, was neither unamiable nor ungraceful. Even he, after long judicial experience, reluctantly confesses their general depravity; and especially the prevalence of perjury, which is perhaps a more certain sign of the general dissolution of moral principle, than other more daring and ferocious crimes, much more horrible to the imagination." Upon a further acquaintance with the Indian character, this excellent recorder adds, "I trust we shall one day have the unspeakable satisfaction of reflecting, that we have not only discharged those duties which preserve the order of civil society; but that by a firm, though moderate execution of just laws, we may have contributed in some slight degree, within the narrow sphere of our influence, to revive those *moral sentiments* which every where naturally spring up in the human heart, but which seem so long to have *languished in the breasts of the inhabitants of India.*"

Dr. Francis Buchanan, who was selected by Marquis Wellesley, governor-general of India, to ascertain the state of arts, agriculture, religion, &c. in different parts of Hindostan, at the commencement of the nineteenth century, says, "The Smartal brahmins allow of no pardon for eating in company with persons of another caste, or of food dressed by their impure hands. In a religious quarrel, the victorious party caused the other brahmins, on account of their obstinacy, to be ground to death in oil-mills. To those who refuse to acknowledge the doctrines peculiar to their own sect, no men can be more intolerant nor violent than the brahmins." This benevolent writer confirms all that has been said of the humiliating and cruel treatment of the Sudra caste by the brahmins; and I fear this assertion of Dr. Claudius Buchanan is but too justly founded: "The Hindoos are destitute of those principles of honesty, truth, and justice, which respond to the spirit of British administration, and have not a disposition which is accordant with the tenor of Christian principles."

I shall close this unpleasant part of the subject with an extract from the Hindoo Pantheon, by Major Moor, a most valuable acquisition to oriental literature. "However difficult it may be for an English reader to believe the hitherto unrecorded story of the flesh-abhorring Hindoos, not only do other castes of the Hindoos, but even the brahmins themselves, eat flesh; and one sect, at least, eat human flesh. They do not kill human subjects to eat, but they eat such as they find about the Ganges and other rivers; and near Benares, they are not unusually seen floating down the river on a corpse, and feeding upon its flesh; and the human brain is judged by these epicurean cannibals to be the most delicious morsel of their unsocial banquet. They are called *Paramahansa*, and are by no means a low despicable tribe; but, on the contrary, are esteemed, at any rate by themselves, a very high one. Whether the exaltation be legitimate, or assumed by individuals, in consequence of penance, or holy and sanctified acts, I am not prepared to state, but I believe the latter; as I have known other instances where individuals of differing sects, by persevering in extraordinary piety, or penance, have been deemed incapable of sin."

The same humane writer fully proves the prodigality of the Hindoos in human destruction. Besides the self-immolation of widows, those of all ranks in religion and life, are in the habit of carrying their aged and diseased parents and friends to the Ganges, or some other holy stream, to perish by hunger, weather, or alligators. "Mothers, incredible as it may seem, revolt not, as the reader must do when he first hears it, at throwing their infants into the sea, or river, to be eaten alive by alligators and sharks. Whole tribes were in the habit of destroying, with but few exceptions, all their female children, until they were reclaimed and reformed by the personal influence and persuasion of Mr. Duncan, governor of Bombay. Human victims were formerly immolated at the shrine of offended or avenging deities; and well-authenticated anecdotes might easily be collected to a considerable extent, of the sanguinary propensity of this people, such as would startle those who have imbibed certain opinions from the relations of travellers, on the character and habits of the "abstinent and blood-abhorring Hindoos; and of the brahmins, with souls unspotted as the robes they wear."

I will add no more on the subject of Hindoo depravity; nor, in contrasting it with Christianity, shall I speak of that blessed *Catholicon* on a limited scale, but place it on the broad basis of divine and human love; its grand objects being to reconcile fallen man to his offended Creator, through the mediation of a Redeemer; and by ennobling his views, enable him to sustain the glorious character of a candidate for eternity; that while passing through the probationary period of time, he may make a proper estimate between the transitory nature of earthly enjoyments, and the delights which await the virtuous in regions of bliss, without satiety, and without end. In such an estimate, engrafted on the principle of faith, hope, and charity, how is the soul raised above sublunary pursuits! how degraded is vice, however gilded by wealth, or sanctioned by fashion; how triumphant is virtue, however forsaken or obscure! Animated by such a prospect, how trifling are the vanities of time, compared with the Christian's everlasting inheritance! To the young and thoughtless, in the morning of life, when the roses of health bloom, and pleasure presents her enticing cup, these may appear unimportant observations; but when the shadows lengthen, the flowers fade, and the mellifluous beverage is exhausted; we see the value of religion, and estimate the wisdom of those who purchase that pearl of price; whose merchandize is better than silver, and the gain thereof than fine gold! Then shall we, like the noble youth who beheld the closing scene of Addison, "see in what peace a Christian can die!"

At that solemn hour, when the fascinations of pleasure, wealth, and power cease, when the drama of life draws to a close, and all its phantoms retire, then shall we experience the excellence of religion, and enjoy that heavenly peace, that divine consolation, which no power on earth can give, nor take away; proceeding from HIM who has promised never to leave us nor forsake us; from HIM who loved us unto death; and, before he drank his own bitter cup, promised to send a Comforter to his disciples, not only then, but in all future periods of the world.

This is neither an imaginary representation nor the language of enthusiasm: these divine consolations have been experienced amid the arduous trials of life, and enjoyed at the awful hour of death by Bacon, Locke, Newton, Boerhaave, Pascal, Hale, Boyle, Lyttelton, and many of the most dignified characters in history; nor have they shone less conspicuous in female life. They supported Jane, queen of Navarre, the second Mary of England, the ladies Grey and Russell, in their trying dispensations; and all the eminently pious women in British biography, have felt their benign influence, from the imperial throne to the peasant's cottage! Shall not such characters be opposed to those Hindoo females, who from educational tenets and custom of caste, have been taught that no sacrifice is allowed to women, apart from their husbands; no religious rite, no fasting; as far only as a wife honours her husband, so far is she exalted in heaven: and that no other effectual duty is known for virtuous women, after the death of their lords, than to cast themselves into the fire. This is enjoined to the higher tribes; among the lower castes the women are included in all the indignities offered to the men, respecting whom the Institutes of Menu declare, that no Chandala nor Swampaca shall live in a town, nor have any wealth besides dogs and asses; that their transactions are to be confined to themselves, and their marriages only between equals; that no man who regards his duty, religious and civil, is to hold any intercourse with them; and that whoever is born a Sopaca is a sinful wretch, who lives by punishing criminals, and is ever despised by the virtuous.—Shall a law-giver who issues such cruel edicts, or his priests and ministers who enforce them, be compared with the Founder of that religion which says, Thou shalt love the LORD thy GOD with all thy heart, and with all thy soul; thou shalt love thy neighbour as thyself; and whatsoever ye would that men should do to you, do ye even so to them?

Such being the laws and established usages of the Hindoos, of what signification are the absorptions, reveries, and mystical intercourse which the religious brahmins and *twice-born men*, are supposed to hold with the Deity? Admitting that some of those devotees, soaring beyond idol-worship, and even above the adoration of the Hindoo Triad, *Brahma*, *Visnoo*, and *Seeva*, (in the attributes of creator, preserver, and destroyer) are by solemn meditation permitted to hold communion with the great mysterious spirit OM, or AUM; that name, which, according to those best versed in the Hindoo theology, is declared to be so sacred, that to hear it uttered by one of an inferior caste is dreadful to the ear of a brahmin; and Major Moor mentions that an English gentleman who had the letters and the sound of the *Gayatri*, something similar to the above, and who, without knowing the result, began to recite it audibly in the presence of a pious pundit, the astonished brahmin stopped his ears, and hastened terrified from his presence. Allowing therefore this spiritual worship, and these sublime conceptions, to the brahmins, which is every thing that can be expected, how few among thirty millions of Hindoos are admitted to this high privilege! how few, comparatively, even worship the triad deity, to whom the Supreme Being is supposed to have delegated his power, from being himself removed above all concern for his creatures! Julius Cæsar assigns it as a reason why the ancient druids would not allow their laws to be committed to writing, that their mysteries might not be rendered common to the vulgar, and profaned by them. The same pride and uncharitableness, pervading the institutes of Menu, enjoins that "if a Suder reads the Vedas to either of the other three castes, or listens to them, heated oil, wax, and melted tin, shall be poured into his ears, and the orifice stopped up; and that if a Suder gets the scriptures by heart, he shall be put to death."

How different is this rejection from the gracious invitation by the evangelical prophet: "Ho! every one that thirsteth, come ye to the waters; and he that hath no money, come buy and eat; yea, come, buy wine and milk, without money and without price! Incline your ear, and come unto me; hear, and your soul shall live!" How opposite is this cruel distinction of the brahmins, to these gentle words of the benevolent Saviour: "Come unto me, all ye that labour and are heavy laden, and I will give you rest! Blessed are ye poor, for yours is the kingdom of heaven!"

From the preceding passages it clearly appears, that a large part of the Hindoos are not only kept in ignorance, but are absolutely compelled to idol worship, and the darkness of paganism. It is probable I exalt them too highly, when I say it places the Hindoos in the condition of the Greeks and Romans, at that period when the Sun of Righteousness arose with healing on his wings, to dispel the darkness in which those elegant nations were enveloped; to whom the truths of Christianity were commanded to be preached, that they might turn from darkness to light, and from the power of Satan unto God! Instead of worshipping Jupiter, Minerva, and Diana, they were to adore the great Jehovah; the balmy comforts of the gospel were to reach their hearts; by a living faith in the merits and mediation of a crucified Redeemer, they were to enjoy a holy intercourse with the greatest and best of beings, and to be at length admitted to his beatific presence, where alone there is fulness of joy, and at whose right hand there is pleasure for evermore!

Sir William Jones has been frequently mentioned in these memoirs with the admiration, esteem, and respect due to his memory. I must here introduce him in another point of view, and express his sentiments on the conversion of the Hindoos, and the other subjects which form the basis of this conclusive chapter. They will be given chiefly in his own words, or those of Lord Teignmouth, his most excellent biographer; whose opinion on these sublime and interesting truths were so congenial to his own exalted mind, and whose words I now use in saying I shall not apologize for these extracts, nor for the reflections to which they naturally lead. Sir William Jones is a host on the present occasion; as such I take the liberty of bringing him forward, without discriminating which are immediately his own sentiments, or which are the words of his noble commentator. The names of Sir William Jones and Lord Teignmouth should not be separated; nor could I hold myself excusable did I not call in the aid of such champions, and shield myself under their panoply.

It was a remark of Sir William Jones, that if life were not too short for the complete discharge of all our respective duties, public and private, and for the acquisition even of necessary knowledge in any degree of perfection, with how much pleasure and improvement might a great part of it be spent in admiring the beauties of this wonderful orb, and contemplating the nature of man in all its varieties.—But his thoughts and attention were not confined to the perishable concerns of this world only; and what was the subject of his meditations in health, was more forcibly impressed upon his mind during illness. He knew the duty of resignation to the will of his Maker, and of dependance on the merits of a Redeemer.

"If we sometimes suffer the humiliation of seeing great talents and extensive erudition prostituted to infidelity, and employed in propagating misery, by endeavouring to subvert the basis of our temporal and eternal welfare, we cannot but feel a more than common gratification at the salutary union of true genius and piety. Learning, that wantons in irreligion, may, like the Sirius of Homer, flash its strong light upon us; but though brilliant, it is baneful;

and while it dazzles, makes us tremble for our safety. Science therefore, without piety, whatever admiration it may excite, will never be entitled to an equal degree of respect and esteem, with the humble knowledge which makes us wise unto salvation. The belief of Sir William Jones in revelation, is openly and distinctively declared in his works; but the unostentatious effusions of sequestered adoration, while they prove the sincerity of his conviction, give an additional weight to his avowed opinions.

" It would be unnecessary to adduce proofs in support of this assertion; but the beauty and piety of his prayers and supplications evince such solemn awe and purity of soul as cannot easily be exceeded. The following sublime address to the Deity is reluctantly curtailed.

" Eternal and incomprehensible MIND! who, by thy boundless power, before time began, createdst innumerable worlds for thy glory, and innumerable orders of beings for their happiness, which thy infinite goodness prompted thee to desire, and thy infinite wisdom enabled thee to know! We, thy creatures, vanish into nothing before thy supreme Majesty; we hourly feel our weakness; we daily bewail our vices; we continually acknowledge our folly:—Thee only we adore with awful veneration; thee we thank with the most fervent zeal; thee we praise with astonishment and rapture:—to thy power we humbly submit; of thy goodness we devoutly implore protection; on thy wisdom we firmly and cheerfully rely.—Impute not our doubts to indifference, nor our slowness of belief to hardness of heart; but be indulgent to our imperfect nature, and supply our imperfections by thy heavenly favour. Suffer not, we anxiously pray, suffer not oppression to prevail over innocence, nor the might of the avenger over the weakness of the just. Whenever we address thee in our retirement from the vanities of the world, if our prayers are foolish, pity us; if presumptuous, pardon us; if acceptable to thee, grant them, all-powerful God! grant them. And as with our living voice, and with our dying lips, we will express our submission to thy decrees, adore thy providence, and bless thy dispensations, so in all future states, to which we reverently hope thy goodness will raise us, grant that we may continue praising, admiring, venerating, worshipping thee more and more, through worlds without number, and ages without end!"

Composed on waking at Sea, in his Voyage to India.

"Graciously accept our thanks, thou Giver of all good, for having preserved us another night, and bestowed on us another day. O grant that on this day we may meditate on thy law with joyful veneration, and keep it in all our actions with firm obedience."

Composed in Sickness, in India.

"O thou Bestower of all good! if it please thee to continue my easy tasks in this life, grant me strength to perform them as a faithful servant. But if thy wisdom hath willed to end them by this thy visitation, admit me, not weighing my unworthiness, *but through thy mercy declared in Christ*, into thy heavenly mansions; that I may continually advance in happiness, by advancing in true knowledge and awful love of thee. Thy will be done!"

Written at Crishnagragur, in 1786.

" As meadows parch'd, brown groves, and withering flowers,
Imbibe the sparkling dew, and genial showers,
As chill dark air inhales the morning beam,
As thirsty harts enjoy the gelid stream,
Thus to man's grateful soul from Heaven descend
The mercies of his Father, Lord, and Friend ! "

" In matters of eternal concern, the authority of the highest human opinions has no claim to be admitted as a ground of belief, but it may with the strictest propriety be opposed to that of men of inferior learning and penetration: and, whilst the pious derive satisfaction from the perusal of sentiments according with their own, those who doubt or disbelieve, should be induced to weigh with candour and impartiality arguments which have produced conviction in the minds of the best, the wisest, and most learned of mankind.

" Among such as have professed a steady belief in the doctrines of Christianity, where shall greater names be found than those of Bacon and Newton? Of the former, and of Locke, it may be observed, that they were both innovators in science: disdaining to follow the sages of antiquity through the beaten paths of error, they broke through prejudices which had long obstructed the progress of sound knowledge, and laid the foundation of science on solid ground; whilst the genius of Newton carried him *extra flammantia mœnia mundi*. These men, to their great praise, and we may hope to their eternal happiness, devoted much of their time to the study of the scriptures. If the evidence of revelation had been weak, who were better qualified to expose its unsoundness? if our national faith were a mere fable, a political superstition, why were minds which boldly destroyed prejudices in science, blind to those in religion? They read, examined, weighed, and believed; and the same vigorous intellect that dispersed the mists which concealed the temple of human knowledge, was itself illuminated with the radiant truths of divine revelation.

"Such authorities, and let me now add to them the name of Sir William Jones, are deservedly entitled to great weight. Let those who superciliously reject them, compare their intellectual powers, their scientific attainments and vigour of application, with those of the men whom I have named: the comparison may perhaps lead them to suspect, that their incredulity (to adopt the idea of a profound scholar) may be the result of a little smattering in learning, and great self-conceit; and that by harder study, and a humbled mind, they may regain the religion which they have left. —The investigation and the propagation of truth, as Sir William Jones has himself declared, in the following elegant couplets, was the fixed object of his whole life.

"Before thy mystic altar, heavenly Truth,
I kneel in manhood, as I knelt in youth:
Thus let me kneel, till this dull form decay,
And life's last shade be brighten'd by thy ray:
Then shall my soul, now lost in clouds below,
Soar without bound, without consuming glow."

I shall conclude these quotations with the remark of Lord Teignmouth, that the friends of religion, who know the value of the "sure and certain hopes" which it inspires, will remark with satisfaction, the pious sentiments expressed by Sir William Jones a few months only before his own death. They will recollect the determination which he formed in youth, to examine with attention the evidence of our holy religion, and will rejoice to find unprejudiced inquiry terminating, as might be expected, in a rational conviction of its truth and divine authority.

Of all modern writers on the subject of Hindoo conversion, I confess myself to be most pleased with the mildness, liberality, and moderation of Lord Valentia. Good sense, nice discrimination, and a knowledge of the Anglo-Indian character, as well as some acquaintance with the prejudices of the Hindoos, are evident to every man who has spent a few years in India. On this subject we must divest ourselves of partiality, and view man as he is. No one can more admire the British character in India than myself. The benevolent and manly virtues which so distinguish it, made an early impression upon my mind, and never can be eradicated. I have taken every seasonable opportunity to impress my readers with a just sense of these amiable characteristics; not from after-thought, and subsequent recollection, but from letters written at the moment—

"Warm from the heart, and true to all its fires!"

alive to every feeling of generosity, philanthropy, and benevolence.

I shall not insert the whole of Lord Valentia's opinion on this interesting subject, but some of his remarks are so truly just, and at this eventful period so peculiarly interesting, that they must not be withheld from those who may not have perused his Lordship's late publication. *Such* sentiments I would rather convey in the language of the noble writer than my own.

" It will hardly be believed, that in the splendid city of Calcutta, the head of a mighty Christian empire, there is only one church of the establishment of the mother-country, and that by no means conspicuous either for size or ornament. It is also remarkable, that all British India does not afford one episcopal see, while that advantage has been granted to the province of Canada; yet it is certain that from the remoteness of the country, and the peculiar temptations to which the freedom of manners exposes the clergy, immediate episcopal superintendance can no where be more requisite. From the want of this it is painful to observe, that the characters of too many of that order, are by no means creditable to the doctrines they profess; which, together with the unedifying contests that prevail among them even in the pulpit, tend to lower the religion and its followers, in the eyes of the natives of every description. If there be any plan for conciliating the minds of the natives to Christianity, it is so manifestly essential it should appear to them in a respectable form at the seat of government, that I presume all parties will allow that the first step should be to place it there upon a proper footing. Since my return to England I find that an episcopal establishment for India, upon a very large scale, has been publicly recommended by the Rev. Dr. Buchanan. Were its expediency in other respects agreed upon, I fear the present state of the revenue in that country would render such a serious addition to the expenditure unjustifiable; but the maintenance of one bishop could not reasonably be objected to; for, with a revenue of eleven millions, it becomes a duty to appropriate a part to religious purposes, and not a mere consideration of eligibility.

" In every view, political as well as religious, it is highly desirable that men of liberal education and exemplary piety should be employed; who, by their manners, would improve the tone of society in which they lived; and by the sacredness of their character operate as a check on the tendency to licentiousness that too frequently prevails.

" The splendor of episcopal worship should be maintained in India in the highest degree our church allows. On the natives, accustomed to ceremonial pomp, and greatly swayed by external appearances, it would impress that respect for our religion, of which, I am sorry to say, they are chiefly by our neglect of it at present destitute. The natural effect of which has been to excite a doubt in the minds of the Hindoo of our own belief in that faith we are so anxious to press upon him.

" The native inhabitants may, indeed, from the sight of one solitary church, believe that we have a national religion, but I know of nothing that can give this information to the rest of our eastern subjects. Whilst the Mussulman conquerors of India have established mosques in every town of their dominions, the traveller, after quitting Calcutta, must seek in vain for any such mark of the religion of their successors."

My opinions do not entirely coincide with those of Lord Valentia respecting the insurmountable difficulty, or rather the impossibility, of converting the brahmins and higher orders of Hindoos, as is evident throughout these volumes; the cause of my differing arises not only from my own observation in India, but from what we know is now actually taking place in favour of Christianity among the brahmins themselves. I acknowledge there is too much truth in his Lordship's remark, that although the Hindoos have adopted from us various improvements in their manufactures of saltpetre, opium, and indigo, and have made rapid advances in the knowledge of ship-building, practical mathematics, and navigation, yet none of these acquirements have interfered with their religious prejudices. The instant these are touched, they fly off from all approximation to their masters, and an end is put to further advancement. Nothing is therefore more to be avoided than alarming their jealousy on this head, and exciting the suspicion that government means, in any manner, to interfere in the business of proselyting. The brahmins are a very powerful body; they are both an hereditary nobility and a reigning hierarchy; looked up to with the highest veneration by the inferior castes, and possessed of the most distinguishing privileges, they will consequently oppose with their whole influence any attempt to subvert that system upon which all their superiority depends. They have already taken alarm at the proceedings of the missionaries in Bengal, and other parts; and, if driven to extremities, will doubtless excite a formidable disaffection to our government among the natives. On the contrary, the former wise policy of treating them with respect, and giving a full toleration to their superstitions, was often attended with the happy effect of making them the instrument of enforcing useful regulations in the country; for they have never scrupled, when required, giving a sanction to the orders of government to suppress hurtful practices, as in the case of the sacrifice of children at Sorgur, and in many other instances. We should also be aware that, although the comparison between the Mussulman intolerance and our contrary spirit, was so much in our favour as to have had a powerful efficacy in attaching them to the British government, knowing that they had only a choice of masters; yet were this difference of policy taken away, their habits and manners, which are more congenial to those of the Mussulmans, would probably induce them to prefer their government to ours.

After a very candid and fair statement of the difficulty in converting the Hindoos, his Lordship draws the following satisfactory conclusion on this important subject.

" Upon the whole, I am fully persuaded that the first step to be taken is that of rendering our own religion respectable in the eyes of our Indian subjects, by an establishment of greater splendor and dignity; and especially by a better choice and more vigilant inspection of the regular clergy; and that government should studiously avoid interesting itself in the conversion of the natives, since it is impossible that they should not connect in their minds the zeal of proselyting, exerted by those in power, with a plan of coercion and intolerance. If placing in the hands of the Hindoos translations of the scriptures into the languages of the country, will not induce them to make unfavourable comparisons between our lives and our doctrines, and consequently expose us to contempt, no objection can be made to such a dissemination of the principles of true religion. To its silent operation the cause of Christianity should be left, and who will not rejoice at its success?"

It must be acknowledged by all, who know how much religion intermingles with the general system of the Hindoos, and pervades the minutest parts of their domestic economy, that the difficulty of converting a man of high caste to Christianity is very great. Such an one must, in every sense, literally fulfil our Saviour's words; he must leave father and mother, brethren and sisters, wife and children, houses and lands, when he becomes his disciple; this is the cross he must take up, the trial he must endure; he must be despised and rejected by his former associates, an outcast from his family and friends. The sacrifice, though great, is transient; the recompence glorious and everlasting. Such sacrifices have been made, and are now greatly increasing. Many brahmins of distinction, who had not previously lost their caste, but on the contrary were looked up to with veneration and love, *have embraced Christianity*. The annals of the pious *Swartz*, the anecdotes of Dr. Claudius Buchanan, and the labours of many zealous and prudent ministers in the Danish mission, prove this assertion. See ANANDA, a learned and respectable brahmin, now become an eminent Christian convert, translating the New Testament into the *Telinga* dialect! Behold SATTIENADEN, a Hindoo disciple of *Swartz*, preaching the gospel in the language of *Tamul!* SABAT, the Arabian, transporting the evangelical books to the gates of *Mecca*, and planting Christianity among the tribes of *Yemen:* while MIRZA promulgates celestial truth throughout the extensive regions of *Persia!* When we contemplate so many Syriac churches in Travencore, which have existed more than a thousand years, under a regular establishment, unaided by European hierarchies, and encompassed by idolatrous nations; when we advert to the patronage given to consistent missionaries by the rajah of Mysore, and other Hindoo sovereigns, we cannot any longer suppose the conversion of the Hindoos impossible.

I have hitherto confined myself to human means, but what are all subordinate agents, compared with the last command of the great founder of Christianity? "Go ye, and teach all nations; baptizing them in the name of the Father, and of the Son, and of the Holy Ghost: teaching them to observe all things whatsoever I have commanded you; and, lo! I am with you always, even unto the end of the world!" If the compassionate Redeemer, who gave this command, and promised to continue with his future teachers, shall bless the present endeavour, if the Lord gives the word, and the Spirit of Truth influences the company of preachers, no earthly power can withstand the heavenly mission; no prince of darkness, no apostatizing emperor, no spiritual wickedness in high-places, can prevail against it. If the DESIRE OF ALL NATIONS is once more to appear in the east, if now is the appointed time, the worship of *Boodha* shall cease, the shrines of *Brahma* be forsaken, and the idols of India fall to the ground, as did those of Greece and Rome in the apostolic age!

I cannot enter upon mathematical demonstrations or metaphysical discussions on the tenets adopted by different Christian churches. There is great beauty and simplicity in the expression of a royal teacher, who well knew the truth of his assertion, "When THY WORD goeth forth it giveth light and understanding to the *simple*." That the poor and simple Hindoos, more than the wise and learned in the higher tribes, now engage my warmest attention, I candidly acknowledge. That the Sudra and Chandala, now deprived of all religious instruction, (by an artificial and cruel degradation of caste) may be taught the plain and simple truths of Christianity, I earnestly plead. That there are higher attainments in its spiritual progress, is readily allowed; there is a continual improvement in religious wisdom; but the apostle seems to limit that superior knowledge to a more perfect class, than he generally expected among the Corinthian converts: " My preaching was not with enticing words of man's wisdom, but in demonstration of the spirit, and of power. Howbeit we speak wisdom among them that are perfect; yet not the wisdom of this world, nor of the princes of this world, that come to nought; but we speak the wisdom of GOD in a mystery; even the hidden wisdom, which God ordained before the world unto our glory!"

These mysteries will, in due time, be revealed; and those inconceivable things, which eye hath not seen, nor ear heard, will be communicated to the pious heart properly prepared for their reception. Those spiritual joys are not the present object, but that millions of British subjects do not share in the common blessings of life enjoyed by the Negroes and Hottentots of Africa, and are deprived of every religious pleasure, is evident in the Pariahs and Chandalas, so numerously dispersed in every part of Hindostan; for *their* temporal and eternal happiness I become an advocate! I know the pride and arrogance of the brahmins must and will militate against every attempt for their liberation: " Procul, O! procul, este profani!" has always been an exclamation among a certain description of people, from Virgil to the present day: " Stand off! for I am holier than thou," is no where more distinctly believed, nor more rigidly practised, than among the brahmins.

Much has been said respecting *compelling* the Hindoos to relinquish the privileges of caste, and embrace a religion which puts all men upon a level. In the first place, it is to be hoped that no compulsion will ever be allowed in the system of their conversion; and in the next, although it be admitted that Christianity in one sense does reduce the whole human race to the same standard, yet in every other, the divine and moral precepts of the gospel enjoin the Christian, in all situations, to give tribute to whom tribute is due, custom to whom custom, fear to whom fear, honour to whom honour. Even regarding the distinctions of meat and drink, the keeping of particular days, and similar non-essentials in religion, nothing can be more liberal or gentle than the admonition of the great apostle to the Gentiles: "Him that is weak in the faith receive ye, but not to doubtful disputations: for one believeth that he may eat all things; another who is weak, eateth herbs. Let not him that eateth despise him that eateth not; and let not him which eateth not judge him that eateth; for God hath received him. One man esteemeth one day above another; another esteemeth every day alike: let every one be fully persuaded in his own mind. Let us not therefore judge one another any more: for I know, and am persuaded by the Lord Jesus, that there is nothing unclean of itself; but to him that esteemeth any thing to be unclean, to him it is unclean. Let us, therefore, follow after the things which make for peace, and things wherewith one may edify another. For the kingdom of God is not meat and drink, but righteousness, and peace, and joy in the Holy Ghost!"

On a fair comparison then, between the Christian and the Hindoo religion, what candid mind can hesitate to pronounce in favour of the former? The religion of Him, who saith "Look unto me, and be saved, all ye ends of the earth!" O! what an ample field is here opened for holy meditation and solemn musing! for pious resolves and holy energies, which are not confined to the brahminical groves, nor the cloisters of a monastery; but are to be found in the heart of every real Christian, who knows that his body is the temple of the Holy Spirit; and that, assisted by divine grace, it is in his power, from that indwelling principle, to perform the relative duties of society, to enjoy the innocent pleasures of life, and at the same time to find himself, at solemn seasons, exalted above this fading scene, in celestial intercourse with his Creator, Redeemer, and Sanctifier!

Under such a view, shall it any longer be said that the Hindoos, who are in a state of spiritual darkness, and practise crimes of the most atrocious nature, do not need the blessings of Christianity? or that their moral and religious codes, even if accompanied by their enjoined virtues, place them above those nations to whom the apostles were immediately sent? Are the inactive brahmins, the idle yogees, the oppressive duans, and cruel zemindars, superior to the active minister of the Ethiopian queen, to whom an evangelist was commissioned to explain the prophecies, and to baptize in the name of that Saviour whom he wished to know and love? Are they coequal with Cornelius of Cæsarea, whose prayers and alms ascended as a memorial before God; whose household was composed of good men, and on whom devout soldiers waited continually? In the opinion of modern unbelievers, such a character needed no conversion; he stood firm on a rock, surrounded by his virtues. But we must not be governed by man's opinion, the Almighty beheld the Roman centurion in a different light, and miraculously sent a messenger to teach him a better way; to proclaim the remission of sins through that name alone whereby we can be saved.

There could not be a more zealous worshipper of God than Saul of Tarsus, under a dispensation which came from heaven, by signs and wonders, and a combination of every thing to render it sublime and awful; yet in his memorable journey to Damascus, the Redeemer of man, having then fulfilled the law, introduced a new dispensation, and ascended into heaven, appeared in a wonderful manner to this zealous champion for Judaism. While he was breathing out threatenings and slaughter against the Christian church, the great Head of that church suddenly arrested him in his career, and sent him, as a chosen vessel, to bear his name before the Gentiles, and to preach his gospel to kings and people; especially to the polished nations of Greece and Rome, whose philosophers believed in the unity of God as much as the absorbed brahmin, or *twice-born man*, among their devotees; but where the mass of the people were, like the Hindoos, given up to polytheism, idolatry, and pagan darkness.

If we place the superior brahmins on an equality with the good Cornelius, more cannot be expected; yet Cornelius was to be taught a better way. And it is granting, perhaps, more than is required, to allow the Hindoos at large to be in the same condition as the Jews, "to whom appertained the adoption, the glory, the covenant, the giving of the law, the service of the sanctuary, and of whom as concerning the flesh Christ came, who is God over all, blessed for evermore!" Yet, after all this superiority over every other nation, the apostle most ardently prays for Israel, that they might be *saved by the gospel of Christ;* because, although they had a zeal of *God*, it was not according to knowledge: and then in the true catholic spirit of that gospel he was so peculiarly selected to preach to the Gentiles, he declares that whosoever shall call upon the name of the Lord shall be saved. This is followed by those questions on which we must now lay the great stress of this argument: "How shall they call on him in whom they have not believed? and how shall they believe in him of whom they have not heard? How shall they hear without a preacher? And how shall they preach except they be sent? as it is written, How beautiful are the feet of them that preach the gospel of peace!"

St. Paul, the learned disciple of Gamaliel, was the apostle chosen to spread those divine truths among the heathen, and was, by high authority, ordained to be the preacher to the gentiles. In obedience to the heavenly mandate, he travelled among the Greeks and Romans, and won over, by the consoling truths of the gospel, thousands of all denominations, from the imperial palace of Nero, to Lydia of Thyatira, and the jailor at Philippi. At Athens, then the most refined and elegant city in the world, the Stoic and Epicurean philosophers brought him unto the Areopagus; where, publicly condemning their ignorance and superstition, he says, on beholding their devotions, he had found an altar erected to the UNKNOWN GOD! "HIM therefore, whom they ignorantly worshipped, he preached unto them; the GOD who made the world, and all things therein; who is Lord of heaven and earth, and dwelleth not in temples made with hands, neither is worshipped with men's hands, as though he needed any thing;

seeing he giveth to all life, and breath, and all things; and hath made of one blood all nations of men, and hathdetermined the times, and the bounds of their habitation: that they should seek the Lord, if haply they might feel after him, and find him; though he be not far from every one of us; for in him we live, and move, and have our being; as certain also of your own poets have said, for we are also his offspring. Forasmuch then as we are the offspring of God, we ought not to think that the Godhead is like unto gold, or silver, or stone, graven by art, and man's device. And the times of this ignorance God winked at; but now commandeth all men every where to repent; because he hath appointed a day, in the which he will judge the world in righteousness by him who he hath ordained; whereof he hath given assurance unto all men, in that he raised him from the dead."

Had a man the power of Demosthenes, or the eloquence of Tully, what could he say more than the apostle preached in that short discourse before the wisest men of Greece? It is equally applicable to the brahmins, and all their deluded followers: for we must not be guided by the opinion of certain modern philosophers, or the superficial observers of local manners and customs in foreign countries; but we must repair to the unerring standard of truth; there we shall see in what these *applauded brahmins* are deficient: and not them only, but their advocates of every description, who, in a christian country, set up the oriental standard of holiness. We shall there also see the situation of Voltaire and his disciples in the eyes of a pure and holy God! for, without REDEEMING LOVE, and the sanctifying influence of the Holy Spirit, what is man? What he is by nature we know from the lives and conduct of the human race, throughout the annals of time. We behold our first ancestor fallen from innocence into a labyrinth of woe, living to see one of his children murder the other. From that unhappy commencement the page of history affords every variety of character. Sailing down the stream of time, we view his posterity, from Nimrod to the Macedonian hero, destroying their fellow-creatures, and sometimes weeping because there were no more worlds to conquer; from Alexander to Cæsar, to Charles of Sweden, and to the present eventful period, we behold the conquerors of the earth pursuing the same career, to end in the same disappointment! In the revolving ages of near six thousand years, if we except the wise and virtuous few, of whatever rank in life, or under whatever religious dispensation; as especially those, who, like holy Enoch, walked with GOD, and were renewed in the spirit of their minds, what a picture do we behold!

> "Sight so deform, what heart of rock could long
> Dry-eyed behold? Adam could not, but wept,
> Though not of woman born: compassion quell'd
> His best of man; and gave him up to tears." MILTON.

I cannot suppose the advocates for Hinduism intend to exalt their favourites above the nations of antiquity. If this humble essay is insufficient to prove their inferiority, many intelligent writers have established the fact; nor can it be deemed irrelevant to produce a few incontrovertible instances from ancient history on this important subject. They are the sentiments of heathens, whose doctrine and practice exalt them in the scale of piety and virtue far beyond many who are called Christians in the present day.

Xenophon thus records the solemn counsel of Socrates to Aristodemus, who doubted of a Providence, and even of a Deity. "O Aristodemus, apply yourself sincerely to worship God; he will *enlighten* you, and then all your doubts will be removed." This divine philosopher, after having drank the deadly poison decreed by unjust judges, in the memorable discourse with his disciples, asserts, "that the soul which cannot die, merits all the moral and intellectual improvements which we can possibly give it. A spirit formed to live for ever, should be making continual advances in virtue and wisdom. To a well cultivated mind, the body is no more than a temporary prison. At death, such a soul is conducted by its invisible guardian to the heights of empyrean felicity, where it becomes a fellow-commoner with the wise and good of all ages." How noble is the sentiment of Plato, a disciple worthy of Socrates, who placed the sovereign good in a resemblance to the Divine Nature, which can flow from God alone! "As nothing is like the sun, but by the solar influences; so nothing can resemble God, but by an emanation of divine light into the soul!" These sublime sentiments of the Grecian philosophers were confirmed by Seneca, one of the brightest ornaments of ancient Rome: "No man is good without God; he dwelleth in every good man. If thou seest a man fearless in the midst of dangers, untainted by riches, happy in adversity, calm in the tempest, looking down as from an eminence on all things sublunary,—dost thou not admire him? Sayest thou not, Virtue is of all things the most great and noble; it is a divine power descended from above? There is a *Holy Spirit* residing in us, who watches and observes good and evil men, and will treat us after the same manner that we treat him." Sen. Ep. 41.

How would such men, with Aristotle, Cicero, and the other worthies of antiquity, have estimated the gospel! What would have been the joy of Confucius, and many oriental teachers, had they been favoured with those divine revelations which are rejected by modern deists! Shall there then be advocates for paganism in a Christian nation, once sunk in greater barbarism than the Hindoos? a nation rescued by the blessing of Christianity from druidical slavery, from sacrificing her children on the unhallowed fires of their sanguinary deities, and all the darkness of idolatry; and restored to reason, to light, and immortality, by that gospel emphatically styled the Light of the Gentiles? Shall there be advocates for withholding the truth from distant regions, composing so valuable a part of the British empire, from millions of fellow-subjects who add so much to her comfort, wealth, and luxury; establishing an intercourse by which this "*Island of bliss*," this seat of commerce, maintains thousands of her industrious sons on foreign shores, and covers the ocean with her sails? Shall that nation, influenced by the noblest motives, emancipate the helpless Africans from bodily slavery, and liberally promote their moral civilization and religious improvement, and leave her Asiatic subjects, shrouded in pagan darkness, in bondage to *their destructive powers*, as some of their deities are truly named; shall she conceal from them the knowledge of Christianity, which is the very cause and support of her own happiness and glory? I shall, I am confident, be supported by the wise and good of every description, in my assertion that Great Britain, amidst the storms and convulsions which have humbled the continent of Europe, and degraded her princes, has been upheld by the arm of Omnipotence, and considered as a *Zoar* by virtuous foreigners; because she is a nation where the Christian religion is preserved; where for more than fifty years it shone the brightest jewel in the diadem of a beloved venerable monarch; and pervading every rank in society, adorns the palace of his nobles, and the cottage of his peasants!

I am aware of numerous exceptions to this delightful portrait. To their own master, such must individually stand or fall: from them the light of truth is not withheld; they have been enlisted under the banner of Christ, and baptized in his name, but allured by various temptations, and led astray by delusive suggestions, they have deserted the sacred standard, and given themselves up to a fading world. To such persons it is hoped the hour of reflection will arrive, ere it be too late; and, awaking them from a fatal slumber to a sincere repentance, they may follow the example of a Rochester, a Gardiner, and other eminent converts, in walking worthy of their high and holy vocation. If this desirable change does not commence in their present state of existence, they must be left to Him who seeth not as man seeth, and has said, "Judge not, that ye be not judged!"

It will not be deemed uncharitable to suppose such persons have not a clear knowledge of Christianity; that they annex certain speculative ideas, which do not appertain to its nature; and therefore, from not understanding its doctrines, they do not practise its virtues. Under one delusion, they say it prohibits the pleasures and enjoyments of this world; discourages the love of fame and glory, and weakens the noblest energies of human action. Another fatal error induces them to set aside the justice, and trust all to the mercy of that God who has declared no unclean thing shall enter into his kingdom. Did they, like the noble Bereans, search the scriptures, and humbly meditate on the Word of God, they would find all the divine attributes to be in perfect harmony; they would know, by happy experience, that under the gospel dispensation, " Mercy and Truth are met together, Righteousnes and Peace have kissed each other." They would see that Christianity does not extinguish the love of fame, the noblest sublunary reward for patriotic virtue; but that it enables its votaries to soar beyond worldly honours, to transcendent glory, to a crown of glory, unfading, eternal, in the heavens! Here, the laurels of the victor, and the wreath of the patriot, often droop from the breath of slander, and wither by the blast of envy: nor, in their best estate, can they long encircle an earthly brow; but the crown which awaits the Christian hero, is celestial and everlasting!

Neither does the Christian religion abolish the natural desires and propensities of the human heart, it only purifies the principle and defines their limits. It is no enemy to pleasure, but chastens and moderates its alluring tendencies. If an earthly parent delights to see his children happy, surely our heavenly Father is pleased to see that heart cheerful which he accepts as his sacrifice. " My son, give me thy heart," is the divine request. The Israelitish monarch, in a state of penitence and humiliation, says, " the sacrifice of God is a broken heart, and a contrite spirit;" such must be the language of every sincere penitent, when he knows the consequence of sin, and beholds the loving-mercy of his offended Maker. But the Word of Truth, which cannot be divided, (nor like the Hindoo Sastras be mutilated for various purposes, suited to different castes) proves that God has given us all things richly to enjoy. In this sublunary sphere there is a tranquil path, untrod by the disciples of Epicurus, and little known to the philosophers of the Stoa, shaded by umbrageous trees, with lovely blossoms and delicious fruits. A perennial fountain refreshes the aspiring passion-flower, the blushing rose, and lowly lily; emblems of faith, hope, and charity, which adorn the borders, and perfume the atmosphere. The rose, it is true, is not always without a thorn; and the lily of the valley is sometimes crushed: but the *passi flora alata* soars aloft, clings to a firm support, and smiles in cerulean ether.

This is that walk on which the Christian pilgrim may safely tread; that happy medium which Stoics and Epicureans missed in ancient times, and Carthusians and libertines equally mistake in the present day; it is the path of piety and virtue, which led to the summum bonum of Plato and Socrates, and conducts the Christian to the throne of God and the Lamb! There we shall find stability and peace; in every deviation from it turbulence, fluctuation, and vanity!

O! how does the Christian character ennoble man! Like the sun, he rises to warm and enlighten all that come within the influence of his rays; in imitation of his divine master, he goes about doing good; he knows that the end of the law is love, and while he contributes to the happiness of others, he secures it within his own bosom. But conscious that clouds and vapours often intercept the brightest beams, he endeavours to anticipate that blissful empyrean, where there shall be a morning without clouds, a day without night, and the Sun of peace and felicity shall shine for ever! Such is the path which convinces us that the Christian has joys with which a stranger intermeddleth not; that he has meat to eat which the world knows not of. To those who have not enjoyed the refined delight of love and friendship, how can they be described? to those who have not experienced the consolations of piety, in the sweet intercourse between the soul of man and his God, how can human language make them known?

When Christianity was first promulgated, the glory of the world had reached its acme. The empires of Assyria, Persia, Greece, and Egypt, were annihilated; Rome reigned triumphant; the nations obeyed her sway. The temple of Janus was shut, and the peaceful olive extended over the civilized world. Art and science flourished, and so superior was that æra for human learning, that in the annals of literature it is eminently distinguished as the Augustan age; yet, so transcendent were the blessings of the Gospel, that then the SAVIOUR of the world was born, and the blessings of his kingdom dispensed; then the angelic choir proclaimed, "Glory to God on high, on earth peace, good-will towards men;" then were those illustrious Romans, those enlightened nations, to be converted to Christianity, and become the disciples of the Messiah, in confirmation of the ancient prophecy, that the Gentiles should come to his light, and kings to the brightness of his rising. Pagan darkness was now to be dispelled, and their idols to be demolished: then was that spiritual kingdom to be established, in which there is one Lord, one faith, one baptism, one GOD and Father of all, who is above all and through all, and in all!

Allowing, therefore, the religion and morality of the Hindoos to equal that of the Greeks and Romans at this memorable period, shall we deprive them of the divine truths and consolations which were commanded to be preached to those enlightened people? Shall we keep our Asiatic brethren from the fold of that heavenly Shepherd who laid down his life for his sheep, and declared that he had other sheep, which were not of that fold; them also he must bring, and there should be one fold, under one shepherd!

This discussion has already far exceeded my intended limits, or it would be easy to produce examples from Eugenius the Roman pontiff, from the emperor Charles the Fifth, and many other sovereigns; from the cardinals Beaufort, Wolsey, Richelieu and Mazarine; and from men in every distinguished situation, whose dying testimony bore witness to the vanity of their former pursuits. Solomon's pathetic motto confirmed the vain regrets of these exalted characters at the termination of their career. They had attained the summit of their ambition, but great was their disappointment and affecting their confessions at the last awful hour! Divine grace, and the influence of the Holy Spirit, can alone conduct us safely through life, and support us at that solemn hour which every child of Adam must experience. Modern philosophy may deny the doctrine and despise the influence of this celestial Comforter; how different were the sentiments of Seneca! To such philosophers, the noble Roman asks this important question, "*Quid aliud voces hunc, quam Deum, in corpore humano hospitantem?*" "*What other canst thou think this internal monitor, than God dwelling in the body of man?*"

The wonderful and sublime subject of the sanctification and redemption of man calls forth all our admiration and all our love! How do the Avatars, or incarnations of the Hindoo deities, recede when we contemplate that awful mystery which even the angels desire to look into, the INCARNATION OF THE SON OF GOD! who left the realms of bliss and glory to take upon him our nature, and to suffer death upon the cross for fallen man! These contemplations require a soul properly prepared. The brahmins seem to have some idea of this kind in their pensive musings; and especially in the absorptions, or trances, of their *twice-born* men, this expression is singular, and on a former occasion an illustration has been attempted. Thus far at least it implies, that a man engrossed by this world, and devoted to its pleasures, is not in a fit state for spiritual enjoyments; but we have higher authority for this assertion, a nobler motive for this delightful preparation. In his memorable conversation with Nicodemus, our SAVIOUR says "Except a man be born again, he cannot see the kingdom of God!" The learned teacher of Israel expressing his surprise at such an assertion, was again assured, that "unless a man be born of the Spirit, he cannot enter into the kingdom of God! He that believeth on the Son of God hath everlasting life: he that believeth not, shall not see life; but the wrath of God abideth on him!"

Let not an ardent desire for the conversion of the Hindoos be deemed a zeal without knowledge. The end is great, noble, and eternal!—the means I do not enter upon. We have liberally introduced our arts and sciences, as far as they choose to adopt them; we have given them wise, just, and humane laws, assimilating as much as possible with their own manners and customs; we have taught them to estimate the blessings of liberty and the security of property. O let us also confer upon them the blessings of TRUE RELIGION from the REVELATIONS of GOD!

We know as much as is necessary of the Hindoo metempsychosis, the brahminical mysteries, and the sensual paradise of Mahomed; as also of the punishments which, in both systems, are denounced against those who are deemed unworthy to enjoy them. We may also, in some degree, judge of their influence in the practice both of Hindoos and Mahomedans; for "by their fruits ye shall know them." They are sufficiently obvious throughout these memoirs. I have read what has been advanced against missions to the East; and remain unconvinced by any arguments yet adduced to prevent them; at the same time I most decidedly agree with those writers, that no compulsive means should be used to effect so desirable an end; on the contrary, no measures too mild, no persuasions too gentle, can be adopted for the Hindoo conversion.

I candidly confess, although I detest the immolation of female victims in the burning cave of death, and abhor the infanticides practised in Guzerat, with many other recited instances of brahmin cruelty; yet I view the innocent flowery sacrifice, the choral song, and the festive dance at the Hindoo temples, with an affectionate liberality, while the disciples of Brahma remain unenlightened by the Sun of Righteousness: but I cannot oppose them, nor any other pagan rites, to the spiritual joys of Christianity! to those heavenly truths, which in prosperity are the delight and the shield of her votary, and in adversity, his support and consolation; which add a zest to his sweetest cup, and extract the wormwood and gall from his bitterest draught; which add a lustre to the splendor of a palace, and cheer the dungeon's gloom. When the Christian is forsaken by all other friends, he has access to

HIM, whose ear is open to his supplication; to the friend of the friendless, and the avenger of the innocent: he goes to that heavenly parent who refuseth not the prayer of the poor destitute, and despiseth not his desire. In the language of the mild and gentle Hannah, who had poured forth her soul in distress, he can join in her grateful hymn "There is none holy as the Lord, neither is there any rock like our GOD! The Lord killeth, and maketh alive; he bringeth down to the grave, and bringeth up: the Lord maketh poor and maketh rich; he keepeth the feet of his saints, and the wicked shall be silent in darkness; for the pillars of the earth are the Lord's, and he hath set the world upon them!"

Could Eli, the high-priest, who rebuked her for an imaginary fault, have formed more sublime conceptions, or clothed them in more exalted language; or can any composition by the most learned student exceed this beautiful prayer? It was, indeed, the prayer of an unlettered female; but that female was the child of God! The wisest and greatest monarch that ever swayed a sceptre, thus addresses the same Jehovah. "O LORD GOD of Israel! there is no God like thee, in the heaven, nor in the earth; who keepest covenant, and shewest mercy unto thy servants who walk before thee with all their hearts; have respect to the prayer of thy servant, and to his supplication! But will God in very deed dwell with men upon the earth? Behold, heaven and the heaven of heavens cannot contain thee! Thou wilt hear from heaven, even from thy dwelling-place, the prayer and supplication of thy people!"

I insert these beautiful effusions from two devoted servants of *God*, in different situations of life; because it has been thought proper to introduce several sublime passages from the Hindoo scriptures into late publications. None can doubt of their sublimity; nor of their pious and moral sentiments, clothed with all the beauty of oriental metaphor: but how few, among thirty or forty millions of Hindoos, contemplate the beauties of the Shasta, or practise the morality enjoined by the laws of Menu! This obliges me to repeat an assertion from that code, formerly mentioned, that "a brahmin, whether learned or ignorant, is a powerful divinity; something transcendantly divine." Such a being, inflated by pride and self-sufficiency, anticipates, no doubt, a glorious situation in the Hindoo metempsychosis; but what becomes of the poor Sudra, in another state of existence, who is not here allowed any share in these spiritual blessings; nor is a brahmin, by the same code, even permitted to give a Sudra temporal advice. Dr. Francis Buchanan, in numerous instances, relates the opinion of the lower castes in India, respecting a future state; from which we learn, that all their ideas of futurity are confused and conjectural, and that some believe in annihilation. In conjectural confusion on this awful subject, the European unbeliever, with all his wisdom and philosophy, is perhaps nearly on a par with the unlettered Chandala. We know what the heathens of antiquity thought of death, from the verses addressed by the emperor Hadrian to his departing soul: and we learn from other records, that the same monarch having asked Secundus what death was, received this memorable answer: "Death is eternal sleep, the dissolution of the body, the rich man's fear, the poor man's wish, an uncertain journey!" The first words of Secundus, as most appropriate for the sad occasion, were placed over the public cemeteries in France, during the reign of terror, infidelity, and atheism.

I always read that affecting passage in Pliny's letter to Calestrius, on the death of Corellius, with renewed pleasure. But it is a pleasure mingled with deep concern. There is not a sentiment in it which I do not feel, from having experienced a similar deprivation. When the noble Roman sues to his friend for *some uncommon consolation, something he had never known nor read of*, how do we wish he had been acquainted with one of those early martyrs in the Christian church, whom, as proconsul of Bythinia, he was then persecuting! The passage alluded to is much to my present purpose; it points out, in one of the most elegant, accomplished, and amiable characters of antiquity, his great desideratum in the hour of calamity, in that trying hour when all human aid is fruitless. Here Pliny must utter his own feelings.

" I now reflect what a friend, what a man I am deprived of! He was sixty-seven years old when he died; a length of age sufficient for men of the most robust constitutions: I know it, he is released from perpetual torture: I know it, he left his relations, nay, he left the commonwealth, dearer to him than all his relations, flourishing and happy: this I know also. And yet I mourn his death, as if he had fallen in the flower of youth, and the full strength of his constitution: but to own to you my weakness; my sorrow is in a great measure occasioned upon my own account. I have lost, O! I have lost the witness, the guide, the master of my conduct. In short, to tell you what, in the first moments of my grief, I said to Calvisius, I fear I shall grow less circumspect than I have been. Administer, therefore, some comfort to me:

tell me not that he was old, that he was infirm, (they are circumstances I have long known) but let it be some new, some uncommon consolation; something I have never heard nor read. All that I have already heard or read occurs to my memory; but that is not sufficient to overcome my sorrow!"

I repeat, how do we wish this noble Roman had known one of those proscribed Christians he punished even to torture; not sparing the female sex, to extort confession of a crime, which, according to his own account, amounted only to an obstinate kind of superstition; in assembling to sing hymns to CHRIST as to a GOD; and binding themselves by an oath, not to be guilty of any wickedness; affirming that these charges, with a refusal to worship the Roman deities, and the image of the emperor Trajan, was the sum total of their fault, or of their error. The earl of Orrery pronounces Pliny to have been one of the best, and one of the greatest men, that any age has produced; second to none in virtue, equal to most in accomplishments; of high birth by his ancestors, but more ennobled by himself—yet, to this dignified Roman, so eminently great and good, the humblest *Christian*, in the season of doubt and distress, would exultingly exclaim, "I know that my REDEEMER liveth! that he hath brought life and immortality to light; and that where HE is, there shall his followers be!"

Pliny's letter unequivocally informs us what were the ideas of death, the hopeless view of a future state, in the great, the wise, the learned philosophers of Greece and Rome. The Christian, in strong faith, humble hope, and holy confidence, beholds the king of terrors in a very different character. He knows that flesh and blood cannot inherit the kingdom of GOD, neither can corruption inherit incorruption; but, in the emphatical language of holy writ, he is shewn the sublime mystery, that at the final dissolution, although we shall not all sleep, we shall all be changed in a moment, in the twinkling of an eye; when the last trumpet shall sound, the dead shall be raised incorruptible, and we shall be changed; for this corruptible must put on incorruption, and this mortal must put on immortality! Then shall the exulting disciple of a crucified Redeemer triumphantly exclaim, "O Death! where is thy sting? O Grave! where is thy victory?" "Then shall he behold a new heaven, and a new earth; he shall see the New Jerusalem, that holy city, where there shall be no more death, nor sorrow, nor pain; neither is there any temple therein: for the LORD GOD ALMIGHTY and the LAMB are the temple thereof."

That the faithful Christian may know who are to be his associates in this heavenly inheritance, the inhabitants of those celestial mansions, he is expressly told, in language which no sophistry can weaken, no philosophy pervert, that he will be there introduced to an innumerable company of angels; to the general assembly and church of the first-born whose names are written in heaven; to GOD, the judge of all; to the spirits of just men made perfect; and to JESUS, the mediator of the new covenant, the Alpha and Omega, the beginning and the end, the first and the last. The faithful witness and first-begotten from the dead; and the prince of the kings of earth. Unto HIM, therefore, who hath loved us, and washed us from our sins in his own blood; and hath made us kings and priests unto God and his Father; unto him, be glory and dominion, for ever and ever! Amen."

Stanmore Hill, 1st *May*,
1812.

" On piety, humanity is built;
And on humanity, much happiness;
And yet still more on piety itself.
A soul in commerce with her God, is heaven;
Feels not the tumults and the shocks of life;
The whirls of passion, and the strokes of heart!
A Deity believ'd, is joy begun;
A Deity ador'd, is joy advanced;
A Deity belov'd, is joy matured!
Each branch of piety delight inspires:
Faith builds a bridge from this world to the next,
O'er death's dark gulf, and all its horror hides:
Praise, the sweet exhalation of our joy,
That joy exalts, and makes it sweeter still:
Prayer ardent opens Heaven, lets down a stream
Of glory on the consecrated hour
Of man, in audience with the Deity!
Who worships the Great God, that instant joins
The first in heaven, and sets his foot on hell!" Young.

FINIS.

EXPLANATION OF THE PLATES.

I.

Humming Birds at the Brazils on a Branch of the Orange Tree.

The infinite variety of these little beauties, hovering over the lemon and orange-blossoms in the groves near Rio de Janeiro, renders it difficult to make a selection. Those introduced in this plate were drawn and coloured from nature. That on the wing is called the Fly-bird, from being the smallest of its species, and consequently the least, hitherto known, of the feathered tribes, in any part of the world.

II.

Blue Banana Bird at Rio de Janeiro, on a Sprig of the Guava Tree.

The beauty and variety of the birds on the coast of Brazil is astonishing: they are all specifically distinguished by naturalists, but the inhabitants of Rio de Janeiro generally call them red, blue, green, and yellow banana-birds, as those colours predominate; especially the birds which feed on bananas and plantains. The guava is one of the most beautiful and best flavoured fruits at the Brazils, and a great favourite with the domesticated songsters among the Portuguese ladies.

III.

Hindoo Peasant ascending the Cocoa-nut Tree, to draw the Tari, or Toddy.

The mode of extracting the Palm wine, or Toddy, is fully described in this work; to the Cocoa-nut tree the pot containing the liquor distilled in the night is affixed, for the peasant to pour into a larger vessel. In the fore-ground is a banana tree; and a Hindoo temple overshadowed by a banian tree, with other oriental scenery, in the distance.

IV.

View taken under Cubbeer-Burr, the celebrated Banian Tree in Guzerat.

This engraving from one of larger dimensions was copied from a drawing made on the spot; and contains about a sixteenth part of that beautiful production the Ficus Indica, growing on an island in the river Nerbudda. This umbrageous canopy is supported by three hundred and fifty large trunks, and upwards of three thousand smaller, all traced to one parent stem: the branches extend over a circumference of two thousand feet, and afford shelter to six or seven thousand persons, as particularly described p. 28, Vol. I.

V.

Monkeys in the Concan and Guzerat.

The Monkey family delineated in this plate was drawn from nature, under Cubbeer-Burr, the celebrated banian tree near Baroche, where they abound, and furnished the interesting anecdote mentioned at p. 27, Vol. I. There seems very little difference in the generality of these animals in the Concan and Guzerat. Malabar affords several varieties.

VI.

The Jaca or Jac Tree and Fruit—The Gardener and the Fruit in just proportion.

The Jac Fruit, *(Artocarpus integrifolia,* LIN.*)* often grows to a larger size than is even here exhibited; and, according to the general œconomy of nature, it has been wisely ordained to grow immediately out of the trunk and strongest boughs of the tree, as it would be impossible for the slender branches to sustain its enormous weight. It is particularly described in the Memoirs.

VII.

The Cobra de Capello, Naga, or Hooded Snake of Hindostan.

The Serpent represented in this engraving is not of the largest size of the Coluber Naga: the drawing was made from the Spectacle or Hooded Snake, mentioned in the Memoirs to have killed the market-woman in the bazar at Bombay. The spots and colours vary in this class of serpents, particularly in the spectacle marks in the expanded hood. The Cobra de Capello selected for this drawing was one of the most common, and one of the highest coloured of its kind.

VIII.

Dancing Snakes and Musicians.

Engraved from a drawing taken on the spot by Baron de Montalembert, when aid-du-camp to General Sir John Cradock in India. It is in all respects an exact representation of the Cobra de Capello, or Hooded Snake, with the Musicians who accompany them throughout Hindostan; and exhibits a faithful picture of the costume of the natives, usually assembled in the bazars on such occasions.

IX.

The Baya, or Bottle-nested Sparrow, on the Rose-Acacia, or Bawbul Tree of Guzerat.

This impression is from a chalk-drawing on stone, afterwards coloured from the original drawing, which was made in the forests of Turcaseer, where these birds abound. It represents the male, with the nest in which he perches and sings to the female during the season of incubation, suspended to a branch of the rose-coloured Mimosa, or Bawbul-tree, which produces a gum similar to the gum-arabic. The baya is fully described at p. 48, Vol. I.

X.

Nests of the Baya, or Bottle-nested Sparrow, with the Mhadavi Creeper.

The Nests here represented are smaller than the nidifications of the Baya, especially in the neck of the bottle, or entrance of the nest, which is generally proportionably longer. The Mhadavi (*Ipomea*, LIN.) is one of the loveliest flowers in the gardens of Hindostan, and a great favourite with the oriental females of every description. It is mentioned in many parts of these Memoirs, and particularly described in the chapter on the Natural History of Bombay.

XI.

The Tailor Birds of Hindostan, Male and Female.

There are many varieties of the *Motacilla Sutoria* in different parts of India. Those delineated in this plate were drawn from a pair, who constructed their nest exactly as here represented, (except being more concealed by the leaves of the Convolvulus), in my garden at Bombay. Few Tailor-birds display more brilliant plumage than the male here selected, and few wild plants in Hindostan are more beautiful than the fruit-bearing Convolvulus.

XII.

The Bulbul, or Indian Nightingale, on a sprig of the Custard-apple Tree.

The Bulbul, called also by the Persians, *Hazardasitaun,* or "the bird of a thousand songs," is one of the most beautiful and melodious in the Indian Ornithology. They differ very much in plumage, some being almost black, and others of a lighter brown than that delineated in this plate with the Custard-apple; both of which were drawn from nature at Bombay, and are of the usual size and colour.

XIII.

A young Hindoo, among the secular Brahmins of distinction.

The different castes of Hindoos are so fully described in the body of the work, that it is only necessary here to observe, this plate represents the usual dress of the younger Brahmins in the house, and a countenance differing very much from that of the Mahomedan youth in another engraving.

XIV.

A Hindoo Family of the Banian caste.

This is engraved from my earliest drawing, attempting to represent the costume of the natives, and the rural scenery in India; it was made in one of those spots frequently alluded to in the Memoirs, whither the Hindoos are fond of retiring with their families.

XV.

Dancing Girls and Musicians.

This is an exact representation of a set of Dancing Girls and Musicians, drawn from the life at Bombay. The costume of these courtezans varies according to their taste, whether Hindoos or Mahomedans, and it seldom happens that two are dressed exactly alike, either in their robes, or ornaments.

XVI.

Manner of travelling in a Palanquin in India.

This was the general construction of a palanquin, until the late improvements by the Europeans settled in Bengal, especially in one kind, which forms almost a small chamber, with windows of Venetian blinds to admit the light and air, as required. The bearers occasionally relieve each other; and on a journey relays of bearers are placed at convenient distances.

XVII.

An Indian Hackeree, drawn by Guzerat Oxen.

This is engraved from a sketch by Baron de Montalembert, of an Indian Hackeree, or chariot, with two wheels, and is an exact representation of that vehicle, as also of the breed of oxen, peculiarly trained for the purpose, as particularly described in the work. Many hackerees have four wheels, and accommodate a small family. The costume of the natives in the back-ground is equally characteristic.

XVIII.

A Mahomedan Youth of Distinction.

This plate represents the usual character, appearance, and dress, of the Mahomedan boys, in the best Mogul families settled in the Western provinces of Hindostan. They do not always wear ear-rings; but when dressed, are adorned with rows of pearl, diamonds, rubies and emeralds; also rings of great value.

XIX.

A Mahomedan of Distinction, with a Dervise on his Pilgrimage.

The sitting figure smoking the Hooka is a Sciad, of a high Mahomedan family, claiming his descent from the prophet of the faithful. He is accosted by a Mahomedan fakeer, or dervise, with his lark and staff, the usual accompaniments of those religious beggars; who, like the Hindoo mendicants, travel throughout Hindostan, living upon alms.

XX.

Parsees at Bombay.

The Parsees, descended from the Persian emigrants who left their country on the Mahomedan persecutions, and settled at Bombay, Surat, and Baroche, are particularly described in the Memoirs. They are a people differing very much in appearance and character from the Hindoos and Mahomedans, among whom they reside, and are in all respects perfectly distinct and separate. The drawing was taken from a Parsee family at Bombay. The back-ground represents one of the common wells in India, with the cocoa-nut, papah, and plaintain trees, and a distant view of a Parsee tomb on Malabar Hill.

XXI.

View of Bombay in 1773, taken from the Harbour.

This view contains the general face of the town towards the harbour; commencing with the dock-yard, and including the Admiralty, Marine-house, English Church, Pier, Bunder, Castle, Dungaree Fort, or Fort George, and other conspicuous buildings, taken from the shipping opposite the Bunder-pier.

XXII.

View from Malabar Hill, on the Island of Bombay.

This View contains the fortified town, and harbour of Bombay, connected with Colaba, or Old Woman's Island; beyond the harbour and shipping are the island of Caranjah, and the high land on the continent. The nearer landscape represents the country on Bombay, consisting chiefly of Cocoanut woods and rice-fields, interspersed with English villas and plantations. Those in this engraving are the Retreat and Tankaville, on the borders of a tank of fresh water, near Malabar Hill; on which is seen one of the Parsee tombs, or large open sepulchres, where the corpses are exposed, to be consumed by vultures and other birds of prey.

XXIII.

View of Bombay Green, taken from the Writer's Apartment at the Bunder.

This View is engraved from a drawing made in the year 1767; it includes part of the Government House, the English Church, Secretary's Office, the residence of the Second in Council, and the scenes daily occurring in this part of the town of Bombay. Among these are introduced the palanquin, hackeree, Bengal-chair, and other objects, which enlivened the spot while the drawing was made.

XXIV.

View on Bancoote River, in the Concan, from Dazagon Hill.

The drawing of this delightful scene was taken from the summit of a lofty hill near the hot-wells at Dazagon, forming almost a birds-eye view. The winding of the river was peculiarly beautiful, forming many islands, cultivated and inhabited; the landscape altogether presenting a pleasing picture of the best part of the Concan, or Cokun, which means the low country, compared with the Deccan, situated above the Gaut mountains.

XXV.

The Golden Lizard, on a Sprig of the Neva Tree.

Nothing can exceed the brilliant colouring of the lizard attempted in this plate; when the sun shone upon the blue and yellow divisions of its body, the richness baffled all attempts at imitation. The Neva tree, when covered with its pensile blossoms, is one of the most elegant vegetable productions in Hindostan.

XXVI.

A distant View of the Hindoo Temple at Alla Bhaugh, with different Natives in the Concan.

This elegant Hindoo structure was drawn from the temple erected by Govindsett, particularly described at p. 226, Vol. I. The men in the foreground, and the women with the water-pots near the well, are in the costume of the better sort of natives in the Concan.

XXVII.

Surat on the Banks of the Tappee.

The engraving represents this celebrated city in the most interesting point of view, from the English factory to the Dutch bunder, taken on the opposite side of the river. In the centre is the castle, with the British and Mogul colours on the towers; the more distant flag surmounts the Portugueze factory.

XXVIII.

The Conclusion of a Cheeta-hunt at Cambay.

The drawing for this engraving was made by Lady Malet, from a picture painted in water-colours by a native of India, taken on the spot, which although deficient in keeping and perspective, exactly described the scene intended: it represents the Cheeta growling over the antelope he has just killed in the chase, and the game-keeper cutting off the haunch to give the hungry animal, to redeem the rest of his prey. Sir Charles Malet and some of his Persian friends at Cambay are spectators. One of the attendants carries a hawk, trained for the chase of antelopes and other game, which formed a principal amusement at Cambay.

XXIX.

View in Goa Harbour.

This pleasing scene embraces the Fort of Alguarda, near the entrance of the harbour; another fortress at the opening of the river leading to the city; with the convents, churches, and villas in the groves and cocoa-nut woods which surround the bay.

XXX.

View of the City of Goa, taken from the River.

The drawing was made in 1772, when the public buildings in the city, with the churches, convents, and villas on the surrounding woody hills, were all in good repair, and added much to the general beauty of the prospect.

XXXI.

The Mango.

The Mango, (*Mangifera Indica*, Lin.) so deservedly esteemed one of the greatest blessings in India, abounds in most parts of its extensive dominions. It is a fruit frequently mentioned in these volumes, as differing in form, colour, and flavour, more than usual in oriental orchards, and far exceeding the variety of apples in Europe. The Alphonso mango at Goa, and that of Mazagon on Bombay, have deservedly obtained the preference to every other sort. The fruit is delineated in its various stages, as is sometimes seen on the same tree, adorned by one of the most beautiful Indian butterflies.

In this plate Mr. Hooker has exhibited a charming specimen of that correct taste and ability in colouring subjects of Natural History, so eminently conspicuous throughout these volumes, as to make me regret that the plan of this work would not admit of a larger selection of embellishments of this description.

XXXII.

Tellicherry, on the Coast of Malabar.

The drawing was taken from a ship in the road, and gives a view of this pleasant and healthy settlement, extending frem Tellicherry to Maylan, a fort about a mile distant.

XXXIII.

Calicut, on the Coast of Malabar.

This humble fishing town scattered among the cocoa-nut woods on the Coast of Malabar, is all that remains of the grand emporium of Calicut, which was esteemed among the first commercial cities in India, when Vasco de Gama arrived there, after his adventurous passage round the Cape of Good Hope, at the end of the sixteenth century; as particularly mentioned in the Memoirs.

XXXIV.

Cochin, on the Coast of Malabar.

This view was taken from a vessel at anchor in the road, and includes the handsomest part of the town, with the entrance of the river. Cochin

Cochin then belonged to the Dutch, who possessed several settlements on this part of the Malabar coast.

XXXV.

Anjengo, on the Malabar Coast.

The drawing was made in 1772; Anjengo was then the most southern settlement belonging to the English on the coast of Malabar. The only public buildings were the Portuguese church and the English fort, which terminate the view north and south.

XXXVI.

A Hindoo Temple, near Eddova in Travencore.

This Temple was selected, as offering a fair specimen of the different style of architecture in the religious structures of Travencore and Malabar, and the Hindoo Dewals in the northern parts of India. The pillars in front of the temple are each of a single stone.

XXXVII.

The Cajew, or Cashew-Apple of Malabar.

This plate represents the Cajew Apple and Nut in all the various stages, displayed at the same time among the leaves and blossoms of this beautiful tree; which is one of the chief ornaments in the Malabar landscape, and is planted on each side of the public roads in many parts of Travencore, to shade the travellers.

XXXVIII.

View of the large Temple in the Island of Elephanta.

This plate is reduced from one of larger dimensions, which was engraved from a drawing taken on the spot in 1774. It gives a general view of the interior of these extraordinary excavations, in which the Triad Deity of the Hindoos is distinguishable at the termination of the central aisle, or avenue. A strong light is thrown into the cave through an accidental aperture in the side of the mountain, the light originally admitted being only from the principal entrance.

XXXIX.

Comparative View of two principal Pillars in the Excavations at Salsette and Elephanta.

The lofty column, surmounted by elephants and something like a bell, was drawn correctly from one highly-finished in the large temple at Salsette. The other is a representation of the fluted pillars in the Elephanta cavern. Its capital seems well adapted to the situation, giving the spectator an idea of its being pressed and swelled by supporting the superincumbent mountain.

XL.

Hill Fort, on the Island of Caranjah.

This island was taken from the Mahrattas in 1774. The fort, built by the Portuguese on the summit of a lofty craggy mountain, contains the ruins of a church, and commands a noble prospect over the island, town, and harbour of Bombay, at a few miles distance.

XLI.

Scene of a melancholy Event on the Island of Salsette.

The little affecting anecdote of a Hindoo mother having her only child carried off by a tiger while gathering fuel on the borders of a forest, is mentioned in the Memoirs at Salsette. The spirit and interest of the original drawing, which is from the pencil of Baron de Montalembert, have been well preserved in the engraving.

XLII.

Ragonath Row, Ballajee, Pundit-Purdhan, Peshwa of the Mahratta Empire.

This portrait, from a drawing made during the campaign in Guzerat in 1775, was thought to be a striking likeness of Ragobah, or Ragonath Row, the Brahmin sovereign of the Mahrattas. On being shewn the original drawing, he said it was rather an unfavourable likeness, but if I would make a sketch of him after gaining a battle, it would be more pleasing, and exhibit his real character. That not according with the general opinion, the drawing remained in its original condition.

XLIII.

The Mahratta Peshwa and his Ministers at Poonah.

My drawing of this interesting party, was made from an original sketch taken in the Durbar at Poonah, in the possession of Sir Charles Malet, bart. during his residence at the Mahratta court; and is an exact representation of the highest order of secular brahmins.

XLIV.

Cambay, from the South.

The drawing was made when the English detachment from Bombay accompanied Ragonath Row from Surat, and a tent was pitched for the reception of the Mahratta sovereign, between the city-walls and the sea, previous to his interview with the Nabob of Cambay. In the centre is the Jumma Musjid and fallen Minar, mentioned in the memoirs.

XLV.

Mohman Khaun, Nabob of Cambay.

The drawing from which this is engraved was made at a public interview between the Nabob and the Mahratta sovereign, near the walls of Cambay; it was thought to be a strong likeness, and an exact representation of the Mogul costume. On that particular occasion the Nabob wore no jewels, nor any kind of ornament, except a fresh-gathered rose on one side of his turban.

XLVI.

Sculpture in a subterraneous Hindoo Temple at Cambay.

This Temple, called by the English Shawuck pagoda, contains some of the most beautiful marble sculpture in Hindostan, of a variety of deities in the Hindoo Pantheon. This compartment, forming the centre in a row of these images, was selected, from being more highly finished and ornamented than the rest; it represents the Deity called Parisnaut.

XLVII.

A Foot Soldier in the usual Costume of the Native Indians.

From a drawing made in the Mahratta camp, of a spear-man in Ragobah's service. Those who carry match-locks, or other Indian armour, are generally dressed in a similar manner, sometimes in a jacket and shorter drawers, according to their own choice; no conformity being attempted, as in the corps of native sepoys in the Company's service.

XLVIII.

A Mahratta Horseman.

Engraved from a drawing sketched in the Mahratta camp; where, as remarked of the native foot-soldiers, few of them are dressed or armed exactly in the same manner; nor is there much distinction in appearance between the officers and the troop they command.

XLIX.

The Table-Land and Cape Town at the Cape of Good Hope.

The Table-land at a distance appears like one long mountain, with a flat surface, a nearer approach discovers its projecting cliffs, craggy sides, and broken precipices. The fortifications and principal buildings in the town being drawn in proportion to the Table mountain, are necessarily on a diminutive scale.

L.

Baroche, on the Banks of the Nerbudda in Guzerat.

This city being fully described in the work, it is unnecessary to add more than that the view was taken from the Melon island in the centre of the river Nerbudda, opposite the south face of the fortifications.

LI.

An English Villa on the Banks of the Nerbudda in Guzerat.

This Villa, situated in the village of Vezelpoor, near Baroche, is particularly described in the Memoirs, with its gardens and accompaniments. The view presents a little scene endeared to the author by many tender recollections; and is introduced into these volumes with a view of giving the European reader some idea of what is called a *Garden House*, in those distant regions.

He that holds fast the golden mean,
And lives contentedly between
The little and the great,
Feels not the wants that pinch the poor,
Nor plagues that haunt the rich man's door,
Imbittering all his state.

HORACE, *by Cowper*.

LII.

Scene in the Garden at Vezelpoor near Baroche.

This varied and beautiful spot, drawn from nature, gave rise to the verses addressed to the Hindoo Naiad *Medhumad'ha*, in the preceding chapter, and forms a pleasing association of Oriental scenery, comprised within a very small compass.

Mellifluous murmurings told the fountains nigh,
Fountains which all the garden's wants supply.

LIII.

The Mausoleum of Bawa Rahan, near Baroche.

A morning scene soon after sun rise; engraved from an oil painting, which I did from my original drawing, to produce a more brilliant effect in colouring. The fore-ground represents the Mahomedan women, on the anniversary of the death of a husband, child, or relative, strewing the grave with mogrees and other fragrant flowers; at the approach of night they place a few lamps round the tomb, and pass the hours in the melancholy pleasure of tender recollection. The pensile nests of the Baya, or bottle-nested sparrow, are suspended to the branches of the Cocoa-nut tree.

LIV.

The Curmoor, or Florican of Guzerat.

The plate represents this beautiful bird of about half its natural size; the plumage is extremely correct: it is of the Bustard genus, and esteemed by epicures to be far superior in flavour to the black-partridge, or any other bird introduced at the English tables in India.

LV.

The Sahras, or Demoiselle of Guzerat. Ardea Virgo.

This bird, drawn from nature, is particularly described, and a singular anecdote related of it, in these Memoirs. The Sahras and Cullum, a similar bird, are very common in many parts of Guzerat, and in their most erect posture generally exceed five feet in height.

LVI.

The Green Pigeon and Cur-Champa.

The bird in the plate is represented about half the natural size; it is of beautiful plumage, and highly flavoured. These pigeons are met with in most parts of Hindostan, and particularly abound in the Banian trees, whose fruit forms their principal food. The Cur-Champa grows to a large tree, with a rich foliage, and at most seasons is covered with white flowers, which emit a delicate fragrance to a considerable distance.

LVII.

Blue Locust, Thorny-nested Caterpillar, and variegated Mimosa, in Guzerat.

These three curious and beautiful specimens in the Natural History of Guzerat are particularly described in different excursions in that province. They are delineated of the exact size and colours of Nature, except in the lively azure of the locust, which it would be difficult for art to imitate.

The caterpillar, and the elegant Baubul-tree, or Mimosa, from whence it instinctively saws off the thorny materials for its temporary asylum, are fully mentioned in p. 272, Vol. II.

LVIII.

Skeleton Mantis, and Oil plant of Guzerat.

There is as great a variety of plants cultivated for the oil which is expressed from their seeds, as there is of the Mantis tribe of insects, in Guzerat. The plant here delineated is one of the most delicate of its kind; and the mantis, or soothsayer, a singular variety among the creeping-leaves, begging-flies, and other insects of the mantis tribe.

LIX.

The Durbar, and adjacent Scenery at Dhuboy.

This plate represents the durbar, or palace of the former Hindoo governors, after being a little altered to the English fashion. It is pleasantly situated on the border of a tank, surrounded by temples and sacred groves of the brahmins. The fore-ground represents that part where cattle were generally led to water. The other sides are enclosed by walls of hewn stone, with steps to the water.

LX.

The Gate of Diamonds at Dhuboy.

The Memoirs contain a particular account of the Eastern Gate at Dhuboy, and assign a reason for this distinguishing appellation. The plate represents its present ruinous state, and the remains of its former magnificence, in the temple and adjoining part of the city walls.

LXI.

Specimen of Hindoo Sculpture on the Gate of Diamonds, at Dhuboy.

This composition was selected to convey some idea of the immense profusion of sculpture bestowed on this celebrated eastern portal, particularly described in the Memoirs. One hundred thousand figures of different kinds would fall far short of the number sculptured on its walls and towers.

LXII.

Peasants at a Well in Hindostan.

The engraving was made from a drawing by Baron de Montalembert, and is an exact representation of the subject. The ox carries a double skin filled with water, hanging on each side, which is sold in the cities and towns throughout India at a very moderate price.

LXIII.

The Indian Squirrel and Tamarind.

These are both of the natural size and colours. There are larger squirrels in India, more like those in Europe; but the little beauty here delineated is common in every town and village throughout Hindostan; perfectly familiar in the houses and gardens of natives and Europeans: the stripes are sometimes of a darker brown. The tamarind leaves and blossoms are of the usual standard; the fruit is shorter than is generally seen, on account of the size of the plate.

LXIV.

Grains in Guzerat. Chena, Buntee, Codra, Natchnee.

The early grains were all drawn from nature, at the commencement of the different harvests in the Dhuboy Purgunna. The Linnean names, and specific distinctions are mentioned in the work: their varied tints, and rich appearance add much to the beauty of the luxuriant plains of Guzerat. These grains are all reaped, in what is called the first harvest, commencing soon after the periodical rains are over.

LXV.

Grains in Guzerat. Juarree, Bahjeree, Batty, or Rice.

These latter grains, whose Linnean distinctions appear in the work, are more nutritive and valuable than those in the preceding plate. They were all drawn and coloured from nature; and when fully ripe, clothe the fertile purgunnas with the most luxuriant and varied beauty, in a province deservedly named the *Paradise of Nations*.

LXVI.

The Wedded Banian Tree.

This tree is so called in Hindostan, where the seed of the Palmyra (*borassus flabelliformis*) has been dropped by a bird, or scattered by the wind into the decaying trunk of a burr, or banian-tree, (*Ficus indica*). The trees thus united form a peculiar contrast, especially when the Palmyra soars loftily above the spreading branches and picturesque trunks of the burr. The trees from which this drawing was made grew near the bottom of the excavated mountains in the island of Salsette; and were much frequented by the Baya, or bottle-nested sparrow.

LXVII.

Hindoo Devotees of the Gosaing and Jetty Tribes.

The various tribes and castes of Hindoo mendicants are fully described in the Memoirs. The Gosaing with his lark is one of the Gymnosophists, who generally travel throughout Hindostan without clothes. The Jetty, or Bramacharee, is another kind of beggar, who always ties a cloth over his mouth, from the fear of inhaling some animalcula with his breath, and thereby hastening a spirit into another state of existence, according to the doctrine of the Hindoo metempsychosis.

LXVIII.

Hindoo Devotees of the Jungam and Byragee Tribes.

These superstitious mendicants have some characteristic difference from those in the preceding plate, the detail of which would be neither interesting nor entertaining to the English reader. Some of the distinctions in the artificial gradations of caste among these people are slightly mentioned in the Memoirs. The contrasted appearance of the well-fed Jungam and the meagre habit of the abstemious Byragee are sufficiently obvious.

LXIX.

Scene on the Banks of the Nerbudda, near Chandode.

Although mentioned near Chandode, this drawing, made considerably more to the westward, contains a view of the village of Succultera, and the sacred groves in that part of the Baroche Purgunna; with the costume of the natives.

LXX.

A Brahmin Woman of Distinction in Guzerat.

This drawing was taken from a brahmin female of high rank, who could not, from religious prejudice, drink water drawn by a woman of inferior caste. There is a grace and dignified air peculiar to these women, arising from the simple custom of carrying jars of water upon the head; sometimes two or three are placed on each other. A Hindoo temple and Ficus Indica in the distant view.

LXXI.

Small Hindoo Dewal on the bank of the Nerbudda.

These little temples, generally shaded by a banian-tree, are built near a Hindoo village, for the convenience of the peasants; and also for the comfort of the boatmen navigating the river; who on festivals, and stated ceremonies, frequently land, and perform their devotions to the deity therein worshipped. The Raje-pipley hills form the distant prospect.

LXXII.

A Banian Tree, consecrated for Worship in a Guzerat Village.

This tree was sketched, not only for its perfect form, and the ramifications and trunks surrounding the parent stems, (from which they did not then extend to a great distance,) but because it gave an exact representation of a village deity often mentioned, in those small hamlets where no building is appropriated to Hindoo worship. To this stone, sometimes rude and shapeless, and sometimes sculptured into the form of a deity, the peasant repairs to perform his daily devotions.

LXXIII.

Scenery among the Sacred Hindoo Groves at Chandode.

This view contains some of the smaller dewals, or temples, under the Ficus Indica and groves of Mango and Pepal trees, on the banks of the river Nerbudda, where the brahmins pass their lives in voluptuous indolence, with the female choristers, and dancing girls. Sacred bulls stray unmolested, and monkeys are cherished, while the poor out-cast Chandalah is not permitted to enter, nor even to breathe the surrounding atmosphere.

LXXIV.

A Coolie Chieftain in Guzerat.

The engraving is from a drawing of a chieftain, or head of the Coolies, a tribe of robbers and pirates settled near the river Mihi, in Guzerat, who are particularly mentioned in these Memoirs: the scene of their depredations is principally in the gulf of Cambay, and the navigation between Surat and Bombay.

LXXV.

Specimen of the Inlaid-work in the Taje Mahal at Agra.

The Mausoleum called Taje Mahal, or the "Crown of the Seraglio," at Agra, erected by the Emperor Shah Jehan, in memory of his favourite Sultana Montazal Zumani, "Paragon of the Age," is so fully described in the Memoirs, that it would be superfluous to add any thing further, than that the plate exhibits a fac-simile of the ornaments inlaid in precious stones on the marble and alabaster of the tomb, for many hundred feet.

LXXVI.

The Jumma Musjid, or Grand Mosque at Ahmedabad.

The engraving is made from a drawing taken on the spot, of one of the most magnificent buildings in Hindostan, still remaining in perfect repair. The minars, or minarets, are uncommonly beautiful; and the plate conveys a complete idea of this style of Mogul architecture.

LXXVII.

Shah Bhaug, a Summer Palace, built by the Emperor Shah Jehan, on the Banks of the Sabermatty.

The palace, park, and gardens, at Shah Bhaug are fully described in the Memoirs. This imperial villa was built in the beginning of the seventeenth century, and is still in complete repair. The external decorations and interior apartments exhibit an excellent specimen of Mogul architecture.

LXXVIII.

Temple of Fountains, at Cambay.

The drawing was taken from a temple of marble, with perforated columns, each supplying a fountain round the dome, as described at large in the work. It stood in the centre of a canal in the garden called Dil-Gusha, or the "Expansion of the Heart," belonging to the Cambay Nabob, surrounded by fragrant flowers and aromatic plants; especially the keurah, mogree, roses, jasmin, and double tube-roses.

LXXIX.

The Keurah Tree, in its common Form.

The Keurah tree, (or rather shrub, as it seldom exceeds eight or ten feet in height,) is a universal favourite with the natives of India, of all castes and descriptions. The flowers and farina of this plant are exquisitely fragrant; and more delicate than the mogree, champaca, and other powerful flowers in the oriental gardens; it is common throughout Hindostan, and planted in many parts for hedges, scenting the atmosphere with a delicious perfume. The Keurah is called by various names in different parts of India; and is the *Pandanus Odoratissimus* of Linnaeus.

LXXX.

A Branch of the Keurah Tree.

This, and the other three plates of the Keurah, are struck off from drawings on stone, made from the sketches taken at Cambay.

LXXXI.

The Flowers and young Fruit of the Keurah.

This shews more distinctly the blossoms and early fruit of a plant so highly esteemed by the Indians. The men wear the flowers falling gracefully from the turban—the women in various ornaments.

LXXXII.

The Fruit of the Keurah.

This plate shews the fruit in a ripe state; it is sometimes eaten by the poorest natives; also the pulp of the stalk in time of famine.

LXXXIII.

A Gracia Chieftain, or Rajah, with his Suaree, or usual Attendants.

This print, taken from a drawing by Baron de Montalembert, gives an excellent idea of the general costume of the inferior Hindoo Rajahs and Princes throughout the greater part of Hindostan; with the usual appearance of their guards and attendants.

LXXXIV.

Ryjee Sihng, a Bhaut in the Zinore Purgunna.

This Bhaut was a native of Serulah in Zinore; the head of one of the chief families in that very extraordinary tribe of bards and heralds, described in the Memoirs: and the principal security for the Gracia chieftains in Guzerat.

LXXXV.

View of Cubbeer Burr, the celebrated Banian Tree, near Baroche.

This sketch, which I drew on stone, represents the general appearance of this wonderful specimen of the Ficus Indica, so often mentioned in these Memoirs, of which a finished engraving has been given in the first volume, to accompany the fullest description. The sketch was taken from the bank of the Nerbudda, opposite to the island on which this beautiful tree has flourished for so many ages, and presents a correct outline of this celebrated oriental production.

LXXXVI.

Ramifications of a Banian Tree, drawn from Nature.

During the many sultry hours passed under the shade of Cubbeer Burr, when the hot winds prevailed in the surrounding atmosphere, I amused myself by sketching the singular roots and extraordinary ramifications of this umbrageous canopy: from a number of these sketches I selected the present, to make a drawing on stone, by way of multiplying the original sketch for my friends. As such, with the Keura, Baya, and a few other polygraphic attempts on stone, it is introduced into this work.

LXXXVII.

Bridge over the River Biswamintree, near Brodera.

This being the only bridge of any consequence I ever saw in India, I have introduced it as a specimen of those structures. —It is built of stone; and during the floods in the rainy season, when the stream frequently rises thirty or forty feet, and rushes with astonishing velocity, through the upper arches, it is of so great use in the province, as to render it astonishing it has not been imitated near other principal towns. This bridge was erected when the Moguls possessed Brodera.

LXXXVIII.

The Red, Blue, and White Lotus of Hindostan.

These Water Lilies were drawn and coloured from nature: they are particularly described in various parts of the Memoirs; and almost cover the Indian lakes. When gently agitated by the breeze, they give them a beauty and freshness not easily conceived by the inhabitants of a colder climate.

LXXXIX.

View of Onore Fort, after the Siege in 1783.

This engraving was made from a drawing taken on the spot by an officer, after the siege by Tippoo Sultan's forces in 1783, when it was most gallantly defended by Major Torriano and a small garrison, as fully related in the Memoirs.

XC.

The Black and White Kingfisher, and Spotted Frog of Malabar.

These are both mentioned in the preceding account of the natural history of Tellicherry. The former frequently varies in its plumage; the black marks being sometimes less regular and more predominant; but it always forms a pleasing contrast to the brilliant azure, green, and golden plumage of the other birds of this species. The Frog, so richly adorned by nature, is not uncommon in the lakes of Malabar; which also abound with the aquatic plant introduced in the plate, and many others of singular beauty.

XCI.

View on the Island of St. Helena.

This is selected from a number of drawings made at St. Helena, some of which, containing the Town and shipping at anchor in the road, would, perhaps, be deemed more picturesque and interesting. The present engraving gives a preferable view of the interior landscape, and manner of enclosing the fields and plantations round the farm houses, to any of the other drawings.

XCII.

Flying Fish, Exocoetus Evolans.

This unfortunate inhabitant of the ocean was drawn of the natural size and colours, from one which alighted on the deck of the ship, in its flight from its watery foes, and pursued by the sea-fowl hovering over the shoal from which it separated. When the oceanic flying fish first emerges from the water, it is of the most beautiful silvery hues, softening the varied shades of purple and blue.

XCIII.

Medusa, or Portuguese Man-of-War.

The latter is the usual appellation to this beautiful production of nature, which expands its light transparent sail at pleasure, and with thousands of its comrades scuds before a light breeze, and enlivens the surface of the ocean in the tropical latitudes.

INDEX.

FINIS.

ERRATA.

VOL. I.

Page 27, line 23, *dele* and.
28, 6, substitute a comma for the period after Baroche, and *for* Putnah *read* which.
32, 7 and 10, *for* kenna *read* henna.
32, 20, *for* Meli *read* Meti.
60, 18, *for* Dewlahs *read* Dewals.
67, 12, *for* soul *read* foul.
114, 16, *for* are *read* is.
153, 7, *for* stood *read* stored.
212, 20, *dele* public.
236, 19, *for* of (2d) *read* in.
294, 8, *for* Satamah *read* Satarra.
307, 22, *for* Caury *read* Candy.
315, 25, *for* Montpellier *read* Montpelier.
337, 18, *dele* I.
348, 16, *for* Cashers *read* Cashew.
466, 1, *for* Sasu *read* Saou.

VOL. II.

Page 10, line 26, *for* Arnan *read* Arrian.
12, 7, *dele* and my life.
18, 8, *for* were *read* was.
31, 22, *for* Sabermally *read* Sabermatty.
101, 18, *after* fleet, *add* mare.
153, 19, *for* depradation *read* depredation.
163, 13, *after* Good *read* Hope.
167, 15, *for* False *read* Falso.
203, 11, *for* Homugas *read* Hormigas.
212, 14, *for* sciences *read* science.
244, 12, *after* is, *add* not.
287, 21, *for* Tops *read* Topes.
343, 19, *for* Junadar *read* Jemadar.
353, *in two places for* per million, *read* per mill: *meaning per thousand*.
416, 16, *for* Vajessa *read* Vajeefa.

VOL. III.

Page 31, line 1, *dele* !
99, 25, *before* inferior *read* oxen.
103, 27, *for* Faje *read* Taje.
124, 21, *for* Saberty *read* Sabermatty.
125, 5, *for* columns *read* domes.
142, 26, *dele* were.
150, 9, *for* Currain *read* Currim.
211, 6, *for* of *read* to.
244, 14, *for* Neber *read* Akber.
332, 22, *after* Concan *put* (:) *after* contrast *put* (,)
364, 16, *for* Manha *read* Mantra.
374, 12, *instead of* (.), *put* (,).
408, 26, *for* Charon *read* Sharon.
441, 18, *for* Nalsey *read* Halsey.

VOL. IV.

Page 123, line 6, *for* Malawar *read* Malwan.
146, 11, *for* prostrated *read* prostrate.
190, 6, *for* south-east *read* south-west.
206, 18, *for* Governor Elliot *read* General Elliot.
207, 9, *for* Allinga *read* Attinga.
237, 8, *after* downy wings, *add* of Time.
237, 13, *after* telescope *read* through.
255, 11, *for* a *read* two.
285, 15, *for* know *read* knew.
326, 21, *for* Yernen *read* Yemen.
334, 13, *for* as *read* and.

Some illustra ion: could not be
included for unavoidable reasons